Electronic Records in the Manuscript Repository

Elizabeth H. Dow

The Scarecrow Press, Inc.
Lanham, Maryland • Toronto • Plymouth, UK
2009

SCARECROW PRESS, INC.

Published in the United States of America
by Scarecrow Press, Inc.
A wholly owned subsidiary of
The Rowman & Littlefield Publishing Group, Inc.
4501 Forbes Boulevard, Suite 200, Lanham, Maryland 20706
www.scarecrowpress.com

Estover Road
Plymouth PL6 7PY
United Kingdom

British Library Cataloguing in Publication Information Available

Library of Congress Cataloging-in-Publication Data
Dow, Elizabeth H.
 Electronic records in the manuscript repository / Elizabeth H. Dow.
    p. cm.
 Includes bibliographical references and index.
 ISBN 978-0-8108-6708-6 (pbk. : alk. paper) — ISBN 978-0-8108-6709-3
(ebook)
 1. Electronic records–Management. 2. Electronic records–Conservation and
restoration. 3. Archival materials–Conservation and restoration. 4. Information
storage and retrieval systems–Management. I. Title.
 CD974.4.D69 2009
 025.17'4–dc22   2009003770

♾™ The paper used in this publication meets the minimum requirements of
American National Standard for Information Sciences—Permanence of
Paper for Printed Library Materials, ANSI/NISO Z39.48-1992.
Manufactured in the United States of America.

To David

Contents

Preface

I write this book for the "Lone Arranger" in the collecting repository who may or may not have a sidekick or two in the office. In my mind I see the curator in a small collecting repository sighing over the electronic media beginning to appear in the collections that have recently come through the door. They include 5.25-inch floppy disks containing data generated by early (and now extinct) computer programs run on old and inoperative hardware. They also include 3.5-inch floppies holding data from unknown sources, CDs holding hundreds of photos, DVDs with home movies, and a wide variety of other electronically produced data, information, and records. Soon they will include storage devices with podcasts, Internet downloads, and personal archives of e-mail and text messages. What in the world should you do with this stuff?

Though I now teach at a large university, I spent my time as an archivist working in small repositories. I sympathize with the fact that you'll never have enough time, money, or staff to do everything you know you should. I also know that if you take my message seriously, you will confront hard choices. But, hard choices are a way of life in the small repository.

All the big institutions concerned about electronic records are still working out the details of experiments and theories, which is as it should be. Regardless, I feel strongly that you need something to get you started. As an academic, I have the time and support I need to read everything about electronic records I can get my hands on and synthesize it specifically to address your problems.

Electronic records have a growing literature. The Society of American Archivists carries over a dozen titles, and ARMA International, a large professional organization for records and information managers, carries substantially more books, articles, online courses, and technical tools. The vast bulk of this literature approaches electronic records from the perspective of a records manager in a large corporate or governmental environment. However useful the curator in a collecting repository might find such publications, she or he will need to wade through a lot of irrelevant information to find what will apply in a collecting repository. I have seen that wading as my job.

The wading was the easy part. The hard part involved figuring out how to organize what I had learned so the information would flow smoothly from one concept to another. I do not want to talk down to you; I don't want to talk over your head; I don't want to overwhelm you with information and concepts. Consequently, I have weighed very carefully what I include and what I leave out. I have left out a lot. I do not pretend to tell you everything you need to know—only what you need to know to get started.

The technologies change rapidly, and a lot of experimenting is still going on. Rather than provide you with what seem like answers, I hope to provide you with concepts, contexts, best practice procedures, and pointers to resources— especially pointers to resources. With those tools in hand, you can address specific technologies yourself; I've provided a fairly extensive list of resources at the end of the book. In time, some of them will go out of date. Others will not.

When I started working on this book, several years ago, most of the research on electronic records came from institutional settings, and for good reasons: they have the money and power to do it, and they have legal concerns. Since then a substantial number of larger public-sector repositories, most of them in academic institutions, have developed projects to test concepts that came from the earlier work. While most of what they have done remains beyond your reasonable reach, it shows us a lot more about approaches a small repository could take, approaches a small repository should avoid, and, most importantly, what a trustworthy digital repository will look like in operation.

In a collecting repository, you may actually play two roles: the role of curator for the collections and the role of institutional archivist for the institution's records. As such, you must operate out of two separate models in relation to digital materials. In this book I deal only with the issues you will confront in your role as curator. While the digital materials problems you face in that role overlap greatly with those you face as institutional archivist, the approach to solutions differs markedly, and I don't want to confuse the two roles here.

Acknowledgments

In the preface I wrote: "As an academic, I have the time and support I need to read everything about electronic records I can get my hands on and synthesize it specifically to address your problems." Here I want to acknowledge the support, which came in many forms. Martin Dillon, of Scarecrow Press, encouraged me to pursue the topic. I have alternately rejoiced at and cursed his name as I worked my way through the fog. Beth Paskoff, my dean, sent me to conferences and smiled encouragingly as I bemoaned my progress. Friends and family all cheered me on, despite the fact that this whole endeavor took approximately a year longer than we expected.

Nothing would exist here but for the work of others. While I have read a fair amount out of actual paper books, far more of my information came from files I found on the Internet. I have repeatedly sent a silent "thank you" to the teams of people who developed the technology of the Internet and those people who have populated it with rich resources. I have thanked the technical people for their vision of what the Web could become and for their work that has made it that. I also have thanked those many researchers and scholars who have allowed their words and thoughts to go out to the public in such an expedient way.

Emotional, financial, and intellectual support count, but eyes on the paper matter a lot. Polly Darnell, my faithful small-repository archivist guinea pig, read this manuscript after just one year. A more ill-conceived, poorly organized mess you can't imagine, but she let me know where she saw hope and what felt most useful to her. Thus she marked the path I should follow. Two years later, Bruce Turner, a very generous colleague whose sense of professionalism has forced him to at least acknowledge, if not embrace, the issue of digital materials, had a go at it. The manuscript had more organization and focus, but parts of it were still practically unreadable. Yet he read it, and offered good feedback. Finally, the publisher's reader offered solid practical advice.

Eyes on the page matter, but nothing goes forward without boots on the ground. In my case, students wore the boots that mattered most. Jennifer Greer, a former student who worked for a records management consulting service, agreed to help me with the research and writing. What she provided amazed and humbled me by its depth and breadth. But for Jennifer, this volume might never have happened; if it had, without her input, it would have been much less precise about the technologies available out there and how they fit into the picture.

Following Jennifer, Mary-Allen Johnson, a scholar in her own right and an extraordinarily talented and detail-oriented student, had the courage to say yes when I asked her to clean up the notes and references. Then she offered to read the entire work. In so doing, she not only provided valuable copyediting support, she shared her perspective as a budding archivist. She had new-enough knowledge that she could remember what she didn't know the previous year when she would have been a member of my intended audience. Given what she had learned in the interim, she could indicate where I needed to do better at bridging the gap for the reader. Finally, at the last possible moment, Dave Gold suddenly appeared and offered important technical clarification and tweaks in the narrative.

If I failed to absorb and execute their help and advice, the fault lies with me, not them.

Introduction

Electronic records and digital documents have become a fact of life in the modern world. ARMA International, the professional association of records and information managers, estimates that more than 90 percent of the records being created today are electronic. A study done by the research firm IDC "sought to account for all the ones and zeros that made up photos, videos, e-mail, Web pages, instant messages, phone calls and other digital content cascading through our world today." They concluded that the world generated 161 billion gigabytes of information in 2006—"three million times the information in all the books ever written."[1]

Like the records managers in corporate and governmental institutions, curators in collecting repositories of historical materials need to take to heart the fundamentals of that message: electronic records will show up everywhere as a wide variety of electronic storage media in personal and business collections. They will eventually become the responsibility of the curator to appraise, acquire, describe, retain, and provide to the researching public as he or she goes about performing his or her archival functions.

Electronic devices have changed the environment that shapes our collections. Hyry and Onuf argue that the term "personal papers" has changed in its meaning completely. The concept of "personal" has grown larger and has fuzzy boundaries, and "papers" no longer refers to hard-copy documents.[2] Although personal and family papers have always revealed the network of people's lives, today we find those networks both wider and more complicated than in the pre-electronic world. In our personal lives, instead of small groups communicating verbally, face-to-face, on both ad hoc and formal schedules and in real time, we find people in social networks communicating across traditional boundaries, ignoring predefined communication paths, involving multidirectional, asynchronous, and ad hoc conversations frequently by electronic means. Likewise, in the institutional world, we used to find small groups communicating verbally, face-to-face, on both ad hoc and formal schedules in real time within hierarchies relying on top-down written orders for command and control of bureaucracies using standard forms, structured rules, and defined communication paths. We now find institutional networks of people communicating across traditional boundaries, ignoring pre-defined communication paths, involving multidirectional, asynchronous, and ad hoc conversations frequently by electronic means.

All of these changes have profound implications for the way we practice our profession. In chapter 1, we review the concept of archival functions from a theoretical perspective. The International Council of Archivists (ICA) defines the archival function as "that group of related activities contributing to, and necessary for . . . identifying, safeguarding and preserving archival records, and ensuring that such records are accessible and understandable."[3] Identifying, safeguarding, preserving, and ensuring that the records in your care are accessible and understandable—that's what historical repositories do.

The definition makes no exception for records in new formats. A document is a document. If it has enduring value, an archivist or manuscripts curator must take care of it. If you are the manuscripts curator or the archivist, you have a professional obligation to stay aware of how to take care of documents in their new formats. The new records aren't nearly as seductive as the old records. They're not pretty, they don't smell "old," they don't make your fingers sigh when you hold them. (They also don't make you sneeze.) None of that matters. An ugly baby needs care and feeding as much as a beautiful baby—and these are the ugly babies of our professional future. As the archivist or curator in a historical repository, it's your job to identify, describe, and preserve them and make them accessible and understandable.

In the early 1990s, the National Archives of Canada started coming to grips with digital materials and conducted a project to identify and develop methods of controlling the digital materials being created as a matter of daily business in the Canadian government. In an article in the *American Archivist*,[4] John McDonald, the project director, outlined "Lessons Learned," which I reworded in chapter 7 to apply to the collecting repository and your work with donors. I repeat here the text from chapter 7 because it very neatly articulates the basics of this book.

Someone, probably you, must be the point person in the repository, taking responsibility for the digital materials, staying abreast of technological developments and the growing sophistication in the archives world about best practices in relation to digital materials. In the collecting repository, this is the person who works with the identified donors as to how those donors should handle their digital materials. This person not only needs to have enough technical knowledge but also must have masterful skills in human communication. In his project, McDonald discovered, to nobody's surprise, that records creators and users resist being told how they should handle "their" records and files. In an institutional setting, the archivist must show creators that "their" records aren't their records: they belong to the institution. In the case of private donors, the materials are in fact the donor's, so the curator works with them only as a consultant, armed with knowledge, but no actual power. As a consultant, the curator must find ways to make sure the donor turns digital materials over in a timely fashion or takes responsibility for their care. The curator must find a motivator, such as a desire to make them available to researchers of the future, to instill a drive to manage digital materials in a way that works for the repository and the creator both. You may find that as donors become increasingly reliant on digital materials, they will welcome guidance in meeting a felt need.

In this book, I attempt to define the problems related to electronic records and digital documents. I then suggest steps the curator should take to manage those electronic records and digital documents and where to learn the specific skills and perspectives needed to do the job well. Finally, I suggest where he or she should keep an eye for future development.

I do not cover the process of digitization of paper- and film-based materials; it has a voluminous literature of its own. I do include the results of that activity, however, as one part of the whole body of digital materials you will face.

How I've Organized This Book

Anyone writing a book intended to teach something must understand that people learn in different ways—some by reading, some by hearing, some by doing, some need all modes. A book largely limits the teaching mode to words on a page and best suits people who learn through reading. But even readers differ. Some like to start with abstractions and move to practical issues after absorbing all the concepts. Others prefer to start with the practical, knowing they will pick up the abstract concepts as they go along. In organizing a book, the author must choose one style over the other.

I have organized this book to move from the abstract to the practical. I start with a review of archival concepts, include a review of archival practices, and then address the problems created by electronic materials in that context. From there I review the research in progress to address the issues. With that framework in place, I move into issues of actual practice in the current climate. If you learn better by moving from the practical to the abstract, I suggest you quickly scan chapters 1 through 4 and then dive into chapters 5 through 8, knowing you can go back to the abstract concepts as you run into vocabulary and concepts that leave you puzzled.

A Few Words

A word about the word *archives*. Like many English terms, *archives* has several meanings, and in conversational use, we generally rely on context to deduce the meaning conveyed in the moment. If we can't figure it out, we ask for clarification. In a published work, the reader can't ask for clarification, so the author must pick a meaning and stick with it. In this work, the term *archives* will refer to those materials of enduring value collected by an institution to document its own history. It therefore refers to governmental archives and various forms of organizational and corporate archives. I will refer to personal and family papers as *manuscript collections* and to organizations that collect historical documents as *collecting repositories.*

Archivists work in archives, bearing the responsibility for the archives of an institution or government body. *Manuscripts curators* work in collecting repositories.

A word about *preservation.* Ross Harvey, professor of library and information management at Charles Sturt University, New South Wales, Australia, made the point at a 2006 conference that the definition of digital preservation really means long-term retention.[5] Liz Bishoff and Tom Clareson, both at OCLC, pointed out that in the world of paper- and film-based materials, cultural heritage institutions "approach preservation as rescue work."[6] While the passage of time will cause analog materials to deteriorate, the deterioration will not happen quickly; if five years go by before the repository initiates some form of intervention to rescue deteriorating newspapers or books, the information they contain won't disappear. The curators can respond to the materials on the curators' schedule. The exact opposite is true with digital materials. Five years can mean the difference between having the information they hold and not having it. The curators must respond to the materials on the materials' schedule.

Furthermore, the term *preservation* has opposite meanings in the world of archives and libraries. Archivists use the term *conservation* to refer to heroic actions to save at-risk holdings, and they use *preservation* to refer to the day-to-day environment and processes that keep the repository running smoothly in a way that will benefit the holdings. Librarians use the terms in exactly the opposite way. Since the readers of this book come from both disciplines, I have decided, when discussing digital materials, to use Harvey's phrase *long-term retention* to represent what archivists call preservation and librarians call conservation. When I discuss physical materials, I use *preservation* as archivists use it, and obviously when I quote other people, I quote them verbatim.

A word about *donors*: in this book I use the term *donor* to refer to your source of collections. Donors come in many guises: grandchildren cleaning out an ancestral home who show up with boxes of "stuff"; small local businesses, about to close their doors, offering you their records; dealers from whom you buy materials. While some provide genuine donations and others expect financial transactions of many sorts, for the sake of simplicity in the language in this book, I lump them all into the category of donor.

A word about *collections*: like archives, in archival circles, *collections* may have several meanings. In this work, it means "a group of papers attributable to a single source." I will use the term *holdings* for the "materials held by a repository."

A word about *records*: while definitions of the concept of a record vary, all include the fundamental concept that a record provides evidence of a transaction between two or more entities, and probably has legal implications. A legally defensible record must be 1) complete in all its final form, content and context, 2) unchanged from its point of final creation, 3) demonstrably related to some preceding transaction, 4) in context, 5) designated as the "official" authority, and 6) unique. Those characteristics make up a record's "recordness."[7] Institutional and governmental archives collect records to document their institution's activities and to defend themselves in case of a legal challenge. Their work focuses on retaining the "recordness" of their holdings.

A word about *documents*: collecting repositories contain a wide variety of documents; some qualify as records, others don't. Except for its own institutional records, a collecting repository has no legal responsibility for the "recordness" of the documents it keeps for research purposes.

A word about *TDR*s: the abbreviation TDR has come to mean a digital repository that you can trust, but what the letters actually stand for varies. Some early users of the concept called it a *trustworthy digital repository*,[8] and others called it a *trusted digital repository*.[9] I've chosen to use the term *trustworthy*; the term implies a status, but does not vouch for it with experience. When I refer to something as *trusted*, I do so because I've had enough experience to test its trustworthiness. As someone new to the world of long-term retention of digital materials, you will be interested in trustworthiness; in time you will talk about trusted technologies and repositories.

A word about the future: the archives education community has begun to address the problem of what the next generation of archivists must know and how to educate them properly. Since 2005, several conferences have met to develop a clear understanding of what a "digital curator" must know to do the job properly. Addressing the attendees of the plenary session at the DigCCurr2007 Conference at the University of North Carolina in 2007,[10] Kenneth Thibodeau, director of the Electronic Records Archives (ERA) Program Management Office at the National Archives and Records Administration (NARA), identified the core problem when he asked: "How do you teach something you don't know? Worse, how do you teach something nobody knows?"[11]

I have two final thoughts to get you started.

First, in the summer of 2007, my husband and I started renovating a nineteenth-century house in northern Vermont. One sunny day, as the crew removed part of the old siding, they found six pages of the Saturday, May 9, 1896, issue of the *Boston Morning Journal*. Brown with age, heavily stained, and fragile, the paper needed tender handling, but it gave up its information as easily as it had the day it hit the streets. Our crew, all devoted young fans of the Boston Red Sox, especially enjoyed the write-up about the shutout the Boston Beaneaters had handed the Louisville Colonels.[12] One of the painters gave us a mini-lesson on the names of baseball teams in Boston, and then everyone went back to work feeling slightly energized by the unexpected discovery and a little awestruck by a newspaper that old. In the quiet of the evening, my husband and I discussed the find: we noted that if we were to download a similar story as a word processor file, put it on a compact disc (CD), and secure it to the side of the house under the new siding, the disk might survive the next century before our new siding comes off, but the information would not.

Second, I once heard Ann Newhall, former head of the National Historic Publications and Records Commission (NHPRC) at NARA, compare the problem of long-term retention of digital materials to leaky plumbing: the longer you ignore it the worse it gets. It won't fix itself.

Notes

1. John Gantz, et al., *The Expanding Digital Universe: A Forecast of Worldwide Information Growth through 2010* (Framingham, Mass.: IDC, 2007), p. 1, www.emc.com/collateral/analyst-reports/expanding-digital-idc-white-paper.pdf (accessed April 12, 2008). There is also a 2008 paper and 2008 summary now available at this URL: www.emc.com/leadership/digital-universe/expanding-digital-universe, www.emc.com/digital_university (accessed June 14, 2008).

2. Tom Hyry and Rachel Onuf, "The Personality of Electronic Records: The Impact of New Information Technology on Personal Papers," *Archival Issues: Journal of the Midwest Archives Conference* 22:1 (1997): 39–41.

3. International Council of Archivists, *Electronic Records: A Workbook for Archivists* (April 2005): 3. www.ica.org/en/node/30273 (accessed June 13, 2008).

4. John McDonald, "Managing Information in an Office Systems Environment: The IMOSA Project," *American Archivist* 58:2 (Spring 1995): 142–53.

5. Ross Harvey, "Cross-Cultural Digital Future Initiatives" (lecture at *Digital Futures: Industry Briefing*, hosted by the National Archives of Australia, November 8, 2006). www.digitalpreservationeurope.eu/trainers/files/Harvey_1197318164.pdf.

6. Liz Bishoff and Tom Clareson, "Digital Preservation Assessment: Readying Cultural Heritage Institutions for Digital Preservation" (paper presented at DigCCurr2007: An International Symposium in Digital Curation at the School of Information and Library Science at the University of North Carolina at Chapel Hill, April 20, 2007). www.ils.unc.edu/digccurr2007/papers/bishoff_paper_8–3.pdf. Accompanying slides available at www.ils.unc.edu/digccurr2007/slides/bishoff_slides_8–3.pdf (accessed July 5, 2008).

7. Ann Pederson, "Basic Concepts and Principles of Archives and Records Management," in *Understanding Society through Its Records*, John Curtin Prime Ministerial Library. john.curtin.edu.au/society/archives/management.html (accessed April 12, 2008).

8. *Trustworthy Repository Audit & Certification (TRAC): Criteria and Checklist*, Version 1.0 (Chicago and Dublin, Ohio: Center for Research Libraries and OCLC, 2007). www.crl.edu/content.asp?l1=13&l2=58&l3=162&l4=91 (accessed April 12, 2008).

9. RLG-NARA, *An Audit Checklist for the Certification of Trusted Digital Repositories* (Mountain View, Calif.: RLG, 2005). This work, originally developed by the Research Libraries Group-National Archives and Records Administration's Digital Repository Certification Task Force, has been revised and expanded. The revised version is entitled *Trustworthy Repositories Audit & Certification: Criteria and Checklist (TRAC)*.

10. DigCCurr2007: An International Symposium on Digital Curation (Chapel Hill, N.C., April 18–20, 2007). http://www.ils.unc.edu/digccurr2007/ (accessed July 5, 2008).

11. Kenneth Thibodeau, "Critical Competencies for Digital Curation: Perspectives from 30 Years in the Trenches and On the Mountain Top" (paper presented at DigCCurr2007: An International Symposium on Digital Curation, in Chapel Hill, N.C., April 18–20, 2007). www.ils.unc.edu/digccurr2007/papers/thibodeau_paper_7.pdf (accessed July 5, 2008).

12. "A Line of Zeros," *Boston Morning Journal*, Saturday, May 9, 1896, p. 4.

Chapter 1

Archival Concepts and Grand Strategies

Archival Concepts and Practices

Traditionally authors begin a work like this with a history of the topic under discussion. In the case of digital materials, the history usually traces the changes in our forms of communication and record keeping from paper-based to a wide variety of magnetic- and electronic-based technologies. While you might find that interesting, as a discrete chapter it does not have a lot of practical value for looking at the issues under consideration here. Rather than create a stand-alone history, I will include lessons from history and explanations based on results of history where it seems useful for your understanding of the concept at hand. For those of you who really want a comprehensive overview of how we got to this state, I'll include references to others' works.[1]

Throughout this book, I will use the phrase *archival function*, a concept the discussion of digital materials has brought to the fore. As I wrote earlier, the International Council of Archivists (ICA) defines the archival function as "that group of related activities contributing to, and necessary for . . . identifying, safeguarding and preserving archival records, and ensuring that such records are accessible and understandable."[2]

The archival profession has developed fundamental perspectives about what each activity entails. For more than a century, archivists and curators have filled periodicals and books with opinions and advice on how to run a modern repository. The Society of American Archivists (SAA) publishes and sells a wide array of books that address the issues in a wide variety of ways.[3] Here I will describe the major functions, though I will not provide a primer to any of them.

Archival Functions

In a collecting repository, the group of related activities involves—usually in this sequence for any given collection—surveying the documents, appraising

1

those with enduring value, acquiring them, arranging and describing them, performing any actions needed to conserve them, and then making them available for public access and use. Though the same function remains, the methods change dramatically when you move from paper to digital materials.

Survey

Survey refers to the process of learning about the materials of a particular donor. Archivists and curators survey materials to determine whether to acquire them or not and what conservation issues they might contain. Before the survey, the archivist or curator looks at the context that gave rise to the materials, and, based on the content and the context, makes a tentative appraisal decision as to whether or not to acquire them.

Traditional Materials

Surveying paper and other tangible documents usually means physically going through an accumulation of materials to get a sense of context, content, and condition.

Digital Materials

No archivist or curator can physically go through an accumulation of digital materials. Surveying digital materials depends on determining the context of the materials' creation and use.

Appraisal

Appraisal refers to the process of deciding what to add—or not add—to a repository's holdings. Deciding what to keep for the historical record raises two distinct questions: 1) do these materials have historical value; 2) if so, do they belong in my repository. An answer of yes to both questions usually means that the curator will want to acquire the materials. A no to the first means nobody will. "Yes" to the first but "no" to the second means that somewhere, another repository should have them. It seems simple enough, but opinions vary widely about how to decide what has historical value.

Traditional Materials

Appraisal theories for traditional materials incorporate a wide variety of factors ranging from philosophical perspectives on the meaning of enduring value to the practicality of surveying large modern business and political collections. Appraisal theory has produced a lot of strongly held and conflicting ideas.[4]

Digital Materials

The introduction of digital materials into the mix has simply intensified those debates. The specter of the certain death of digital documents skews the decision-making time frame and therefore the curator's discretion—especially to say no. In the paper world, the curator can weed out a predecessor's bad decisions and reopen the negotiations about others. In the digital world, you must assume you do not have that luxury. Imagine this: you're new at your job. While looking through the files you inherited, you notice that in the 1980s some local feminists offered your predecessor papers documenting the local feminist movement of the 1960s and 1970s. Your predecessor politely declined the offer. With several decades' hindsight, you recognize the value of those papers, and you decide to reopen the conversation, knowing that unless the women threw the materials away, you can still add them to your holdings.

Now imagine a time shift. The work those feminists did with typewriter and hectograph machines in the 1970s would almost certainly be done with a word processor today. While some paper copies of widely circulated materials would probably survive, the e-mail or word-processed correspondence among the organizers would exist in electronic format only. Consequently, that correspondence has a lifetime limited to the amount of time the file formats, the software that produced them, and the hardware that ran the software remain viable. In the digital world, if your predecessor rejected the offer, thirty years later you would reopen the conversation about a much thinner, less revealing, and less accessible collection of materials.

Acquisition

Acquisition involves transferring legal control and physically moving collections to the repository where they will stay and serve the needs of researchers. Proper acquisition ensures the repository has physical custody and legal ownership.[5]

Traditional Materials

Acquiring traditional materials involves legal paperwork in the form of a deed of gift, administrative paperwork in the form of acquisitions records, and actually moving boxes, file cabinets, and other storage units holding the contents of the collection. The process of packing the materials for moving gives the archivist an opportunity to get better acquainted with the contents of the collection, as does the moving itself.

Digital Materials

Acquiring digital materials involves legal paperwork in the form of a deed of gift and administrative paperwork in the form of acquisitions records as well. Digital materials come to a repository on a variety of storage media, but they will not occupy the amount of physical space traditional materials do, nor will the curator have as clear an understanding of the contents of the collection: she or he can only hold up the devices and wonder what's on them. The packing process reveals the storage media, but not the contents.

Arrangement and Description

Once a repository has ensured that it has legal and physical control of a collection, it will seek intellectual control as well. Intellectual control comes through arrangement and description.

Traditional Materials

After a traditional collection arrives at the repository, someone will physically arrange the contents in an order that makes them most useful to researchers while maintaining, as much as possible, the order and context that reflect their creation and use. Physical arrangement will involve, among other processes, saving original documents and weeding out copies or duplicate material. The arranger will create a finding aid to the collection; it will describe the creators, the circumstances of the documents' creation, uses which the materials served, and their content. This description will first provide an overview of the full collection and its creators and creation. Below this overview, the finding aid will describe the component series, subseries, and filing units. Occasionally description includes specific items, but more likely getting no more specific than the filing unit level.[6] This description will clearly reflect the way documents relate to each other and their creation and use, and how they might relate to other collections. The curator will always keep the collection as a discrete unit, never intermingling it with others that the repository holds.

Digital Materials

After a digital collection arrives at the repository, the need to arrange and describe it raises a lot of complicated issues because many concepts we rely on in the paper world simply cease to have any meaning. We see the organization of digital materials on a storage medium through a series of codes and symbols that make the contents appear to have an organization that humans recognize. On the actual storage medium, however, no such order exists. So, even as we maintain the creator's original directory structure we know that it's all an illusion created by metadata. I'll go into this more deeply in chapter 3.

Rather than arranging the digital materials, the archivist or curator will focus on describing the contents to make them most useful to researchers, including an explanation of the order and context of their creation and use. As with a traditional collection, the arranger will create a finding aid to the collection that describes the creators, the circumstances of the documents' creation, uses which the materials served, and their content. This description will first provide an overview of the full collection and its creators and creation. Beyond that it will become much more detailed than a description of traditional archival materials. As you'll see when you get to discussions of metadata, much of the description of digital materials relates to the technical details of their creation, use, and relationship to other digital objects.

Consider this: when we copy a computer file we create two identical files. Computer files do not degrade down through the generations as photocopies do. If it weren't for the time and date stamp (metadata) the computer attaches to each file, we could not determine which file represents a "copy" of another. Duplicates present slightly different problems. The first has to do with identifying the version of an electronic document that a "duplicate" represents. If you find one of a series of letters written by a traveler detailing the adventures of a trip to New Zealand to a mailing list of family and friends, can you assume that each, like a photocopy, contains exactly what all other copies of the same file in the family collection contain? Unless the time and date stamp on each exactly matches all the others, you shouldn't assume that's the case. Further, files that carry the same file name but appear in different directories may or may not be genuine duplicates. In writing this book, I have a set of chapter-defining file names I work with. As I write, I add a time and date stamp to a header of the file as a way of keeping track of which "version" of a chapter I'm working with. Periodically I copy the entire series of files to another directory named "archives" and then to subdirectories within it to capture versions as the work progresses. A manuscripts curator could easily assume that the "duplicate" files all contain the same text; it would be a very wrong assumption.

Public Access

With good intellectual control established, the curator can open collections to researchers. Opening them includes providing some device through which the researcher can know what a given collection contains—the finding aid. Curators know that allowing researchers access to unique original documents puts them at risk of alteration, and typically have reading room policies to protect them.

Traditional Materials

Access to traditional materials nearly always comes through the use of a traditional finding aid and/or a conversation with a staff member. Protecting traditional materials means protecting the physical object from harm: theft and wear. Policies to address the problems start with providing secure storage and a well-supervised reading room. Protecting specific materials involves policies that range from limiting access to a small number of items at one time to providing photocopied or scanned copies of vulnerable materials.

Digital Materials

Access to digital materials may involve a traditional finding aid, but it might also include a search engine that will locate the desired materials. While a user can't tear or dirty a digital object, a user might alter or delete a digital object if the system does not guard against it. Since the data live on a computer system, rarely will the researcher actually work with the "originals."[7] The standard in the field recommends that repositories make copies of digital materials available to researchers, keeping the originals safely stored away.

Preservation and Long-Term Retention

While making the materials available to the public, the archivist or curator will do so in a way that gives maximum priority to the safety and integrity of the materials as the public handles them.

Traditional Materials

While the soundness of the archival repository as a physical unit and the atmospheric conditions and management practices maintained within it work together to provide most of the preservation its holdings need, occasionally the curator will notice some portion of one or more collections that need conservation of some sort—cleaning, mending, additional protection, etc.—and have those needs looked into and taken care of.

Digital Materials

The trustworthiness of the digital repository provides the protection that digital materials need. Establishing a trustworthy repository presents challenges far more subtle and difficult than those presented in the preservation and conservation of traditional materials, and I devote substantial space to it in chapter 2.[8]

That about sums it up: the archival function calls for appraisal based on circumstances of creation and content, honoring the provenance of each collection, maintaining, as much as possible, the original order of the materials, describing them so researchers can understand what each collection holds, providing an environment in which researchers can use the materials, but will not alter or damage them in any way, and conserving materials when necessary and continuing to make them usable. The rest is details. Details matter, but they all merely support the larger archival principles for performing the archival function.

As I've tried to show above, those basic archival functions do not change with the format of the materials in hand. However, the way the archivist or curator understands and executes them has to change in response to the format of the materials. Theorizing and research into how to perform archival functions on digital materials has gone on for more than two decades with few fully developed answers yet. That doesn't mean we don't know anything. We do have some answers on some issues, and we obviously know more about all aspects of the challenge they pose than we did twenty years ago. But, we still have a lot of fundamental issues to sort through.

When Does Something Become "Historical"?

When do documents reach the stage in which they belong in a historical repository? Until recently archivists thought in terms of the life cycle of records. The metaphor divided the life of a record into three stages. A record was created and functioned as an *active record*. As such, its user kept it near until its function ceased to have immediacy. At that point the record became an *inactive record*. In that phase, it had some potential use, which is to say, functional value, but its creators didn't expect to need it enough to provide it prime real estate in their files; frequently they moved it to a records storage center somewhere. In its third phase, the record became dispensable. If it had archival value, it moved to an archives; there it belongs to history. If it had no archival value, it became trash.

From the life-cycle theory came the concept of *life-cycle management*, an abstraction that had real meaning only in large institutional settings. There it referred to the need for records managers to work with records creators as they develop records retention schedules so that only materials of truly lasting value arrived in the institutional archives. The life-cycle management perspective served to keep the archives from becoming a dumping ground and to shift initial appraisal to records managers and records-creating departments working with the archivist.

Manuscript curators typically did not think in terms of life-cycle management. They tended to appraise materials when someone walked through the door with a collection to donate or sell. Similarly, they pored over catalogs and websites looking for documents or collections to acquire. In both cases, the creator had emotionally let go of the documents before the curator noticed them. If manuscript curators applied the concept of life-cycle management at all, they did so when they approached a significant donor and arranged to receive materials during the donor's years of active creation.

When all documents came on paper, we could work from the assumption that the archivist's or curator's job really started when documents had ceased to have active value and had come to the point of disposition—either to a recycle center or to a historical repository. Regardless of repository affiliation, nobody worried that the records would self-destruct or become obsolete before they had reached an age to enter a historical repository.

The fragility or impermanence of digital documents has changed much of that. The records continuum model from Australia[9] focuses on the need for an evolving system for managing electronic records throughout their existence, and it has called into question the "stages" defined by the life-cycle theory. The creators of the continuum model argue that some records have archival value from the moment of their inception and that archivists should somehow participate in the management of the whole extent of a record's existence. That position, which has growing acceptance in the profession, implies that archivists should identify digital materials of archival value and assert some authority over them at creation, or before.[10] I'll go into this much more in chapter 7 when I discuss the archivist's relationship with donors.

What Do We Call Them?

Throughout the literature, one runs into two terms: *digital document* and *electronic record*. A digital document can be any complete intellectual statement that exists as a series of electronic impulses—a digital photograph, a blog entry, a text document, a spreadsheet, an e-mail message—anything created or existing digitally is a digital document. While most digital documents are not electronic records, all electronic records consist of one or more digital documents.

That brings us to the definition of a *record*. When all records were paper-based, we didn't ask what a record was. However, having to explain to computer systems designers and other information technology (IT) people the archival perspective on records forced archivists to think beyond the paper document. IT people don't think about records: they think about data. They use the term *record*, but apply a meaning very different from records managers, archivists, or curators. In order for them to develop systems that will produce and preserve records—as archivists think of records—we had to find a way to explain the concept. So, if its physical format didn't make a document a record, what did? What's a record?

Definitions vary, but all include the fundamental concept that a record provides evidence of a transaction involving two or more entities. On paper, most of a record's "recordness" exists on one physical document—date of creation, content, signatures, etc. But in a computer, a "record" has no physical reality. Its various parts exist as logically related bits of data scattered all over the storage medium (literally). Computers put data anywhere they find room, but use an index called a file allocation table to keep track of which bits relate to each other. So, in that environment, archivists and curators have had to define what the computer system must produce and track to retain a valid legal record; in other words, define the functional requirements we need in a records creation and management system to ensure it creates and retains legally valid records, not just retrievable data and files.

Clearly not every digital document qualifies as a record—that is, evidence of a transaction between two or more entities. Just as clearly, curators in a collecting repository will have to deal with digital material, whether it fits the definition of a record or not. Well, what shall we call them?[11] In this book, I will borrow a term used by Maggie Jones and Neil Beagrie in their *Preservation Management of Digital Materials*, and use *digital materials* to refer to digital objects created by digitizing another format, such as a photograph, and *born digital materials* that refers to digital objects that do not, and may never have, another format, such as an e-mail message and electronic records.[12]

Archives and Collecting Repositories: Their Differing Perspectives

Institutional archivists and curators in collecting repositories can have two different attitudes about digital materials. Here's why: an institutional archivist exists as part of the team of legal custodians of the records, and his or her shop may at some time have the legal duty to produce archived electronic records in response to some legal action. That's not the situation the curator of someone else's collection will face. Collecting repositories, and their curators, deal in information, not records. While they hold a lot of records, they do not have the legal responsibility for the documents' recordness that institutional archivists have. Courts have ruled that electronic records must remain in their original (electronic) form to serve as legal evidence.[13] An electronic document has a great deal of metadata surrounding it that does not print out, and proof of authenticity of the document lies in the metadata. Therefore, institutional archives have a legal obligation to preserve e-mail, for example, in its original form. However, unless you serve as the official archives for the creators of your holdings, you do not have the legal obligation to preserve legally valid evidence. The curator's responsibility does not extend beyond the terms of the deed of gift.

In another area, however, I see no difference between the institutional archivist and the curator of a collecting repository: they must both involve themselves with digital materials early on. Everyone who has given more than about two minutes thought to the long-term retention of digital materials agrees that archivists and curators must get involved at the records-creating level. That is not an issue of debate.

When all records came in paper, we assumed that the manuscript curator's job really started when records were ready for disposal—either to a recycle center or to the archives. In the world of digital materials, we have come to see that to fulfill the archival function, we *must* become involved with the manner in which our institutions or donors create records, lest there be nothing for us to collect and retain. Unless manuscript curators get involved with the way creators create and manage their materials, the materials may not exist when they've reached the archival stage in their lives.[14] This is also true for the organizational and business collections we take in. The records management world has developed a sense of urgency about managing electronic records during their active life, but archivists and manuscripts curators care about management and retention over the long term. That concern has made donor relations extremely important in the digital world. I go into those issues in chapter 7.

How Do We Start Addressing the Problem? Steps and Strategies

You already have. By picking up this book, you have acknowledged the issue and begun to think about your response to it. Good for you; you've just put yourself ahead of the curve. A 2007 study of 126 collecting repositories in academic institutions, historical societies, and some public libraries in forty-three states and Washington, D.C., shows that while almost half (44 percent) saw digital materials as a very important issue for the profession, fewer saw it as a significant issue in their repository. Less than half accept digital materials into their repositories, about a fifth know they plan to accept them "someday," and the rest haven't decided. If they accept digital materials, only about a fifth have policies on the subject in place.[15]

McLeod and Hare refer to taking on digital materials as "playing the long game."[16] They point out that a long game requires someone to establish a vision, raise awareness, establish benchmarks for accountability, design an architecture that includes both human and technical capacity, and start building the capacity to do the work. The long game requires you to develop a strategy and make it work within your own context. It's a huge undertaking, and you will measure success as an accumulation of small victories.

In this section I present steps you will need to go through to bring your archival concerns about digital materials to your repository's attention and to set up a program that can actually function within all the constraints you must accommodate. I've drawn my suggestions from a wide variety of sources. While I will present a very broad outline, I will point you to resources and strategies to help you fill in the many layers below what I have to say here.

Step one, create two "motivational" signs for yourself, one from the *Pirke Avot* ("It is not up to you to complete the work, nor are you free to desist from it"[17]), and another from the 1987 movie *The Princess Bride* ("Listen, sonny, you rush a miracle man, you get rotten miracles"[18]). Put them somewhere handy so you can read them as circumstances warrant.

It will serve you well to start thinking about change, how people react to it, and how to manage it. In a session introducing the National Archives and Records Administration's (NARA) Electronic Records Archives (ERA) initiative at the 2006 SAA annual meeting in Washington, D.C., Fynnette Eaton from NARA presented a paper on managing change.[19] She made the point that people typically resist the psychological shift that change requires more strongly than they resist the actual change itself. She presented expert opinion to the effect that the transition period can cause a sense of loss of identity and place in a known world; people feel disoriented as they move from a known to a not-yet-known existence. The disorientation compounds their anxiety about failing in the new order of things. Eaton did not deny the disruption to workflow that change can cause. She simply indicated that the savvy curator, before she or he starts advocating for serious change, will become familiar with humans' resistance to change and the disruption it can cause in an organization. The business world has an extensive literature on the topic; don't expect yourself to become expert on it, but don't ignore it either. Change management falls outside the scope of this book, but I'll include a couple good websites to get you started. The "Resistance to Change" website provides a clear and easily readable introduction to the topic.[20] The U.S. Department of Transportation's Federal Transit Administration also has a good place to begin.[21] I've included additional resources in the list of resources in the back of this book.

Terry Cook, formerly of the National Archives of Canada and now at the University of Manitoba, observes that unless you get substantial new financial and human resources, you will need to stop doing important work you are now doing, and reallocate significant resources to digital documents, period. There is no other way. Stopping what you're now doing and reallocating your time and resources requires "an act of personal will and professional commitment, not technological infrastructure or digital expertise. The will to change must come first, and it will be your hardest decision."[22] According to the signs you've just made, you don't really have a decision. You must address this issue, and you must address it deliberately.

Question your priorities. Next week, figure out when to work on this. Reprioritize your work in light of your repository's and researchers' needs. It may be, as Cook suggests, you will stop doing something important to free up the time you need. Nevertheless, if you're going to start a program, you must start the work. The McLeod and Hare book on my list of essential tools has case studies. Read them and learn how others have done it. Read also Priscilla Caplan[23] and Liz Bishoff and Tom Clareson,[24] but don't get bogged down in details, and don't get discouraged. Don't be surprised that setting up some of the systems took five years from start to fully functioning; Cook suggests ten years. You're making miracles: don't rush.

Step two, look for the best partners you can find. At the 2007 meeting of the Best Practices Exchange, an opening-session exercise broke the 120 people in attendance into groups and asked each group to create a motto for people working with digital materials. Two mottos stand out from that exercise. One read, "Collaboration, Collaboration, Collaboration." It's true. Most of the successful research projects have involved collaborations of large organizations that shared common problems and common interests in solving them, but did not come from the same discipline. The differences they brought to the collaboration broadened their ability to address the problem they sought to solve. I will mention them throughout the book, in the context of the problem they sought to gain some understanding of.

Another motto read, "Go to conferences: Network," which is also true. Since attending all the professional conferences you might like can become very expensive, consider attending them after they are over. Most professional organizations now publish their programs on the Web. If you become aware of a conference that looks like it might have something to offer, search the Web for presenters and topics after the conference has ended. Undoubtedly you'll find at least some of the materials made publically available. Most conferences, and more presenters, make their papers and presentations available on the Internet or through recordings. SAA has its sessions recorded, although not section and roundtable meetings. For less than $200, you can purchase the entire set of recordings to listen to at your leisure.[25] In addition, wikis related to each meeting contain papers and PowerPoint presentations from the sessions.

You have a long learning curve ahead of you, and Richard Pearce-Moses offers very sound and practical advice:

> Assess your own level of readiness, your own comfort with working with digital materials. If you don't have a good understanding of the general issues of electronic records, read the literature. Don't limit yourself to archival literature; a lot of important work is being done in other fields. Ask your friends to recommend articles, especially if you're just starting out. [See note 26] Start a reading group so you don't work in isolation. . . . Continuing education is no longer a luxury we indulge in once in a while; it's a necessity. . . . Take a workshop or . . . an introductory computer course at a community college.[27]

You need a variety of partners, and the further you go in the process, the more partners you'll need. Partners bring with them a broader base of support than you can muster alone. They also bring a wide variety of skills, perspectives, and contacts. Getting your goals met requires knowing how to work with people: how to create a vision of what you want, how to communicate what's needed—and why—in a way that decision makers buy into it, how to negotiate so that everyone feels like a winner, and how to work the politics of a situation—the timing, the power flow, the agendas, and the personalities. Your partners will fall into three large groups: professional, political, and technical.

While you start learning all you can about archiving digital materials, you will want someone in your professional network with whom to bat ideas around, share resources, and swap war stories. Look for people in similar repositories or locations and investigate the notion of informal partnerships, reading groups, or support groups to help each other's learning curve and political acumen. These will become the friends Pearce-Moses refers to above. Phil Bantin, archivist at Indiana University, recommends that you look for partners in positions that share your mission.[28]

Throughout the process of developing a way to archive digital materials you need to get your concerns addressed by people who have the political power to change the things that need changing: decision makers and funds allocators. To reach them, you may need to create political alliances both within and outside the work environment. Inside the workplace, start with an alliance with another office in your institution that has the same concerns you have. Look at the mission statements of offices responsible for accountability and risk management of various sorts. Bantin has worked to create a partnership with the department in charge of internal audits by recognizing that his need for good electronic record keeping matched their need for accountability. Approach your potential partners willing to learn their languages and willing to teach them yours. They may not realize how much your two areas have in common, so be prepared to explain that. Outside the workplace, you may need to educate one or more members of the board of directors who will support your concerns in high places. Approach your institution's legal advisor with issues you know put the institution at risk. Granted, political alliances take time and tact to develop, but without them, you will hoe a very tough row, indeed.

Ultimately you must work closely with technical staff. Archiving most digital materials means storing them in a digital repository of some fashion. Unless *you* manage the technology in your institution, you will need to work with an IT department somewhere. The IT department may work in your institution or it may work at a repository you've hired to hold your materials. While I don't address your actual interaction with IT folks at length in any one place in this book, it's clear that IT staff of some sort will play a role at almost every turn. Your interaction with them will depend on a wide variety of human and technical variables.

Like most of the skills and perspectives under discussion here, you can find conference papers, seminars, workshops, full courses, and published materials in some abundance that will sort this out for you. In the past few years, e-records "camps" and workshops have begun to appear. Camps and workshops provide the participants with opportunities to interact with instructors and fellow students in ways they can't interact with written materials. They cost more (fees typically hover around $250 for registration, plus travel and subsistence costs), but in many ways they're more efficient. On the other hand, you can't go back and refer to a camp experience, except through memory and notes, the way you can refer to a written document. You will want to replace or supplement a conference or camp experience with published (electronic or hard copy) guides.

Jones and Beagrie[29] address the issue of partnering most directly. Section 3.1 of their manual on preservation management discusses different approaches. They first review the pros and cons of internal collaboration, noting its benefit for building teamwork within the institution. They also acknowledge the frustration that can arise from turf guarding and other negative internal dynamics.

When Jones and Beagrie write about external collaboration, they focus on the pros and cons of formal agreements and informal agreements with outside parties. Depending on the size of your institution, you should probably consider the points about formal and informal agreements when you're looking at internal collaboration as well. Jones and Beagrie discuss at length the need for outreach to your two stakeholders——management and your donors.

Further, Jones and Beagrie take an organized look at the issues that might lead you to consider hiring third-party services, including a table that addresses pros and cons of outsourcing in five different circumstances: 1) where you have limited practical experience in preserving digital materials, 2) where having access to the stored materials is important, 3) where rights management issues are particularly complicated, 4) where security has a high priority, and 5) where loss and distortion of data are a major concern. The bibliography Jones and Beagrie put together provides you a rich portal to larger, more focused, resources on all the topics they cover.

As soon as you begin to think in terms of partners or collaborations, you'll find them everywhere. A browse through the resource guides at the back of this book will reveal a wide variety of partnerships and collaborations for you to use as models. A very nice little paper delivered at DigCCurr2007 by Kathleen Murray and Mark Phillips called "Collaborations, Best Practices, and Collection Development for Born-Digital and Digitized Materials" includes sections on key lessons learned. Among others, they point out that "the downstream implications of requirements stated in memorandums of understanding with resource providers can be hard to anticipate and modifications are sometimes necessary." Also, "clear communications and expectations among many collaborators are critical." Those are not really new thoughts, but it's good to see how they apply to a digital repository initiative.[30]

Step three, start reading the publications created by the Paradigm Project of the academic research libraries at the Universities of Oxford and Manchester.[31] Between January 2005 and February 2007, the project explored the long-term retention of private digital "papers." As a test case, the project worked with a young British politician to explore the issues involved with archiving private papers. As part of the project, the participants have written a very good workbook on collecting private papers. Most other workbooks, including the ICA's, address electronic records as an institutional archivist. The Paradigm Project looks at private papers. While you will learn much of a general nature from the electronic records literature, the Paradigm Project will focus your attention on the specifics of establishing an electronic repository for private papers.

Step four, develop or refine your policies to ensure the long-term retention of digital materials. After you have established policies, you will need to translate them and instructions on digital-document management and retention to your donors. Cornell University Library started with a "Digital Preservation Policy Framework" in which they laid out their mandate as a library, followed by their objectives in terms of fulfilling that mandate, stated their priorities of concern for various digital materials, and then established their operating principles. It's very nicely done, and it could save you a lot of time.[32] For more detail, go to chapter 3 of Charles M. Dollar's book, *Authentic Electronic Records: Strategies for Long-Term Access*. Dollar gets very precise about what policies you should have and what they should contain.[33] Furthermore, the Paradigm Project addresses the issue of policies and practices very specifically.

Step five, beef up your records management (RM) knowledge. When repositories took in nothing but paper- or film-based documents, what the creator did with them concerned us, but rarely did we think it appropriate to assert any sort of management role in the life of those documents. Today we know that if we want digital materials to survive, we will probably have to work with their creators. That means that we're entering into conversations with known donors about still active digital materials—and that's the realm of RM. You don't need to become an expert, but you will benefit by understanding the fundamental concepts and vocabulary. Shepherd and Yeo's book in the list of essential tools provides an excellent introduction to RM, as do David O. Stephens's books. Further, membership in ARMA International gets you access to a lot of documents and tutorials you can't get otherwise.

Step six, find out what's going on in electronic records research. The ICA asserts that archivists must have the knowledge and skills to apply archival principles to digital materials, which means knowing how to do what we do with paper records when we're working with digital materials.[34] While we have some answers, we need many more. We now have some short-term strategies, but long-term solutions still exist largely as theoretical models; that's what all the research is about, and you need to pay attention as groups work through the problems. That does not mean that when something that started as a research project grows into a mature protocol you must embrace it completely. Choose from it what you can incorporate into your situation and don't feel guilty about what you can't. Anything you do with the research findings will produce better results than doing nothing or inventing a system completely on your own. Start with chapters 3 and 4 of this book, and follow the leads in them.

Step seven, learn the language used by the IT departments and the conceptual tools they employ. The ICA points out that we must know the language and concepts of the people we approach in the IT department if we want to come across as credible in our conversations with them. You don't have to know how to build the system, but you must know how to talk and understand the language of the builders who do. If we don't have an IT department to work with, we still need to know the language so we can read the literature, or work with a consultant or contractor.

Gregory S. Hunter, who has consulted and written widely on electronic records, reminds us that "we will not have the cutting-edge information technology available in other organizations or elsewhere in our own organization."[35] Some of the most creative work you will do will involve developing workarounds for problems you just can't address with the right tools. Networking with the IT folks may help you tap into other people's workarounds as well. Here's another topic on which "camps"and workshops have begun to appear. I've listed them as part of the resources at the back of the book. The same advantages and disadvantages apply here. The same "workaround" strategies can apply as well. Conferences that focus on real-world implementation projects have begun to appear. Whereas the first wave of implementation came from the private sector, academic and digital library interests have begun to develop test projects and post online everything they learn. Watch for them and take advantage of what they offer in the way of tools, strategies, insights, and cautions.[36]

Step eight, become familiar with some functional requirement models that exist for digital repositories. Learn the language. Learn to think in terms of digital materials' authenticity, reliability, integrity, and usability and accessibility from storage with current software and hardware capabilities; develop an image of the functions and processes that produce them and will retain them for the long term. Be patient with yourself. Buddy up with a colleague and work on this together. The Paradigm Project,[37] which I refer to throughout this book, provides good guidance, as do other projects I refer to in the text and in the lists of resources at the back. Conference papers, seminars, workshops, and published materials will sort this out for you. Look through the resources at the back of the book and follow those leads. This topic really requires that you try it out so you can really get a sense of how it works.

Step nine, get familiar with emerging metadata schemes and standards. In McLeod and Hare's anthology (2005), Hans Hofman argues that standards set a recognized level of quality, improve efficiency (thus reducing costs), offer a framework for implementation, accountability, and certification, and provide stability and authority for decisions—a certain amount of political cover.[38] As a practical matter, anything you can do according to a standard is something you don't have to invent for yourself. Further, using the standards the metadata world has to offer will allow you to standardize your own protocols to conform to the larger environment. Seminars, workshops, courses, and published materials will get you started, and I've included reference to several in the resources section and scattered throughout this book. Practice will teach you the most, however.

Notes

1. For an overview of the changes electronic devices have made in our way of conducting business and our daily lives, see Phil Bantin's "Electronic Records Management—A Review of the Work of a Decade and a Reflection on Future Directions," *Encyclopedia of Library and Information Science* 71, suppl. 34 (2002): 47–81, www.libraries.iub.edu/index.php?pageId=3313, and any of David O. Stephens's books, especially *Records Management: Making the Transition from Paper to Electronic* (Lenexa, Kan.: ARMA International, 2007). For an overview of the research into archival management of electronic records and digital objects, see the first section of David Bearman's "Moments of Risk: Identifying Threats to Electronic Records," *Archivaria* 62 (Fall 2006): 15–24.

2. ICA Committee on Electronic Records, "Guidelines for Managing Electronic Records from an Archival Perspective," *ICA Study* 8 (February 1997): 24, www.ica.org/en/node/30019 (accessed July 6, 2008).

3. The SAA Publications and Products catalog is available online: www.archivists.org/catalog/index.asp.

4. Helen Willa Samuels, "Who Controls the Past," 193–210; Frank Boles and Julia Marks Young, "Exploring the Black Box: The Appraisal of University Administrative Records," 279–300; Timothy L. Ericson, "At the 'Rim of Creative Dissatisfaction': Archivists and Acquisition Development," 177–92; Mark Greene, "'The Surest Proof': A Utilitarian Approach to Appraisal," 301–44, all in *American Archival Studies: Readings in Theory and Practice*, ed. Randall C. Jimerson (Chicago: The Society of American Archivists, 2000).

5. Typically archives negotiate to get the copyrights for materials that still fall under copyright protection. The creator or creator's estate might hold them for themselves for a variety of reasons, including royalties that might accrue, or the power to control reproduction of the materials.

6. A single archival folder may hold a group of documents that have such a strong relationship with each other that we think of them as a single unit—all the letters from a soldier at war, for instance—and we call that single folder a filing unit. If the soldier wrote more letters than we should put in a single folder, we would house them in several folders. Regardless, those letters from that soldier still constitute a single filing unit: "Letters Home, 1972."

7. For reasons I'll discuss later, the concept of "original" has little meaning in the digital world.

8. Phil Bantin presents a fuller and more sophisticated analysis of archival theory on the issues of acquisition, appraisal, description, and life-cycle management of digital materials in "Strategies for Managing Electronic Records: A New Archival Paradigm? An Affirmation of Our Archival Traditions?" *Archival Issues* 23, no. 1 (1998): 17–34, www.libraries.iub.edu/index.php?pageId=3313 (accessed April 12, 2008).

9. Ann Pederson, "Australian Contributions to Recordkeeping," *Understanding Society through Its Records*, John Curtin Prime Ministerial Library, 2004, john.curtin.edu.au/society/australia/index.html (accessed July 6, 2008).

10. Mike Marsh, et al., "The Nexus and Praxis of Records Management and Archives: Is There a Difference?" (lecture at Internationaler Archivkongress: Archive, Gedächtnis und Wissen, in Vienna, Austria, August 23–29, 2004), www.wien2004.ica.org/imagesUpload

/pres_186_MYBURGH_B-ARMA01.pdf (accessed April 12, 2008).

11. The SAA's *Glossary of Archival and Records Terminology* does an outstanding job of parsing out many aspects of the digital world that archivists or curators must deal with, but does not provide an umbrella term for digital materials as a general category. Richard Pearce-Moses, *A Glossary of Archival and Records Terminology* (Chicago: The Society of American Archivists, 2005), www.archivists.org/glossary/index.asp (accessed July 21, 2008).

12. Maggie Jones and Neil Beagrie, *Preservation Management of Digital Materials: A Handbook* (London: British Library, 2001), 10, www.dpconline.org/graphics/handbook/reviews.html (accessed July 21, 2008).

13. *Armstrong v. Executive Office of the President*. See Gregory S. Hunter, *Preserving Digital Information: A How-To-Do-It Manual*, How-To-Do-It Manuals for Librarians, no. 93 (New York: Neal-Schuman Publishers, Inc., 2000), 80–81.

14. Greg O'Shea and David Roberts, "Living in a Digital World: Recognising the Electronic and Post-custodial Realities," *Archives and Manuscripts* 24, no. 2 (November 1996): 294.

15. Susan E. Davis, "Electronic Records Planning in 'Collecting' Repositories," *American Archivist* 71, no. 1 (Spring/Summer 2008): 167–89.

16. Julie McLeod and Catherine Hare, *How to Manage Records in the e-Environment*, 2nd ed. (London: Routledge, 2006): 186.

17. *Pirke Avot, the Sayings of the Jewish Fathers*, II:21.

18. Billy Crystal as "Miracle Max" in *The Princess Bride*, DVD, directed by Rob Reiner (1987; Santa Monica, Calif.: MGM Home Entertainment, 2001), and based on the book by William Goldman, *The Princess Bride: S. Morgenstern's Classic Tale of True Love and High Adventure: The "Good Parts" Version, Abridged* (New York: Harcourt Brace Jovanovich, 1973), www.imdb.com/title/tt0093779/ (accessed April 12, 2008).

19. Fynnette Eaton, "Managing Change in an Ever-Changing Electronic Environment" (presentation at the SAA Annual Meeting, Washington, D.C., August 5, 2006), www.archives.gov/era/pdf/2006-saa-eaton.pdf (accessed April 12, 2008).

20. *Changing*Minds.org, "Resistence to Change," changingminds.org/disciplines/change_management/resistance_change/resistance_change.htm (accessed June 16, 2008).

21. University of Wisconsin-Milwaukee, "Resistance to Change," Center for Urban Transportation Studies, University of Wisconsin-Milwaukee, www.uwm.edu/Dept/CUTS/bench/change.htm (accessed June 16, 2008).

22. Terry Cook, "Byte-ing off What You Can Chew: Electronic Records Strategies for Small Archival Institutions" (presentation at Archives and Records Association of New Zealand, ARANZ 2003, *Past Prospects: Future Reference* conference, September 4–6, 2003, Otago Museum, Dunedin, NZ), www.aranz.org.nz/Site/publications/papers_online/terry_cook_paper.aspx (accessed July 6, 2008).

23. Priscilla Caplan, "How to Build Your Own Dark Archive (In Your Spare Time): A Talk for the Cornell Digital Preservation Management Workshop" (lecture given at the Cornell Digital Preservation Management Workshop, Cornell University Library, November 2004), www.fcla.edu/digitalArchive/pdfs/Howtobuildyourowndarkarchive.pdf (accessed June 16, 2008).

24. Liz Bishoff and Tom Clareson, "Digital Preservation Assessment: Readying Cultural Heritage Institutions for Digital Preservation" (paper presented at DigCCurr2007:

An International Symposium in Digital Curation at the School of Information and Library Science at the University of North Carolina at Chapel Hill, April 20, 2007), www.ils.unc. edu/digccurr2007/papers/bishoff_paper_8-3.pdf (accessed June 16, 2008). Accompanying slides available at www.ils.unc.edu/digccurr2007/slides/bishoff_slides_8-3.pdf.

25. Convention Recordings International, Inc., 6983 Sunset Drive South, St. Petersburg, FL 33707, www.conventionrecordings.com (accessed April 14, 2008).

26. Check the bibliographies in the back of the books, especially the beginner bibliography in this book.

27. Richard Pearce-Moses, "The Winds of Change: Blown to Bits" (address presented at the closing plenary of the Society of American Archivists' 69th annual meeting, New Orleans, 19 August 2005), www.archivists.org/governance/presidential/rpm2005.pdf (accessed April 15, 2008).

28. Philip Bantin, Rosemary Pleva Flynn, Terry Radke, and Stacie Wiegand, "Protecting Organizational Information: Developing Partnerships for Managing University Information Systems" (presentation at EDUCAUSE 2001, Indianapolis, Indiana, October 28–31, 2001), net.educause.edu/ir/library/pdf/EDU01115.pdf (accessed April 15, 2008).

29. Jones and Beagrie, *Preservation Management of Digital Materials*, Section 3.1: Collaboration, www.dpconline.org/graphics/inststrat/collaboration.html (accessed April 15, 2008).

30. Kathleen Murray and Mark Phillips, "Collaborations, Best Practices, and Collection Development for Born-Digital and Digitized Materials" (presented at DigCCurr2007: An International Symposium in Digital Curation at the School of Information and Library Science at the University of North Carolina at Chapel Hill, April 20, 2007), www.ils.unc. edu/digccurr2007/papers/murrayPhillips_paper_9-3.pdf. Accompanying slides at www.ils. unc.edu/digccurr2007/slides/murrayPhillips_slides_9-3.pdf (accessed July 21, 2008).

31. Paradigm Project, *Workbook on Digital Private Papers*, www.paradigm.ac.uk/ workbook/ (accessed July 21, 2008).

32. Cornell University, *Cornell University Library Digital Preservation Policy Framework*, December 2004, commondepository.library.cornell.edu/cul-dp-framework. pdf (accessed June 16, 2008).

33. Charles M. Dollar, *Authentic Electronic Records: Strategies for Long-Term Access* (Chicago: Cohasset Associates, 2002), 91–116.

34. ICA Committee on Current Records in an Electronic Environment, *Electronic Records: A Workbook for Archivists*, ICA Study 16 (Paris: ICA, April 2005), www.ica.org/en/node/30273 (accessed April 15, 2008).

35. Hunter, *Preserving Digital Information,* 114.

36. National Digital Information Infrastructure and Preservation Program (NDIIPP), www.digitalpreservation.gov/; Collaborative Electronic Records Project, siarchives.si.edu/ cerp/index.htm (accessed April 15, 2008).

37. Paradigm Project, *Workbook on Digital Private Papers*, www.paradigm.ac.uk/ workbook/oais (accessed July 6, 2008).

38. Hans Hofman, "The Use of Standards and Models," in *Managing Electronic Records*, ed. Julie McLeod and Catherine Hare (London: Facet, 2005), 18–33; Marcia Lei Zeng, "Metadata for Digital Collections" (lecture notes for Metadata for Digital Collections Workshop, School of Library and Information Science, Kent State University), www.slis.kent.edu/~mzeng/metadata/lecturenote.htm (accessed June 16, 2008).

Chapter 2

What's the Problem with
Digital Materials?

To understand the issues that digital materials raise, you must understand their essential nature. All digital data, regardless of origins, share the same basic structure that we speak of as a series of binary digits, or bits, and are represented as a series of 1s and 0s. The bit actually represents an electrical state of on or off. If we represent a bit as a 0, we mean the electrical impulse doesn't exist—it's off. If we represent a bit as a 1, we mean the electrical impulse exists—it's on. Any document or image on our screens and any sound from our speakers occurs because several layers of hardware and software have made sense of a series of electrical impulses presented in a coded format. In other words, digital documents aren't real documents. Clifford Lynch explains it best:

> Bits are not directly apprehended by the human sensory apparatus—they are never truly artifacts. Instead, they are rendered, executed, performed, and presented to people by hardware and software systems that interpret them.[1]

Digital materials depend on the technologies that create them. Technology changes, and electronic technology changes rapidly. It has to, because it's based on market forces that, generally speaking, run exactly counter to archival needs. Change will continue, and we must learn to change to keep up. That's the first problem.

Other problems come from the perils of the world around us: unstable media filled with inherent vice, improper storage environments, infrastructure failure (e.g., failed plumbing, failed HVAC systems, failed roofs, etc.), overuse, inadequate hardware maintenance leading to hardware malfunctions—and just the perversity of inanimate objects. Natural disasters (flood, earthquake, fire, hurricane), human error, and the perversity of human nature that leads to vandalism in the form of data corruption, theft, and destruction also play a part. All these threaten digital materials just as they threaten traditional collections, but digital materials lack the inherent strength of most traditional historical materials and cannot defend themselves effectively.

To retain digital materials over long periods of time, you must face five issues.

Preserving the Hardware: Think about the most recent upgrade of your computer(s) or sound system(s). Could you use your old data storage devices (vinyl, film, tape, disks) on the new system? Maybe, for a while, as the manufacturers of the new equipment go out of their way to accommodate the old media. But eventually they stop and a generation or two away from the creation of your old data devices, you have no way to play them. So, unless you can maintain the old hardware, you cannot access the old storage devices. As we all know, old equipment breaks down and wears out. Who will repair it? Where will you get a replacement?

Preserving the Software: You know how this works: the new version of an old beloved piece of software turns out to be completely rewritten and uses a new file format. The new program cannot read your old files made by a program with the same name. Or, a better product comes along and yours disappears. Or, the one you choose never gains viable market share and dies. Or a competitor buys it and "retires" it, leaving you with old data files written in a format that nothing can read.

Preserving the Storage Medium: Let's say you can play your old data storage devices on your new system. How long will the devices last? Eventually they will wear out in one way or another. We clean the heads of our VCRs because they pick up dirt and magnetized iron filings from the tapes that go through them. Those iron filings carry the information on the tape, and playing the tape wears them out more or less the same way that phonograph needles wear out the vinyl disks they play. What's the life expectancy of a floppy disk, regardless of size? A CD? A Zip disk or flash drive? Is it a decade? A century? A millennium? Forever?

Preserving the Skills: Even if you have a system that can read your Harvard Graphics, VisiCalc, and Javelin files,[2] do you have someone who can use the programs and make sense of the data? Could you afford to have that person do the work of the patron who can't?

Preserving the Information: It comes down to this: while most of us cannot establish a collection of functioning old equipment, old programs, and old users, we must preserve the information. Combine the factors described above and you see obsolescence made possible many different ways: *it takes only one broken strand in the web of hardware, software, data, and user knowledge needed to retain digital materials for them to be lost forever.* That makes the window through which we can reach out and save them very small—only a few years at most. Even as you read this, chances are you have digital materials in your holdings that neither you nor a researcher can read. That's why this issue has such urgency. If we don't identify digital materials of enduring value almost at the point of creation and appraise them as having enduring value then, we may never see them in our repositories. It's that critical.

The Emergence of Digital Information

The emergence of digital information—information transmitted as a series of electrical impulses and stored as a string of code—actually began long before the computer appeared. While the telegraph used Morse code to convey text in an electronic form beginning about 1840, it relied on the duration of the electrical signal as the code rather than a combination of on/off electrical states. The first real encoding of text into an electronically produced but human-readable form occurred in 1874 when Emile Baudot created a 5-bit code for each letter of the alphabet with each bit having two possible states—on or off. While the telegraph relied on humans to translate the code to a human readable format, Baudot's code and later modifications could create its own visual form as paper tape punches.[3]

With the emergence of the computer and binary code (a binary or Base 2 numbering system),[4] came the American Standard Code for Information Interchange (ASCII). ASCII (pronounced "AS-kee") uses a 7-bit code to represent upper- and lowercase letters, numbers, common punctuation marks, and a handful of telecommunications signals. It remains the most popular standard for text encoding today. However, documents in ASCII consist of only text; they have no formatting. The desire for a more "published" look led to the rise of word processing programs and "what you see is what you get" (WYSIWYG) computer interfaces that rendered font shapes and variations like italicized or bold text. No matter how fancy, however, all encoded information stored on a computer depends on bits and bytes.

What Are Bits and Bytes?

We call the smallest unit of information that can be stored in a computer a *bit*. It consists of an electrical state of either on or off, represented as either a 1 or 0. All computer calculations happen at the bit level. We combine bits in groups of eight and coordinate their on/off states to form a *byte*. By coordinating the on/off state of the first seven bits in each byte—and saving the eighth bit to check the accuracy of the first seven—we can create the 256 different combinations of characters of the standard ASCII table.[5] For example:

01000001 for A
01000010 for B
01000011 for C

01000100 for D
01000101 for E
01000110 for F
01000111 for G

Bits aggregate to bytes. Common aggregations for bytes come in multiples of 1,000, such as kilobyte, megabyte, gigabyte, and so on:

Bit (b) 1 or 0
Byte (B) 8 bits
Kilobyte (KB) 1,000 bytes
Megabyte (MB) 1,000 KB
Gigabyte (GB) 1,000 MB
Terabyte (TB) 1,000 GB
Petabyte (PB) 1,000 TB
Exabyte (EB) 1,000 PB
Zettabyte (ZB) 1,000 EB

We use the term *bitstream* to refer to the flow or transmission of the bits as an undifferentiated sequence of binary numbers. When we "digitize" something, we convert an analog object (paper-based or film-based) into series of bits.

As you can imagine, digitizing an image creates more bits than digitizing a page of written text, especially if you make a color image; they can create genuinely huge files.[6] While the number of audio files born digital and digitized from analog formats has kept pace with the creation of visual files, sound files do not result in the same enormous file sizes of image or video content. *The Expanding Digital Universe: A Forecast of Worldwide Information Growth through 2010*, a privately commissioned study, predicts that between 2006 and 2010 new information added each year to the digital universe will jump from 161 to 988 exabytes—with one quarter of that growth coming from digital cameras and camcorders.[7]

But how does this translate into "real world" terms regarding space and size for an archival repository? It's pretty easy to grasp the size of a byte—equivalent to a character on a page—or even a megabyte, which includes about the same amount of information as a small novel. But what about an exabyte—a million million megabytes? The same IDC study reports that

> the digital universe in 2006 could be likened to 12 stacks of books extending from the Earth to the sun. Or one stack of books twice around the Earth's orbit. By 2010 the stack of books could reach from the sun to Pluto and back. . . . However . . . bits and bytes themselves are getting smaller. That is, the circuits or media that store them are increasingly able to pack more into the same amount

of space. In 1956, when IBM introduced the first disk drive, it could only store 2,000 bits per square inch, a measure commonly referred to as areal density. Today disks routinely store 100,000,000,000 bits per square inch. Over the last few years, and for the foreseeable future, areal density is expected to double every 2 to 3 years.[8]

So while the content within the digital universe grows, the actual space needed to store that content shrinks, making it even harder to visualize the actual amount of information a modern storage device holds.

Comparing Digital and Analog Materials

Analog materials have three consistent qualities that curators have come to rely on. First, the information is tied to a physical medium. We can remove writing from a page, but when we do, it disappears. We cannot lift the writing from the page and put it someplace else, as we can cut and paste bits of text in a digital file. Second, the information appears in a linear representation. One word or number follows another; one line follows another. A ledger has one and only one format. Put the data into the ledger and the reader can see them only that way—unlike a database that the reader can manipulate to show many different presentations of the data. Third, analog materials degrade when copied. Photocopy a copy of a copy of a copy of a copy of a page of text, and you have a mess to look at. Copy a copy of a copy of a copy of a copy of a file with the system that created it, and you may have trouble detecting any difference.

Common digital materials, such as personal letters, reports, school papers, presentations, and business documents such as memoranda, correspondence, reports, and e-mail, all closely reflect similar paper documents. They serve the same function, and you can think of them as directly analogous. Electronic systems will track them in ways similar to paper systems, and you will find it relatively easy to assess which elements of the document you must preserve. Likewise, databases often have equivalent forms in paper record systems such as registers, logbooks, or catalogs. But, unlike simple ledgers, the power of computers allows us to create databases that have much more complexity than we could create with paper, with many more information types within them and complex interrelationships between those information types.

In addition to the characteristics mentioned above, digital materials have characteristics that analog materials do not. First, we can link a digital document to many other types of documents to create multimedia content; for example, we can link text to moving image with sound. Second, we can store digital materials in a variety of ways—hard drives, CDs, or DVDs, for instance—and search them electronically at the word or phrase level, providing a quality of intellectual access almost impossible to deliver in an analog document. Third, we can compress very large amounts of digital data into a relatively small unit for more efficient storage. All these differences make digital materials very attractive.

What Must a Digital Curator Do?

Given the differences between analog and digital materials, what must a curator do to fulfill his or her archival responsibility? Terry Cook did a wonderful job of summing up the challenges a curator must consider when archiving digital materials.[9] I paraphrase Cook here, using much of his original language and the order in which he presented the issues.

> Captured [electronic] records must be comprehensive: [in other words] the who, what, when, where, why, and with whom, etc. must be created for every business transaction, between humans and machines, or between machines. Records must be uniquely identifiable [which means] (numbered, [and] labelled) and linked to each and every specific transaction. Records must be complete in terms of preserving a content, structure, and context for the transaction they document. [Records must be] accurate, including values imported from separate authority files. [Records must be] understandable [which requires] all screen views, data placement in virtual documents, and logical relations to other physical records must be maintained and represented. [The system must also capture all] system functionality. [Records must be] meaningful, [which means that] the business rules that generated the transaction and the links between records of one transaction [must be] preserved. Records moreover must be authentic: the access, permissions, and authorizations to the data, or parts of it, must be recorded, and traceable to each record and transaction.[10]

You can see that this makes sense. If Cook were describing the needs of paper documents, he would have the same archival requirements, but they would seem less daunting. You would nod, knowing that you have practices in place that *capture* records in a way that includes the circumstances that produced them and their links to other records and "business transactions." You know how to give them unique identifiers, file them in a predictable and documented way, and protect them from alteration.

Cook had this to say about the maintenance of digital materials:

> Records must be *maintained* in an integral way, protected from accidental or deliberate destruction or modification. No deletion or alteration to a record can occur once the transaction to which it relates has taken place. Records must be coherent and reconstructible in terms of their migration and functionality across hardware and software generational changes. Records must be auditable to represent all processes to which the record has been subjected. Each use, viewing, indexing, classifying, filing, copying, etc., of a record is also a transaction and thus must generate its own record. And records when removed from the system

under proper authority must leave contextual audit trails documenting the deletion.[11]

Again, you know how to *maintain* records so no harm comes to them, even as
you move them from one storage area to another, and have other people handling
them and using them. And you document those activities.
Here Cook covers the usability of archived digital materials:

> Finally, records must be *usable* in terms of being exportable to other systems
> without loss of information and especially functionality. Records must be ac-
> cessible in presenting over time to new users the content, structure, and con-
> text as they appeared originally. Each such new presentation of the information
> [must] create an audit trail and another transaction record. And records must
> be redactable, allowing anonymized or [censored[12]] versions where appropri-
> ate, with such actions also being recorded as separate transactions linked to the
> original record.[13]

Again, you know how to make them available to users in a way that protects
them and tracks who has used them. If you must, you know how to redact and
censor them. It's all a known process. However, executing that process usually
depends on your ability to see, hold, and file the record itself. With that ability,
you can track its use relatively easily using very unsophisticated technology. So
the archival functions Cook describes come as no surprise, but the nature of digital
materials makes performing them a challenge.

What Makes a Good Digital Document Good?

Before you put a lot of time and effort into archiving digital materials, you
need to know that, at a technical level, the materials you want to capture and
archive are worth the resources they will require over time. So, what makes a
good digital document "good"? As do most writers on electronic records, I have
relied heavily for definitions and descriptions on the first edition of ISO 15489,
the standard for records management.[14]

General

A "good" digital document, when captured into an archival system, correctly
and completely retains its structure, content, a record of the context in which it was
created and used, and links to other pertinent documents. In other words, the who,
what, when, where, why, and with whom, etc. of a document's "life" must exist
for every transaction that involved it, whether between humans and machines or
just between machines. Further, each document must be uniquely identifiable in
each and every specific transaction that included it. Documents will be complete

in terms of preserving a content, structure, and context for the transaction they document, including values imported from separate authority files.

We use the term *completeness* to mean that a single digital document or a collection of digital materials contains everything it should—no more and no less. Determining what it "should" contain can raise issues, as it does in hard-copy collections. Digital document systems can make the question more complicated. For instance, some e-mail systems automatically strip out attachments and store them elsewhere. A collection of e-mails created by such a system should have the attachments somewhere, and we want it to have a way to determine which attachment or attachments belong to which e-mail message.

Authenticity

An *authentic* digital document can be proven 1) to be what it purports to be, 2) to have been created or sent by the person purported to have created or sent it, and 3) to have been created or sent at the time purported. That usually means that the access, permissions, and authorizations to the data, or parts of it, must be recorded and traceable to each record and transaction.[15]

Archivists and manuscript curators have long relied on several strategies to prove authenticity in the hard-copy world. First, given a letter, we look to *physical characteristics* of the letter to confirm that we have an authentic document—a letter dated "London, August 13, 1797" for example. We look at the paper: does it conform to what we know about paper at that time? What about the ink? Do we find any additional evidence—a seal, perhaps, watermark, or a manner of folding? If we have doubts, we could find a laboratory that can run chemical tests on the paper and ink to date them. Other experts could testify to the human elements, like format, handwriting, spelling, punctuation, etc.

Second, we rely on *provenance*—the custodial history. Do we know for sure the provenance of the letter? Someone found it in a box in an attic and brought it to us. When did the box arrive in the attic? Who put it there? Where was it before that?, etc. If we can trace the chain of custody back to the original recipient, we express confidence that we have a really authentic letter written by the person whose signature it bears.

Third, we might consider the letter's *suitability*.[16] Does what it conveys make sense in the context of the sender and receiver? Here we're looking for anachronisms and other internal problems in the content of the letter.

Fourth, for mass-produced and distributed materials, we *compare* our copy to others, trusting that at least one is a "true copy." These methods work just fine in the physical world, but since digital materials have no physical manifestation, only the third and fourth tests, suitability and comparison, can have any application at all. Given what we know about how easily we can alter or fake a digital document, we realize that curators have a pressing need to find a way to establish an authentic provenance for digital materials.

Reagan Moore, while at the San Diego SuperComputer Center, listed the metadata that digital material requires just to ensure its authentic identity:[17]

- Date record is made
- Date record is transmitted
- Date record is received
- Date record is set aside (i.e., filed)
- Name of author (person or organization issuing the record)
- Name of addressee (the intended receiver, whether a person or an organization)
- Name of writer (person or organization responsible for the articulation of the record's content)
- Name of originator (electronic address from which the record is sent)
- Name of recipient(s) (person or organization to whom the record is sent)
- Name of creator (person or organization in whose archival fonds the record exists)
- Name of action or matter (the activity in the course of which the record is created)
- Name of documentary form (e.g., e-mail, report, memo)
- Identification of digital components
- Identification of attachments (e.g., digital signature)
- Archival bond (e.g., classification code)
- Assertions about the creation of the record
- Assertions made by the archivist about the creator of the record and the creation process

While Moore created an impressive list, he did so in addressing only one small part of the process. We should not proceed into the digital future thinking that we can reduce the concept of authenticity to a simple test or set of procedures. We can't, as Clifford Lynch makes very clear in his outstanding essay on the concept.

> Virtually all determination of authenticity or integrity in the digital environment ultimately depends on trust. We verify the source of claims . . . and, on the basis of that source, assign a level of belief or trust to the claims. . . . It is important to recognize that trust is not necessarily an absolute, but often a subjective probability that we assign case by case. . . . This suggests that our ability to manage and understand authenticity and integrity over long periods of time will require us to manage and preserve documentation about the evolution of the trust and identity management infrastructure that supports the assertions and evaluation of authenticity and integrity.[18]

Reliability

A reliable digital document can be trusted as a full and accurate representation of the transactions, activities, or facts to which it attests and can be depended upon in the course of subsequent transactions or activities.

Integrity

Integrity in a digital document refers to its being complete and unaltered, regardless of format or technological change.

Usability

A usable digital document can be located, retrieved, presented, and interpreted. In the end, we may find usability the most fundamental of all characteristics. Complete and authentic collections of digital material have no value if we cannot access and use them. To provide usability, we must have hardware and software that allows us to locate records of interest and translate them into a human-readable form. The materials must make sense to someone with the skills to understand them. If your researchers can read Greek, the digital materials you have in Greek must make sense to them, even if you personally can't read Greek. This understandability may require technological assistance (in the case of Greek, your computer must have a screen driver that will display Greek characters) as part of the access system. Usability goes to another level if we strive to facilitate a researcher's ability to use the records as the creator did.[19]

Some documents depend on other documents and cannot stand alone. In those cases, we must make sure that all supporting documents stay with them in our archives. For instance, most maps need keys. If the key exists in a separate document, the maps have substantially less research value if we don't make the key readily available. We may think of the key as part of the map, but a computer system may not. To ensure the computer saves the key with the map, we must make sure that we can process the computer-based record, that we preserve any paper- or computer-based ancillary information, and that we preserve the conceptual or electronic link between the record and the ancillary information.

As you see, accessibility can become pretty complicated. Much of what we collect will interest researchers only for the data it contains: what does the e-mail or word-processed document say? As with paper, researchers may make note of the visual context—hmmm, interesting letterhead—but they will turn fairly quickly to the text. However, "text" that takes the form of a web page goes beyond just text to tell the complete story: the background, visual images, sound effects, and interactive features, etc., matter, and understandability requires that we provide the researcher all of them along with the actual text. Here it gets tricky. We may capture the text and contextual codes perfectly, but differences in our hardware and software may render them substantially different from their original form. According to Lynch,

This raises questions about how to define and measure authenticity and integrity. In the most extreme case, we have objects that are rendered experientially—video games, virtual reality walk-throughs, and similar interactive works—where the focus shifts from the bits that constitute the digital object to the behavior of the rendering system, or at least to the interaction between the digital object and the rendering system.[20]

Lynch identifies a hierarchy of digital objects from the simplest to the most complicated to capture and render as data, documents, sensory presentations, interactive, and/or experiential works. Obviously as we move up the hierarchy from data to interactive experiential works, the questions about integrity and authenticity become more complex and more subjective, involving human perception and experience in relation to documentary content. Even more subjectively, the researcher often seeks to discuss the *essence* of a work rather than the exact data that create it or that may represent it in a specific context. Again, the further up Lynch's hierarchy we move, the more problems we run into. That doesn't mean we don't have problems at lower levels. Even there we run into imprecision and ambiguity that confounds our attempts to preserve these materials.

If we have authentic, reliable, and usable digital materials, we want to manipulate, select, and display them in a manner congruent with our reason for preserving them. Doing that may require using facilities similar or identical to those that created them. This requirement of usability sets a high bar.

If digital materials are usable, we will find the documents potentially reusable. That means we can copy information from the document or have it interact with modern information-processing systems in some other way. In that context, we want the system that holds the documents to maintain and clearly show all screen views of any given digital document, its placement in any virtual documents, and its logical relations to any physical records. The systems in which we store digital materials must also have the critical functionality of the systems that created them. We may not give patrons access to all these functions, but we should have them. Consider materials created on an ancient word processor, for example. While we will need to preserve the word-processed documents so researchers can locate and read them, we do not need to provide the researcher the ability to edit them or to carry out other actions that the original software might have permitted.

Reusability strikes me as the most professional goal to strive for. We cannot today predict how a researcher might want to reuse data in the future; knowing that, we do well to keep it reusable. Further, by aiming for reusability, we also ensure the record's accessibility and comprehensibility.

So, if we set reusability as our goal, we must find a way to maintain documents in an integral way, protected from accidental or deliberate destruction or modification. We cannot allow any deletions or alterations to a document once the transaction to which it relates has taken place. We must keep our documents coherent, reconstructible, and functional as we migrate them across hardware and software generational changes. We must be able to audit documents to track all processes to which they have been subjected while in our custody. As Cook says, "each use, viewing, indexing, classifying, filing, copying, etc.," must generate its own record as a transaction. "Our document must be redactable, *allowing anonymized or [censored] versions where appropriate, with such actions also being recorded as separate transactions linked to the original record*."[21] Finally, when we remove documents from the system under proper authority, we must leave contextual audit trails documenting the deletion.

If all this were describing the needs of paper documents, these same functional requirements would seem less daunting. But, I repeat, digital materials are invisible: they're not real items. All digital materials consist of raw data plus all the logical links that point to the data's storage locations. The storage locations may be scattered all over the storage media. The digital document also includes the logical structure file that controls the data's physical or intellectual representation. To accurately capture, maintain, and make available a digital document means documenting everything that happens to it, and you must depend on the computer hardware and software to do that.

Functional Requirements of a Digital Archives

To get systems that will meet our needs, we have had to educate systems developers about what functions to build into the system. Explaining the archival perspective on records to computer systems designers has forced archivists and curators to think beyond the paper document. If its physical format didn't make it a record, what did? What's a record?

As I also said earlier, definitions vary, but all include the fundamental concept that a record provides evidence of a transaction involving two or more entities. Therefore, a good records management system keeps all the logical links and bits of content that create the impression of a record on the screen or in print, and it keeps them in a way that the full record can be retrieved over time. IT people are agreeable about creating such a system, but they need to know, in fairly fine detail, exactly how the computer should function. What must they program it to do? That leads archivists and curators to start thinking about the functional requirements essential in computers so we could be sure they maintain archive-able records.

The concept of functional requirement is not new to any of us. When we set out to buy something, we think in terms of what we want it to do—think about your next car, your next HVAC system, your next vacation, your next hire, your next meal—you know with more or less precision what you want—what your functional requirements include. The work of defining functional requirements for electronic records systems has gone on since the early 1990s, and we now see consensus developing around a number of functions. We have also come to understand the role of metadata in the process.

What Is Metadata?

When we archive physical documents we do it in such a way that the researcher can understand the roles that the materials originally played in the world of their creator. That seems an equally compelling principle as we work to retain digital materials. Further, in some cases a researcher might want to use the materials as the creator did.[22] To make that possible, we will need to rely on metadata in large measure.

Metadata may seem like a new concept, but it isn't; only the word is new. We now use *metadata* as a generic term to describe a type of information we have known about all our lives. In a book, the index provides metadata about the content of the pages. In a library, the card catalog or online catalog provides metadata about the holdings of the library. The owner's manual for a stove or refrigerator provides metadata about the appliance.

All documents[23] have three features that we can describe through metadata: content, context, and structure. We have more experience with metadata that describe the *content* of something—the catalog record describes the content of a book in a library and finding aids describe the content of a collection. Finding aids provide more *context* for the creation of historical materials, though a catalog record will place a title in a publisher's series if it belongs there. Both also describe *structure* in terms of how big, how many pages, boxes, folders, or items, the presence of images, maps, etc.

The author's intention to create a unified intellectual effort holds a book together as a book, but what holds a collection of letters together as a collection? A shared characteristic. The characteristic usually has to do with the creation process: all the letters were written by one person, or to one person, or in the same place, or at the same time, etc. While the shared creation characteristic relates to the content, that creation data aren't, strictly speaking, part of the content—they are metadata. The metadata reveal a group of documents as a collection.

The metadata we need when we work with paper documents pale in comparison to the metadata we need when we work with digital materials. Think about Moore's list above. Let's revisit Cook. Every time Cook says "documents must," he implies the use of metadata. I'll repeat a couple of paraphrased sections from above:

> A good digital document, when captured into an archival system, will correctly and completely retain its structure, content, the context in which it was created and used, and links to other pertinent documents. In other words, *the who, what, when, where, why, and with whom, etc.* of a document's existence must exist for every transaction that involved it between humans and machines or between machines. Further, *each document must be uniquely identifiable in each and every specific transaction that included it.*[24]

The "who, what, when, where, why, and with whom" are metadata; the "unique identifier" is metadata. Think about the details that your computer can supply you about every file you have. That's metadata, and, except for the name of the file, you didn't create any of it. As Cook says,

> We must keep our documents coherent and reconstructible and functional as we migrate them across hardware and software generational changes. We must be able to audit documents to *track all processes to which the document has been subjected while in our custody. Each use, viewing, indexing, classifying, filing, copying, etc., of a document is a transaction and must generate its own record.*[25]

All that history gets collected in the form of metadata—time stamps and the like. In the perfect system, almost all metadata come from the system itself, and there is much work under way across a wide variety of disciplines to develop standard metadata schemes for systems to work with.

Archival Metadata

Archivists and curators have chewed on the problem for more than a decade, and have achieved some success. Anne Gilliland divides archival metadata for archives into five types:[26]

1. administrative metadata, used in managing and administering information resources, for example, acquisition information, rights and reproduction information, location information, etc.;
2. descriptive metadata, used to describe or identify information resources, for example, cataloging records, finding aids, and indexes;
3. preservation metadata, used to manage preservation activities for holdings, for example, description of the physical condition of resources on receipt, scheduling of conservation treatments, description of conservation treatments, etc.;
4. technical metadata, used to document how a system functions or metadata behave, for example, hardware and software documentation, information on digitization formats, compression ratios, scaling routines, etc., security data such as encryption keys, passwords, etc. Technical metadata, such as file format and date of last format migration, define the characteristics of the system that created or processed the documents. One could consider them record-keeping metadata, since they come from the original system. Typically we don't regard technical metadata as information the end user needs to have access to, but computer programs that manage and retain the documents must create and manage it or there is no record. Occasionally, users may need to have access to technical metadata, if, for instance, the creator used a particular version of software with documented "bugs." Some users would then want to know which documents might reflect the "bug" in some way;
5. use metadata, which describe the usage of holdings, for example, user records, exhibit records, published references, etc.

All that metadata will constitute a database, albeit a small and often relatively simple database. Once we have created the metadata, we must retain *it*, often using the same techniques that we would use to retain a database.

Metadata about a digital object accrue. The creator and the creator's system apply a layer of metadata in the original environment: file name, format, directory structure, etc. When the digital object moves to a repository, the repository staff and systems may add higher-level descriptive metadata in the form of registration information, descriptive information, legal status information, repository location information, use logs, etc. This accrued metadata will take many forms, such as file names based on the creator's personal file-naming whim or scheme as well as professionally assigned controlled descriptors. Some of these metadata will never change—the date of creation, for instance. Some may change erratically, for example, I've changed the name of the word processing file that held the various drafts of this exact text several times. Some change routinely, such as technical transaction status information. That's true for all the accruing levels of metadata. Some of the metadata will conform to a prescribed structure and format, such as most machine-generated metadata or a MAchine-Readable Cataloging (MARC) record describing a digital object. Some will consist of unstructured notes. Finally, some metadata refer to individual items in a collection and some refer to the collection as a whole.[27]

Computers don't understand concepts, but we've come to appreciate how powerfully they can manage consistently coded information. With that in mind, various groups have developed a wide range of metadata schemes. With good metadata, we can have reliable audit trails that log transactions so we can know what the system or outside forces did to all or portions of a record. Again, audit trails aren't a new concept in repositories. You use audit trails in your work every day—patron sign-in/sign-out sheets, call slips, and "pulled slips." In the paper world, our audit trails can track activities and people at a fairly basic level of information. Not so in the electronic world. Further, audit trails are records themselves and need their own sets of metadata and audit trails.

Metadata and audit trails call for standards, both official and *de facto*. Only if everyone uses essentially the same information will one system understand the records created by another. As I mentioned in chapter 1, Hans Hofman argued that standards set a recognized level of quality that improves efficiency (thus reducing costs), offer a framework for implementation, accountability, and certification, and provide stability and authority for decisions—all of which provide you a certain amount of political cover.[28] As a practical matter, anything you can do according to a standard is a process you don't have to invent yourself.

In the long term, the information professions, to which archivists belong, envision a genuine information age in which all types of information resources link together. Imagine a system which will allow a user to locate primary documents (archival materials), secondary documents (library materials), and physical documents (museum materials) that all relate to the question of the moment. People use Internet search engines for that purpose today, but the results come back as a very large number of hits, with very little precision within that set of hits. To create a system that will provide good precision in identifying materials across repositories around the world—including yours—requires a variety of different types of metadata. We need different types of metadata to develop effective, authoritative systems that can work together, grow, and remain stable for generations to come as we preserve the world's cultural heritage information. I go into this in more detail throughout the book.

Notes

1. Clifford Lynch, "Authenticity and Integrity in the Digital Environment: An Exploratory Analysis of the Central Role of Trust," in *Authenticity in a Digital Environment: May 2000*, ed. Charles T. Cullen (Washington, D.C.: Council on Library and Information Resources, 2000), 44, www.clir.org/pubs/reports/pub92/lynch.html (accessed July 6, 2008).

2. Three widely used programs in the 1980s.

3. Wikipedia contributors, "Baudot Code," *Wikipedia: The Free Encyclopedia*, en.wikipedia.org/wiki/Baudot_code (accessed April 12, 2008).

4. For an explanation of Base 2 as a concept, see Wikipedia contributors, "Binary Numeral System," *Wikipedia: The Free Encyclopedia*, en.wikipedia.org/wiki/Base_2 (accessed April 12, 2008).

5. For a rendering of the full ASCII table, see The Basement, "ASCII Table: 7-bit," Basement Computing, www.neurophys.wisc.edu/comp/docs/ascii (accessed April 12, 2008).

6. For more on digital imaging, see Howard Besser, *Introduction to Imaging*, rev. ed., ed. Sally Hubbard with Deborah Lenert (Los Angeles: Getty Institute, undated), www.getty.edu/research/conducting_research/standards/introimages/ (accessed July 6, 2008).

7. John Gantz, et al., *The Expanding Digital Universe: A Forecast of Worldwide Information Growth through 2010: An IDC White Paper* (Framingham, Mass.: IDC, 2007), 1, www.emc.com/collateral/analyst-reports/expanding-digital-idc-white-paper.pdf (accessed April 12, 2008).

8. Gantz, et al., *The Expanding Digital Universe*.

9. Terry Cook, "The Impact of David Bearman on Modern Archival Thinking: An Essay of Personal Reflection and Critique," *Archives and Museum Informatics* 11, no. 1 (March 1997): 15–37.

10. Cook, "The Impact of David Bearman," 25.

11. Cook, "The Impact of David Bearman," 25.

12. This bracketed word corrects an obvious typographical error in the published document.

13. Cook, "The Impact of David Bearman," 25–26.

14. International Standards Organization, *International Standard 15489: Information and Documentation—Records Management, Part 1, General*, 1st ed. (Geneva: ISO, 2001), www.iso.org/iso/catalogue_detail?csnumber=31908 (accessed April 12, 2008).

15. Remember, to prove a digital document's authenticity does not guarantee the truth or accuracy of all information within the record any more than it does for paper letters or diaries.

16. Jeff Rothenberg, "Preserving Authentic Digital Information," *Authenticity in a Digital Environment: May 2000*, ed. Charles T. Cullen (Washington, D.C.: Council on Library and Information Resources, 2000), www.clir.org/pubs/reports/pub92/rothenberg. html (accessed July 27, 2008).

17. Reagan Moore, et al., "Building Preservation Environments with Data Grid Technology (NARA Research Prototype Persistent Archive)" (presentation at the Society of American Archivists Annual Conference, Washington, D.C., August 5, 2006), www.archives.gov/era/pdf/2006-saa-moore.pdf (accessed April 12, 2008).

18. Lynch, "Authenticity and Integrity," 46–48.

19. Jeff Rothenberg, "Digital Preservation: The State of the Art" (presentation at the Digital Preservation Technology & Policy Workshop, Koninklijke Bibliotheek, Nationale bibliotheek van Nederland, December 13, 2002), 10, www.kb.nl/hrd/dd/dd_links_ en_publicaties/workshop2002/rothenberg.pdf (accessed April 12, 2008).

20. Lynch, "Authenticity and Integrity," 36.

21. Cook, "The Impact of David Bearman," 25–26.

22. Rothenberg, "Digital Preservation," 10.

23. We don't generally think of a chair in a museum as a document, but we can. If we define a document as something that provides information in some way, every type of information source fits the definition. Using the largest possible definition of document in this context simplifies my writing substantially in this book.

24. Cook, "The Impact of David Bearman," 25, emphasis mine.

25. Cook, "The Impact of David Bearman," 25, emphasis mine.

26. Anne J. Gilliland, "Setting the Stage," in *Introduction to Metadata: Pathways to Digital Information*, online ed., version 2.1, ed. Martha Baca (Los Angeles: Getty Institute, undated), www.getty.edu/research/conducting_research/standards/intrometadata/setting. html (accessed July 6, 2008).

27. For a more fully developed exploration of this information, see Gilliland, above.

28. Hans Hofman, "The Use of Standards and Models," in *Managing Electronic Records*, ed. Julie McLeod and Catherine Hare (London: Facet, 2005), 18–33.

Chapter 3

Solving the Problems: Systems and Tools

Today all digital materials depend on some sort of electronic system to take a digital document (like an image from a digital camera) and make it available to whomever. Adrian Cunningham has argued that archivists must understand the underlying systems that create the historical documents we collect. He has asserted that the biggest challenge for us remains "developing and implementing comprehensive regimes for capturing and managing records as evidence in context from before the point of creation for as long as those records are required by their creators and by society at large."[1] While he has focused on "evidential records" from an institutional perspective, his observation holds true for all of us; our future donors create content on systems like the ones Cunningham refers to. Therefore, we must all understand those systems well enough to capture the content and its provenance.

Capturing digital materials and moving them from their home system to an archival system requires that we set up archival systems that can preserve them. In this chapter, I discuss the information technology (IT) concepts that explain the IT environments that create digital materials and which a digital archival repository must have. Frankly, I find this chapter difficult to read from end to end. Of necessity it throws information at you in a relentless stream of terms and definitions—no plot, no character development, no atmosphere—just facts. I suggest you skim through it, note what it contains, and return to it as you need to know more about a specific term or concept.

Information Architecture

We call the framework of computing systems, storage devices, and networks that our donors use the *information architecture*. The concept includes all related policies and procedures, documented or not. Computing systems include the hardware and software of any desktop or laptop computers, e-mail systems, networks, Internet access and security, and related components. Our donors have an information architecture they work in, and so do you. To successfully move digital materials from their systems to yours, you must understand both.

Think of your system as having four layers. First, its hardware—the physical components such as servers, network components, and storage devices. Second, the operating system—software that controls data movement among the computer's central processing unit, memory devices, and peripherals. Third, the application software—programs that enable specific functions. Fourth, design and architecture—the overarching model that determines how all the above connect and work together.

To make the best use of the potential of the technology—and avoid its dark side—we must understand at least the basics of how the systems' components interact and communicate. That understanding may provide you with a new sense of resolve and the courage to step into the choppy waters of the digital universe. While we do not need to transform ourselves overnight—we're creating miracles here—we *do* need to build a firm IT knowledge base, which begins with learning a bit about the components that will create the perfect archival system, which will have 1) rapid access, 2) fast read/write rates, 3) low cost per stored byte, and 4) stable storage across time, ensuring unalterable content.

Hardware

Computers

We can define the computer as a machine that can execute a programmed list of instructions and respond to new instructions as given. Today, when we think about computers, we usually think of the desktop and laptop computers that most people use. When referring to a desktop model, the term *computer* refers to the box itself—not the peripherals, such as the monitor, keyboard, mouse, external storage devices, printers, external speakers, etc. Laptops encase most peripherals in one complete unit.

Storage Media and Devices

Archivists have more interest in storage devices than they have in other peripherals, so I'll focus on them here. I'll start by making a distinction between the storage media and storage devices. *Media* refers to the object that stores data, such as CDs, floppy disks, and magnetic tape. *Device* refers to a piece of equipment, such as a tape drive or hard drive, that reads the data stored on the media. Today we have a growing array of storage media. Each has strengths and weaknesses we must work with.

Hard Disk Drive

A hard disk drive consists of an integrated system of media and device that provides the primary storage on personal computers. Hard disk drives provide high capacity (greater than 100 gigabytes) and moderate access times relatively cheaply. Because hard drives within computers serve as integral parts of the system, currently we cannot remove a hard disk drive from its host system and easily connect it to another system and expect it to store the data it contains the way we can remove and store other storage devices. Nor can we guarantee that the content of a hard drive will remain safe from alteration. So, while most of the content we may want to store exists on the hard disk drive of a donor's system, we will have to move that content to an archival medium.

Floppy Disk

The earliest removable storage devices, floppy disks are made up of a disk of thin, flexible ("floppy") magnetic storage medium encased in a square or rectangular plastic shell. From the mid-1970s to the late 1990s, "floppies" were the standard form of portable data storage and exchange. Today universal serial bus (USB) and optical devices have taken their place for storage.

Magnetic Tape

Magnetic tape is a mature, removable, and stable medium that dates back to the 1950s. Magnetic tape offers the highest capacity of all storage media, and at very affordable prices. Many producers of extensive digital materials still use tapes for backup storage copies. For archival purposes, we remove a tape from the device and place it on a tape-reading device to access its content. Tapes store information sequentially, and the user must start at the beginning and run the tape until reaching the desired content—a process that both wastes the user's time and causes wear to the tape; wear may alter the content or render it unreadable.

Compact and Digital Versatile/Video Discs

Compact discs (CD) and digital versatile/video discs (DVD): CDs and DVDs are two optical media that hold a large amount of content on a removable device. We can configure an automatic disk changer (jukebox) to access a large number of optical disks relatively quickly. Further, we can protect the content on optical disks from alteration. Accessing the content takes longer than accessing content on a hard disk drive, but less time than accessing content on a tape system. However, both types of disks have known fragility. We don't have sure knowledge of their "shelf-life," but we do know they scratch easily, and can break.

USB Sticks

USB storage devices, known as jump drives, flash drives, thumb drives, flash sticks, and memory sticks, consist of memory chips in a device that has no moveable parts and plugs into a USB port on a computer. They provide a very affordable and portable way to store a large amount of content in a very small device. Unfortunately the very compact nature of these storage devices makes them easy to lose and steal. Further, unlike optical media, which we can access through an automated jukebox, we must manually attach each individual device to a machine that can read it, and then manually locate and retrieve its contents.

Holographic Storage

Holographic storage devices are an emerging optical method of storing large quantities of data by writing data as light patterns. While still in the testing stage, holographic storage will add to our arsenal of media that can store a large quantity of data in a dense format on a small device—with both the advantages and disadvantages that entails.

Storage Location

Regardless of the media we choose for storing digital materials, we have a number of options for configuring our system. Like the media itself, each system model has advantages and disadvantages.

Online Storage

Online storage is a system in which we use server hard drives for storage either in a network or on a stand-alone computer's hard drive. Generally, we keep online storage active and immediately accessible. Online storage systems can support sophisticated automated techniques for record control, monitoring, and backup procedures. Unfortunately, online storage systems are expensive to maintain, and the contents may be at risk of alteration or deletion without good security parameters and records management practices.

Nearline Storage

Nearline storage is a system in which we store content on physical storage media (DVDs, CDs, and magnetic tapes) on an intermediate device, such as a storage tower or jukebox, semi-separate from our network or computer. Towers and jukeboxes can hold many different disks and provide automatic retrieval from them all. The automated nature of nearline systems means that they share many of the advantages of online systems, and provide an environment that protects the content from alteration.

Offline Storage

In offline storage, we store our media completely away from a computer or network, not immediately available for use. To access the content, someone must physically retrieve and load it. While offline storage provides good security and disaster recovery, the inconvenience of access makes it suitable for storing only highly important materials that need the security or infrequently used low-value materials. Someone must also take responsibility for monitoring offsite materials for environmental degradation and changes in technology that may adversely affect the storage media.

Storage Configuration

For access to digital materials, online storage provides the fastest and most convenient option. However, storing everything on a working hard drive can heavily tax the power of a single server, so people have turned to remote storage systems that behave like online storage systems. Remote "online" storage appears in at least three different arrangements that archivists and curators should know about. The first two rely wholly on online storage, while the third approach leverages the unique qualities of all three models described.

Redundant Array of Independent Disks (RAID)
RAID is a generic term for a variety of data storage schemes that divide and/or replicate data among multiple hard drives that appear to the user as one logical unit. RAIDs increase the capacity, reliability, and backup capability of the system.

Storage Networking
Storage networking is a generic term used for two common configurations: storage area networks (SAN) and network attached storage (NAS). Unlike RAIDs, both types acknowledge their remoteness to the user; beyond that the technical details matter only to the computers.

Tiered Storage
Tiered storage is an architecture that places the most important information online, while keeping less critical data in either nearline or offline storage space, with the least important data being kept on magnetic tape.

Software

Operating Systems

Operating systems function as traffic cops controlling data management among the hardware and the application programs. Since operating systems are themselves programs, developers of applications target an operating system to interact with. We all know about the operational barriers between the Mac and Windows worlds. Typically every operating system has a distinct user graphical user interface (GUI, pronounced "gooey") that relies heavily on pictures and icons, rather than words and numbers.

Applications

Applications dominate the world of the user. Information creation and management applications include:

1. Word processing
2. Spreadsheet
3. Presentation management systems
4. Correspondence management systems
5. E-mail management systems
6. Database management systems
7. Forms management systems
8. Internet website content management systems
9. Imaging systems
10. Workflow systems
11. Case file management systems
12. Customer relations management systems
13. Computer-assisted design/computer-assisted manufacturing (CAD/CAM) systems

Network Architecture

When we link computers and their peripherals together so they can "talk" to each other and exchange information, we have a network. The term *architecture* refers to the hardware, software, or combination of hardware and software comprising a computer system or network. We use the term *open architecture* to describe computer and network components that readily connect and operate with other systems with no restrictions beyond basic hardware requirements. Conversely, the term *closed architecture* describes components that require specific software components to join.

The most common network architecture creates a client/server relationship among computers, where the client computer requests data or a service and the server fills the request. The Web works on a client/server architecture. When you click on a link, your machine, the client, opens a connection and sends a request to the server that holds the file you've requested. The server sends the file and closes the connection. Frequently we include an external storage device that maintains the data the client wants. With client-server architecture, work that takes a lot of computing power happens on a server computer, while less intensive applications activities occur on the client computer. This configuration dramatically reduces traffic on the network and protects the speed with which the network can function.

A peer-to-peer (P2P) network, a second popular configuration, has all computers providing or requesting services among computers without a central server. A cluster network creates a collection of individual computers that appear as a single logical unit. Clusters may also be referred to as matrix or grid systems.

Middleware

In a networked computer environment, the middleware is the layer of software that lies between the operating system and the applications on each site of the system. It serves as the data pipeline that acts as a go-between for data sources (server) and applications requesting the data for use (client). Middleware compensates for the heterogeneity and/or distribution of the underlying hardware and operating systems.[2]

Network Components and Types

Network components communicate in the various system configuration and architecture models through a variety of networks protocol languages. You may recognize some of the initialisms: FTP (File Transfer Protocol) for moving files from one machine to another, TCP/IP (Transmission Control Protocol/Internet Protocol) for connecting to the Internet, or HTTP (Hypertext Transport Protocol) for working with hypertext files on a network. You don't need to know a great deal about how the protocols work, only that each of those initials stands for a particular network language that performs a particular network function.

Bandwidth is the rate at which one computer can communicate with and transfer data to another. We measure bandwidth in bits per second (bps). The International Network (Internet) is a worldwide system—the biggest network of all. Metropolitan area networks (MANs) are networks used primarily to provide free wireless Internet access to a given city or metropolitan area. Wide area networks (WANs) are networks used to share server access across a large, distributed organization. Local area networks (LANs) are networks used to connect clients to a central server in an office or to provide Web connection to multiple computers in a home.

Intranets are private networks, internal to an organization, that restrict access to designated personnel within the organization. In any given shop, the intranet may include publicly accessible areas called *extranets*. A related network type called a *virtual private network* (VPN) allows authorized users access to content on a private intranet through a secure pathway on the Internet.

Digital Materials

An issue you must take into consideration early on relates to the organization of the content of various files. Typically we divide content into three types: structured, unstructured, and mixed.

Structured Data

We call data that resides in the fixed fields or cells of a record or file *structured data*. The contents of relational databases and spreadsheets, for example, conform to and operate within the structure of the database or spreadsheet, which defines exactly what data each part holds and where it holds it relative to all other parts. The value of every cell in a database has a clearly defined meaning established by the structure of the database. Structured data appears in spreadsheets, financial programs, databases, bibliographic citation managers, etc.

In the institutional world of information technology, structured data usually resides on mainframe computers, servers, or powerful workstations. The IT and database management specialists in institutions run the IT department and rarely consult archivists about designing their systems. As a result, they may have little awareness of issues that concern archivists: data alteration, deletion, and archival transfer. As Terry Cook states, in IT departments, "the focus is on reliable, accessible, efficient, up-to-date data, not time-bound records wrapped in context-rich transactional metadata reflecting changes over time."[3] Programs for personal computers, designed and created on the model developed by the mainframe world, all suffer from all the weaknesses Cook points out about structured data on mainframes.

Unstructured Data

Unstructured data has no internal descriptions or definitions comparable to the parameters created to form a spreadsheet or database. The world of e-mail, word processing documents, images, presentations, calendars, and other features common to "office suites" of integrated software produces far more unstructured data than structured. According to an IDC report, unstructured data accounts for over 95 percent of the global digital universe.[4] In the world of unstructured data, everyone does more or less as she or he chooses, having virtually no general and/or enforced rules about how to manage the files. While the brain of the beholder may discern the structure of a business letter, the computer sees it as unstructured data. Most unstructured data requires interpretation by humans or specific programs to determine what a file might actually contain. Further, the content of unstructured files may vary—text, images, sound, etc. Because unstructured data has no self-description, we must consciously apply a wide variety of metadata to it so we can manage and then archive it. The chaotic world of unstructured data has begun to show up in historical repositories. Archivists have no choice but to impose some order on the chaos.

File Formats

All computer programs create files that have organized the data in a particular way. We call that particular way its *file format*. The file name extension (the suffix beginning with a period) often indicates the file format by three standard letters that represent the format. For a program to use the data in a file, it must understand

and know how to work with the file format. For example, Corel WordPerfect can read and display the Microsoft Word .doc file format, but Word cannot read and display the WordPerfect .wpd file format.

There are as many different file formats as there are different programs to process the files. A few of the more common include:

- Microsoft Word documents (.doc or .docx)
- Image files (.gif, .tif, and .jpg)
- Adobe [Postscript] files (.ps)
- Adobe Acrobat Portable Document Files (.pdf)
- Executable programs (.exe)
- Audio files (.mp3)
- Microsoft PowerPoint (.ppt or .pptx)

Compound Digital Objects

As the name implies, compound digital information objects come from aggregating multiple file formats into a logical whole, for example, an aggregation of scanned pages that form a chapter; an aggregation of chapters that form a book; an aggregation of text and supporting materials such as data sets, software tools, and video recordings of an experiment that form a scholarly paper; multipage Web documents with an HTML table of contents linked to multiple interlinked images, databases, and HTML pages that make up a single website. All such compound digital objects result from an intention to create them according to a plan, drawn from an overarching vision; they don't happen spontaneously.

Digital Repositories

When it became obvious that digital materials would need long-term care and feeding, both by the creators and the caretakers, those with something at stake began developing functional models for a repository in which to store them. We now have a robust model, and various groups have begun to develop or adapt software to provide the functions outlined in the model. I look at all that below, briefly, and in more depth in chapter 5.

The OAIS Model: Functional Requirements for Repositories

The Open Archival Information System Reference Model (OAIS) originally came from NASA's Consultative Committee for Space Data Systems,[5] and it has become an ISO standard.[6] The model defines the modules and functions of a digital repository at a very high level; it defines the components such a repository must have and how the components relate among themselves and with the outside world of donors and users. The OAIS developers took particular pains to keep the language of the model free of any professional or discipline imagery so anyone could adopt it, thus making it a shared language across all disciplines. They succeeded; the language of the OAIS does not have an aerospace ring to it—which NASA wanted to avoid—but it also doesn't sound like anything archivists or curators would say on a normal day.

When they published the model, the developers included a conceptual diagram to explain it, but unless you're used to reading such things, the diagram can confuse you more than a verbal description. In chapter 5 I describe the OAIS model in some detail and tell you where to go to find the diagram, but I deliberately don't include it anywhere in this book. Right now I want to simply introduce the OAIS concepts to inform your reading for the next couple of chapters. As you read through the discussion below, just roll with the language and go with the images—don't think you have to understand in any detail: there will be no quiz.

According to the OAIS model, a digital repository must have six major units: 1) ingest,[7] 2) archival storage, 3) data management, 4) administration, 5) preservation planning, and 6) access.

Ingest

The repository must have a defined routine for moving digital materials from the creator's system to the repository's storage devices. The ingest process needs hardware and software and a well-defined set of processes to work smoothly. The OAIS model assumes that the repository will set certain parameters for the materials it can accept and that the creator will meet those requirements before submitting its Submission Information Package (SIP). However, most collecting repositories today accept whatever donors provide.

Archival Storage

The repository must have the facilities—hardware, software, and peripherals—to store authentic materials across time. The OAIS model assumes that the archived materials will have certain characteristics that protect its integrity, making it an Archival Information Package (AIP).

Access

The repository must have facilities—hardware, software, and peripherals—that will allow researchers to retrieve the contents. The OAIS model assumes that researchers will not work with "original" documents or systems. Instead, researchers will work through a system that provides them with "use copies," called Dissemination Information Packages (DIP). The access system will not allow users to corrupt the repository's data in any way.

Planning for Long-Term Retention

The repository must have people and policies that stay current with technological development and routinely question the long-term retention facilities and policies in use. The repository upgrades the facility, equipment, policies, and/or personnel skills as needed.

Data Management

The repository must have people, policies, and facilities to manage the archival storage in a way that protects the integrity of the materials. This undoubtedly means periodic migration of all data and could mean the use of emulation systems. Only with rigorous management of the data and its related metadata can the repository fulfill its mission.

Administration

The repository will need an administrative structure to manage personnel, policies, facilities, and finances. The OAIS reference model provides an overview of a repository's need, but no specific details beyond defining and describing processes and basic requirements for the various information packages. Any repository can adopt the whole system, or parts of it, as seems needed to improve its own operation. Below, I describe some of the details a repository must take into account.

Management Systems

The OAIS provides the model for the components a digital repository must have in place to function, but what hardware and software must a historical repository have to create something akin to what the OAIS calls for? Obviously, it will need the hardware for acquiring, storing, manipulating, and accessing the contents of the repository. Here I will make no suggestions, stressing that if you go in this direction, you'll want to get your software needs addressed and then get the hardware and peripherals you will need to support it. That is to say, *first* you determine what software tool(s) will best meet the requirements of your repository. While there are numerous commercial e-record/content/digital asset management systems and digital library software packages available, most cost too much for the average historical repository to consider. If you plan to create your own digital repository (I examine this option in chapter 5), most of you will have to turn to open-source software as a basis for building digital repositories. Below I examine the advantages and disadvantages of proprietary and open-source software.

Proprietary Systems

Commercial products have many positives. They usually come ready to use with minimum customization. Vendors often offer support during product installation and/or ongoing support and maintenance. Further, vendors will usually react quickly to address bugs in their software and provide patches and updates. Despite the cost, those of you who lack a strong technical support system may find that a proprietary system serves your needs best.

However, a proprietary system also has negatives. Commercial products using a unique file format may only respond to a narrow selection of programs— sometimes only one. To other programs, the files remain a mystery. When companies die, users find themselves without backup support and with potential problems in migrating files. Some commercial vendors do not make information about their code sequences readily available, nor do they guarantee accuracy of some information they provide. So, without that deep technical information, nobody can develop tools to keep such files alive over time. Other problems include high installation and license fees that increase over time and upgrade costs that may outweigh the value of what you will receive from the improved functionality.

Open-Source Systems

On the plus side, open-source programs typically come free and without restrictions on modifications, upgrades, and free redistribution, making the real benefit of using open-source software the fact that your system doesn't rely on a proprietary code and that you will not have license or usage restrictions. Nobody owns the code, so nobody has the right to take it off the market. Further, open-source systems have the flexibility that allows you to tailor them to your organization's requirements.

There is, however, no such thing as a free lunch; with the benefits come issues you should consider very carefully. While the software itself doesn't cost anything to acquire, it may come with no organized technical support. Instead, new users count on the community of seasoned users and consultants who can support the products. Typically, the user community takes the place of extensive documentation, though a growing number of books on open-source products have begun to appear. In theory, hundreds, if not thousands, of developers work with the most popular open-source products, and members of the user community can be reached through e-mail groups and other collaborative applications. Therefore, implementation, training, and maintenance may cost dearly.

Open-source communities of users call on members to share the discovery of bugs and to offer fixes to the community, free, for the benefit of all. However, individual institutions must integrate the fixes into their systems. Further, it is one thing to send out a request for help to the community, and quite another to get a response. Nobody *must* respond to your call for help. Software developers in other organizations are likely to be busy, and a question may either get no response or many different responses offering different solutions. Further, the general trend of development in the community of users you choose to join may not go in the direction you want, or the deeply tech savvy in that community may find something else they prefer, leaving you high and dry.

Management System Types

Recognizing the issues regarding open or proprietary systems, you will want to pick a type of system to use. By now you see that a digital repository involves much more than just computer hardware networked to enough storage devices to hold content. It must have the power to acquire, manage, preserve, and provide access to its digital holdings—all those OAIS functions.

As the private sector became aware of the need to manage its electronic records at least as well as its paper records, it created a market for systems designed to capture and manage electronic evidence of business transactions. These systems manage the content and structure of electronic records, provide access to them over time, and maintain linkages between records and the activities they document. A variety of disciplines has contributed to the current thinking about how to provide that functionality. The disciplines include: records management (RM), electronic records management (ERM), documents management (DM), electronic documents management (EDM), digital asset management (DAM), digital libraries management (DLM), enterprise content management (ECM), web content management (WCM), and knowledge management (KM). Some of these have potential as digital repositories for archival materials.

Electronic Document Management and Imaging Systems

Electronic document management and imaging systems (EDMS) first appeared as a way to reduce the amount of paper businesses had to store. Early EDMSs allowed a business to scan paper records and store the images in the EDMS. In time, EDMSs evolved into systems that could manage both digitized records and born digital records. While EDMSs ensured that captured records were unalterably fixed in time, this very characteristic turned out to also be a drawback. It proved inefficient to transfer an electronic document from the system that created it to the EDMS. Hence the rise of electronic records management systems (ERMS) that include a system to automatically pull records from their source and store them safely.

Electronic Records Management Systems

Electronic records management systems (ERMS) provide the control and management functions to provide comprehensive auditing and control over the access to and actions on records as records, not as scanned images. Typically they include rigorous retention controls, prevent records modification, prevent records deletion, and include rigorous arrangement structures and classification schemes to provide a secure repository. As you might expect, ERMSs aren't cheap, but they do offer one form of digital repository. Before you set out to acquire one, do your homework as to what you need and what you don't—it's one of those times when you must have a full grasp of your functional requirements. At a minimum, an ERMS should manage electronic documents in the context of a classification scheme. An ERMS should also manage versions of an electronic document as separate but related entities. It should work with related systems, including image-processing and scanning systems, while retaining full control of existing digital materials. An ERMS must copy the contents of an electronic record to an access system while ensuring retention of the original record intact. Undoubtedly we will have "closed" digital materials just as we have closed paper materials, and an ERMS should allow you to hide those records from public view. It should also set times, sometimes far into the future, when certain closed materials can return to the public view.

According to the 2006 National Archives of Australia's *Guidelines for Implementing the Functional Specifications for Electronic Records Management Systems Software*,[8] an ERMS should have the functionality to:

- Maintain records and files according to an applied classification scheme;
- Manage all required metadata of folders and records;
- Declare an electronic document as a business record and maintain its integrity as evidence of a business action or decision;
- Provide mechanisms and interfaces to search for and retrieve records;
- Manage retention and disposal of folders and records according to an applied retention schedule;
- Control access to folders and records and maintain an audit trail of actions taken on them; and
- Provide manageable, usable, and robust mechanisms to carry out core functions.

As businesses acquire ERM systems, they need to integrate ERM capability into their IT architectures and basic business procedures. While this integration continues to spread in the business world, it has been a bit slower to be customized to the archival environment and requirements.[9]

Digital Asset Management Systems

Digital asset management systems (DAMS) grew out of the media and entertainment industry, whose digital assets have substantial financial and intellectual property value. DAMSs have functionality similar to document management systems in that they focus on the storage, tracking, and use of media-rich documents. Like EDMSs and ERMSs, DAMSs require support or management by technical staff.[10]

Digital Library Systems

Digital library systems (DLS) grew out of the online world of repositories wanting to post digitized versions of their holdings on the Web. A DLS may include the following functions:

- Acquisition: the collecting of library materials through purchase, exchange, or license. As part of this function, the system should facilitate the acquisition of the digital rights that relate to the acquired materials, if only permission to use them. It should also have a mechanism for enforcing of those rights.
- Cataloging and indexing: the proper and consistent description of digital materials enables users to search for and retrieve those assets using cataloging standards such as MARC format and Dublin Core metadata.
- Storage of digital content: the management, naming conventions, and tracking of digital materials, and the ability to retrieve them easily. Unfortunately, to date, DLSs have not put a high priority on long-term retention of the digital materials they contain.
- Circulation and distribution: the management of digital materials like a traditional integrated library system. This includes the ability to record items issued and returned, items overdue, and items requested. These include the recording of user data, reading, and service preferences.

Institutional Repositories (IR)

"An Institutional Repository is an online repository for collecting, preserving, and disseminating—in digital form—the intellectual output of an institution, particularly a research institution."[11] The idea grew out of the dissatisfaction academics felt about the management of digital output that various research efforts had created. It was further fueled by their dependence on the academic publishing industry. Why didn't the institution create a repository through which researchers could make their work available to the public without depending on its being published in an academic journal?

The concept gained popularity with the development of a standard metadata scheme—the Open Archives Initiative (OAI) and its Open Archives Initiative Protocol for Metadata Harvesting (OAI-PMH)—which facilitated links among similar documents among many institutions through one search service—OAIster, which describes itself as a union catalog of digital resources.[12] Institutional repositories, much like digital libraries, involve collecting, housing, classifying, cataloging, preserving, and providing access to digital content. Unlike digital libraries, however, the institutional repository model makes provisions for institutional members to "deposit" their materials themselves. Over time, then, institutional repositories may acquire materials with significant historical value, but typically that has not motivated their development.

Nor have the developers always factored archival concepts into the development of the systems.[13] A variety of software suites for institutional repositories has appeared. According to a project called Repository66, the most popular IR software platforms are Eprints, DSpace, and bepress, with a handful of Fedora and Open Repository users.[14]

Metadata

As our understanding of the value and need for metadata has grown, so has our understanding that we need many different types of metadata to represent the many different facets of a document. To keep the types and schemes well organized, we need a "framework" for capturing and applying them to any given digital document and the activity around it. Several of these so-called frameworks have appeared.

Resource Description Framework (RDF) provides a framework for descriptive metadata that enables researchers to find something in a repository. Using RDF, a repository with published materials, digital materials, paper primary documents, and three-dimensional artifacts can use several different descriptive metadata schemes in one record in a way that keeps everything sorted out and easy for the computer to understand. A repository could add that metadata record to a union database of such records where researchers could discover it along with records from repositories all over the world. Tony Gill does a nice job of explaining how that works.[15]

The Open Archives Initiative (OAI) provides another framework for discovery metadata. Whereas RDF came from the W3C organization's work on the "semantic web,"[16] OAI has its roots in the institutional repository movement. Like RDF, OAI promotes broad access to digital resources through projects like OAIster, a union database of records describing more than sixteen million digital resources in more than a thousand repositories using the OAI protocol.[17]

While RDF and OAI provide frameworks for descriptive metadata, Metadata Encoding and Transmission Standard (METS) provides a framework for descriptive, administrative, and structural metadata, which is to say that METS provides a format for holding metadata used to manage, retain, display, and exchange digital materials.[18] It can handle complex, reformatted digital materials.

At the turn of the twenty-first century, OCLC and RLG combined their efforts and developed PREservation Metadata: Implementation Strategies (PREMIS), a framework for capturing the so-called preservation metadata that documents the life of a digital object across time. PREMIS "addresses provenance (who has had custody/ownership of the digital object?); authenticity (is the digital object what it purports to be?); preservation activity (what has been done to preserve the digital object?); technical environments (what is needed to render and use the digital object?); rights management (what intellectual property rights must be observed?)."[19] Without this information, we could not adequately keep track of our digital material with any certainty about its authenticity and integrity.[20]

New Media and Web 2.0

Just as we have begun to come to terms with long-term retention and format normalization of digital materials, new challenges emerged under the labels new media and Web 2.0.[21] The Web has undergone a number of major evolutions. Today's users comfortably work with Google Maps, GMail, Blogger, Flickr, Delicious, and Wikipedia. These new services have reset expectations about the Internet environment, creating a fundamental shift in both technology requirements and associated managerial requirements for archiving the results. In addressing the Netherlands Commission for UNESCO in November 2005, William Urrichio described "social media" as including "blogs (web logs), wikis, massively multi-player role-playing games, and various on-line social spaces."[22] He went on to assert that, unlike traditional archival objects or texts, social media are not "stable and fixed in the way that we think of photographs or films or books [and] fall outside of the familiar limits of our cultural habits and expectations." These new technologies have had a fundamental effect on users' expectations in the areas of rich user interfaces, participation, community services, categorization, and trust.

A number of web-based services and applications demonstrate the foundations of the Web 2.0 concept. Not really new technologies, the services (or user processes) apply capabilities inherent in the technologies and open standards that support the Internet and the Web, but use by the general public has only recently caught on. But it has caught on with the young—that is, donors of the future—really strongly. The services include blogs, wikis, multimedia-sharing services, content syndication, podcasting, and content-tagging services. Many of these applications of web technology are relatively mature, having been in use for a number of years, although new features and capabilities are being added on a regular basis.

Blog

The term *blog* has become the standard abbreviation of web log. A "blog is a Web page that serves as a publicly accessible personal journal for an individual. Typically updated daily, blogs often reflect the personality of the author. (v.) To author a Web log."[23]

Wiki

The term *wiki*, from the Hawaiian slang for "quick," applies to a collaborative website that "comprises the perpetual collective work of many authors. Similar to a blog in structure and logic, a wiki allows anyone to edit, delete or modify content that has been placed on the Web site using a browser interface, including the work of previous authors. In contrast, a blog, typically authored by an individual, does not allow visitors to change the original posted material, only add comments. The term wiki refers to either the Web site or the software used to create the site."[24]

From an archival standpoint, the main difference between blogs and wikis lies in the fact that wikis generally have a *history* function. History allows previous versions of an entry to be viewed through a *rollback* function; blogs don't.

Both wikis and blogs illustrate the new networked and collaborative forms of cultural creation. They abandon the traditional idea of authorship of a finished work and embrace a process of creating an organic and constantly evolving work that includes both original work and content copied from others. While characteristic of the collaborative mentality of the new social media, the results raise the question of how the archivist will evaluate such content and when to freeze it for capture. As Urrichio says later in the same 2005 article, "even if we accept the social [media] and acknowledge that patterns of interaction are as important as the text, how do we go about documenting them in meaningful ways?"[25]

Social Bookmarking Tools

Traditional ways of describing information have generally relied on well-defined and pre-declared vocabulary schemes ranging from simple controlled vocabularies to taxonomies to thesauri to full-blown ontologies. This orderly approach to cataloging allows for both the validation and quality control of known terms in the information system. By contrast, social bookmarking links are generally annotated with *tags*, which are free-form labels assigned by the user and not drawn from any controlled vocabulary. Describing intellectual property this way creates a "bottom-up" (or personal) approach compared with the traditional "top-down" (or organizational) approach to subject classification. This free-structured utility creates a vocabulary and classification scheme known as *folksonomy, social classification, open tagging, free tagging,* and *faceted hierarchy.* A formal subject classification system generally needs to prescribe the ordering of terms used in it, and the terms that will be allowed by it. By contrast, a free-tagging approach to subject classification has no order or limits, but produces vocabularies and relationship links recognized by most users. Further, like other Web 2.0 technologies, the more people use social bookmarking tools, the more value accrues to the system itself and to all who participate in it.[26]

Multimedia Storage and Sharing Services

Multimedia storage and sharing services allow users to contribute actively to the production of Web content on a massive scale.[27] Well-known examples include YouTube (video), Flickr (photographs), and Odeo (podcasts). Millions of people now produce and share their own podcasts, videos, and photos.

Audio Blogging and Podcasting

Audio blogging and podcasting services present talks, interviews, and lectures that the user can play either on a desktop computer or on a wide range of handheld MP3 devices. This ability has given rise to the growth of people's *personal catalogs*—digital collections of music, photographs, and videos from a growing range of services.

An additional dimension comes to this new world in the form of the Application Programming Interface (API). APIs provide mechanisms for programmers to use a set of programming modules without having access to the source code. An API that doesn't require the programmer to license or pay royalties is often described as *open*. Such open APIs have helped Web 2.0 services develop rapidly and have facilitated the combining of data from various sources with two technologies in one virtual space.[28] The unintended and novel synergies of services are informally referred to as service *mash-ups*. Service mash-ups are part of a wave of innovation on the Internet. Google Maps' API, for example, allows Web developers to embed Google maps within their own sites.[29] Amazon has started to allow access to its database through Amazon Web Services (AWS) API.

Much of this social media content is available for copy and use under Creative Commons[30] or similar "free use" copyright licenses. So by identifying online content that falls under such a "free use" license, a user can create a virtual collection of multimedia digital content to call his or her own. Archivists can also use it to create test environments and as a way to keep abreast of how social media tools are being used by our particular community of interest.

If content within media such as blogs or wikis derives much of its meaning from the very technology and media in which it is created and maintained, archivists face a huge hurdle in deciding how to capture such content. However, given the work we have already reviewed in the current landscape of digital curation, as well as all related fields with interest in this area, no doubt professionals and experts will create solutions and tools for the task. Keep in mind that you don't have to build the solutions to all these problems—large research universities and consortia will do that. Rather you must keep abreast of the issues surrounding new technologies and of attempts by others to address them. In this rapidly changing digital landscape, one of the most important skills required for success is learning to use and adapt the success of others.

Notes

1. Adrian Cunningham, "Digital Creation/Digital Archiving: A View from the National Archives of Australia" (paper presented at DigCCurr2007: An International Symposium in Digital Curation at the School of Information and Library Science at the University of North Carolina at Chapel Hill, April 20, 2007), www.ils.unc.edu/digccurr2007/papers/cunningham_

paper_7.pdf (accessed April 17, 2008). Accompanying slides available at www.ils.unc.edu/digccurr2007/slides/cunningham_slides_7.pdf.

2. OW2 Consortium, *ObjectWeb: Open Source Middleware*, middleware.objectweb.org/.

3. Terry Cook, "Byte-ing Off What You Can Chew: Electronic Records Strategies for Small Archival Institutions," *Archifacts* (April 2004): 1–20. See also: Archives and Records Association of New Zealand (ARANZ), www.aranz.org.nz/Site/publications/ papers_online/terry_cook_paper.aspx (accessed July 22, 2008).

4. John Gantz, et al. *The Expanding Digital Universe: A Forecast of Worldwide Information Growth through 2010: An IDC White Paper* (Framingham, Mass.: IDC, 2007), 1, www.emc.com/collateral/analyst-reports/expanding-digital-idc-white-paper.pdf (accessed April 17, 2008).

5. Wikipedia contributors, "Consultative Committee for Space Data Systems," *Wikipedia: The Free Encyclopedia*, en.wikipedia.org/wiki/CCSDS (accessed November 29, 2008).

6. International Organization for Standardization, *ISO 14721:2003, Space Data and Information Transfer Systems—Open Archival Information System—Reference Model* (Geneva: ISO, 2003), www.iso.org/iso/iso_catalogue/catalogue_tc/catalogue_detail.htm?csnumber=24683 (accessed July 20, 2008).

7. See what I mean about the language? Stay with it; after a while the gastronomic association fades.

8. National Archives of Australia, *Guidelines for Implementing the Functional Specifications for Electronic Records Management Systems Software* (February 2006), www.naa.gov.au/Images/ERMSguidelines_tcm2-1018.pdf (accessed April 17, 2008) or www.naa.gov.au/Images/ERMSguidelinesupdated_tcm2-1019.rtf (accessed April 17, 2008).

9. Carl Lagoze and Herbert Van de Sompel, "Object Reuse and Exchange Compound Information Objects: The OAI-ORE Perspective" (May 28, 2007): 2, www.openarchives.org/ore/documents/CompoundObjects-200705.html (accessed April 17, 2008).

10. Magan Arthur, "Intro to Digital Asset Management: Just What Is a DAM?" *CMS Watch* (April 30, 2005), cmswatch.com/Feature/124-DAM-vs.-DM (accessed April 17, 2008).

11. Wikipedia contributors, "Institutional Repository," *Wikipedia: The Free Encyclopedia*, en.wikipedia.org/wiki/Institutional_repository (accessed June 25, 2008).

12. *OAIster*. www.oaister.org/ (accessed June 25, 2008).

13. Michael Day, Maureen Pennock, and Julie Allinson, "Cooperation for Digital Preservation and Curation: Collaboration for Collection Development in Institutional Repository Networks" (paper presented at DigCCurr2007: An International Symposium in Digital Curation at the School of Information and Library Science at the University of North Carolina at Chapel Hill, April 20, 2007), www.ils.unc.edu/digccurr2007/papers/dayPennock_paper_9-3.pdf (accessed April 17, 2008). Accompanying slides available at www.ukoln.ac.uk/ukoln/staff/m.pennock/presentations/digccurr2007.ppt (accessed April 17, 2008).

14. Repository66, *Repository Maps*, maps.repository66.org/ (accessed June 25, 2008).

15. Tony Gill, "Metadata and the World Wide Web," in *Introduction to Metadata: Pathways to Digital Information* (Los Angeles: Getty Institute, 2000), www.getty.edu/research/conducting_research/standards/intrometadata/metadata.html (accessed April 17, 2008).

16. W3C. *Semantic Web Activity*, www.w3.org/2001/sw/ (accessed April 17, 2008).

17. Open Archives Initiative, www.openarchives.org (accessed April 17, 2008); OAISter, www.oaister.org (accessed April 17, 2008).

18. Library of Congress, *Metadata Encoding and Transmission Standard*, www.loc. gov/standards/mets/ (accessed April 17, 2008).

19. Online Computer Library Center (OCLC), "Preservation Metadata for Digital Materials," OCLC, www.oclc.org/research/projects/pmwg/background.htm (accessed April 17, 2008).

20. OCLC/RLG PREMIS (PREservation Metadata: Implementation Strategies) Working Group, "Implementing Preservation Repositories for Digital Materials: Current Practice and Emerging Trends in the Cultural Heritage Community" (Dublin, Ohio: OCLC Online Computer Library Center, September, 2004), www.oclc.org/research/projects/pmwg/surveyreport.pdf (accessed April 17, 2008); OCLC/RLG PREMIS Editorial Committee, "PREMIS Data Dictionary for Preservation Metadata, Version 2.0" (Dublin, Ohio: OCLC Online Computer Library Center, March, 2008), www.loc.gov/standards/premis/v2/premis-2-0.pdf (accessed April 17, 2008).

21. Paul Anderson, "What Is Web 2.0? Ideas, Technologies and Implications for Education," *JISC Technology and Standards Watch* (Feb. 2007), www.jisc.ac.uk/media/documents/techwatch/tsw0701b.pdf (accessed June 25, 2008).

22. William Urrichio, "Moving beyond the Artifact: Lessons from Participatory Culture," in *Preserving the Digital Heritage: Principles and Policies*, ed. Yola de Lusenet and Vincent Wintermans (The Hague: Netherlands National Commission for UNESCO, 2007), 16, www.unesco.nl/images/preserving_the_digital_heritage.pdf (accessed April 17, 2008).

23. JupiterOnlineMedia, "Blog," *Webopedia: An Online Information Technology Encyclopedia*, www.webopedia.com/TERM/b/blog.html (accessed June 17, 2008).

24. JupiterOnlineMedia, "Wiki," *Webopedia: An Online Information Technology Encyclopedia*, www.webopedia.com/TERM/w/wiki.html (accessed June 17, 2008).

25. Urrichio, "Moving beyond the Artifact," 17.

26. Tony Hammond, Timo Hannay, Ben Lund, and Joanna Scott, "Social Bookmarking Tools (I) A General Review," *D-Lib Magazine* 11, no. 4 (April 2005), www.dlib.org/dlib/april05/hammond/04hammond.html (accessed June 17, 2008).

27. Anderson, "What Is Web 2.0?" www.jisc.ac.uk/media/documents/techwatch/tsw0701b.pdf (accessed April 17, 2008).

28. The Programmable Web website (programmableweb.com/) keeps track of the number of APIs available and what people use them for—it recently registered over three hundred. Programmable Web claims that over 50 percent of data mash-ups use Google Maps.

29. Google, *Google Maps API*, www.google.com/apis/maps/ (accessed July 23, 2008).

30. Wikipedia contributors, "Creative Commons," *Wikipedia: The Free Encyclopedia*, en.wikipedia.org/wiki/Creative_Commons (accessed July 23, 2008).

Chapter 4

Long-Term Retention and Access

So now we come to the core of the problem—how do we preserve digital materials across decades and centuries? The question periodically appears on archives and electronic records listservs I've monitored for more than a decade. Though the responses change as technology evolves, nobody claims to have a foolproof answer. We know that doing nothing guarantees digital materials will not survive; we can't guarantee that what we do will ensure their survival across centuries. The knowledge raises a number of questions: 1) What do we mean by long-term retention of digital materials? 2) How will we keep the digital materials? What form will we keep them in? How can we guarantee and prove they haven't changed or disappeared? 3) Who will do it? 4) Where will they do it? I will address the first two issues in this chapter, and take up the second two in chapters 5 through 7.

What Do We Mean by "Retaining" Digital Materials?

Archivists think in terms of "forever." We all recognize that most documents will not truly last forever, but we hear tales of ancient documents that have survived millennia and we take up the challenge to establish policies and practices that will carry our collections to that degree of longevity. We may have a shot at doing that with some paper materials, but what about digital materials? The truth is, we don't know, but our commitment to the archival function compels us to proceed as if we can find a way. After all, if we accession something into our holdings, aren't we effectively promising it immortality?[1]

Further, we have a reason for wanting to retain the digital materials and records we acquire: they fit our collecting policy and will support the work of the researchers who use our repository. At a minimum, we expect digital materials will provide the researcher with some information or evidence[2] that will forward his or her work. Optimally, we may see the researcher actually using data to answer the questions that she or he might have under investigation. With this in mind, we must do what we can to keep our long-term retention decisions from impeding use of the materials, within the terms of the deed of gift.

Therefore, we know that we will have to keep the data and the links that create whole digital documents far longer than we need to preserve the hardware and software that produced them, and far longer than anyone can reasonably predict the direction or rate of technological change. The uncertainty of the future strongly influences the strategies we should adopt to ensure effective long-term retention. That understanding brings us back to the observation by Clifford Lynch in chapter 2: not all digital materials will find immortality in the same way.

How Will We Retain Digital Materials?

By now you know that you can't just put digital materials into a box, put them on a shelf, keep them in the dark with meticulously controlled temperature and humidity, and expect the contents to last for the next few centuries. They won't. We cannot retain them like we can preserve a bundle of letters or a collection of photographs, which is why I prefer not to use the term *preserve* in relation to digital materials. We must copy them in some way. To copy means to change, to transform the original in known and unknown ways. "Differences will always be introduced in copying: the trick is to regulate the process sufficiently so the resulting differences are of little or no consequence and that the properties of greatest consequences are shared"[3] between the original and the copy.

Convert to Analog

I've seen several discussions on the Archives listserv over the past decade in which curators discuss how they handle computer-dependent materials that show up in collections. Some attempt to save them in the original form; others reformat them to paper and then treat them as paper. I'm sympathetic to the latter. There's no question that a printout of an e-mail is not the original, but neither is a preservation photocopy of a deteriorating news clipping. Provided that the essential contextual information appears as part of the printout, a researcher fifty years from now will probably not care about the internal metadata that the printout does not contain. He or she will just be grateful that the content and essential context still exist in a usable format.

Converting digital materials to analog provides a technique for retaining the content of some digital materials, but we cannot think of it as a long-term retention method for all digital materials. That said, converting digital materials to a stable analog format—printing a document to paper or a film-based medium like microfilm or microfiche or a nickel disk[4]—has much to recommend itself as a strategy for small repositories. The strategy does not receive a lot of respect in the world of large well-funded repositories and research centers, but as an immediate response for small shops, I think it has a lot of merit.

Analog formats do not suffer from the same fragility that digital formats do; they keep well. Once you have made the conversion, you *can* put the materials into a box, put the box on a shelf, keep it in the dark with meticulously controlled temperature and humidity, and expect the contents to last for the next few centuries. Digital media need refreshing and migrating periodically to keep up with technological advances. Analog formats need only a light source, perhaps a magnifier, and a human eyeball to read the content.[5] Digital materials need a "machine" that understands them. As someone observed during a listserv debate, "Which is of more value to society: Protecting the intrinsic value of the records and severely limiting access, or foregoing intrinsic value in favor of making the information available to a wider audience?"[6]

However, the cumulative cost of converting one or more large digital collections of text documents to analog may run high. Further, not all digital material lends itself to conversion to analog. While analog materials may preserve the content of a document, they do not preserve the functionality. After we have converted them, we can no longer exercise the powerful search engine tools for querying a textual collection. Nor can we manipulate a database we've converted to analog. Converting to analog kills any hyperlinks that a file may contain. Finally, conversion to analog may not preserve as much metadata about creation and use as we would like or need. So, while the decision to convert to analog makes a lot of "quick and dirty" sense in a lot of cases, do revisit the decision when any of the issues above appear.

Ordinarily, "convert to analog" means print to paper, but it can also mean copying computer data to microfilm or microfiche. Obviously storing microforms takes less space than paper, but computer output microfilm (COM) requires specialized equipment to both create the forms and read them. Therefore, COM can provide a very cost-effective analog format for very large volumes of data, but may not for smaller collections.[7]

Retain Digitally

If we don't convert to analog, how do we retain digital materials over time? As I pointed out in chapter 2, all digital material amounts to a stream of electrical states of on and off, called *bits*, represented by 1 for on and 0 for off. We organize the individual signals into consistent units of eight (00000001, 00000010, 00000011) called *bytes*. Then we refer to series of bits that flow through a computer or over a network as a *bitstream*. Retaining digital materials means retaining collections of bitstreams. Retaining a document digitally comes down to retaining bitstreams, their relationship to other bitstreams, and maintaining a system that can read and manipulate them.

As you can imagine, retaining bitstreams across time depends on hardware and software. To retain bitstreams reliably, we must carry out several fundamental actions in response to the way computers work. We start by recognizing that every bitstream has a unique identifier, called a *checksum*—a small piece of information of fixed size, independent of the size of the bitstream. The computer calculates the checksum based on the contents of the bitstream. We can assume the checksum exists because computers create them for their own purposes. It *will* be there, and it is difficult for any accidental or deliberate alteration of the file to take place without altering the checksum. If we can show, using files' checksums, that we have every bitstream given to us (and no more), we can show completeness of the materials being moved—the fixedness. Fixity refers to the concept that what we have is exactly what the creator created; nothing has changed. We can trust the authenticity of digital materials only if we routinely confirm their fixity through regular checksum monitoring.

Although computers create checksums for their own use, we may have a hard time finding and using them, so we can create our own; indeed, we should. We should calculate a checksum upon initial receipt of the digital material and then periodically recompute and compare it to the original to make certain nothing has changed. We should schedule checksum comparisons on a routine basis, including any time an object is retrieved, transferred to new media, transmitted over a network, or processed in any way that allows for change to its bitstreams. We usually use encryption to create a checksum.[8] Two well-known examples are MD5 (Message Digest 5) and SHA-1 (Secure Hash Algorithm 1). MD5 comes as a standard component on most Unix and Unix-like systems, including Linux. MacOS X has a component called Md5sum. In addition, you can find a number of freeware MD5 generators for Windows.

You can see how this would work: as soon as new digital materials arrive, we calculate the checksums. We maintain, somewhere outside our long-term retention system, one or more lists of bitstreams and checksums, and we add this information about the new materials to that. Periodically we compare the information in both systems. Any difference between the numbers we get at the check and the numbers we have on file indicates that either the system has failed or someone has tampered with the files. Regardless, the situation needs investigating. Whenever we alter the format of our preserved files, we alter the bitstreams. After each reformatting, then, we recalculate all the checksums on the data and store the numbers. We place access controls on the checksum system so that no one person can simultaneously alter the information in both systems.

Fortunately modern hardware for storing, manipulating, and transmitting digital content has intrinsically low error rates, so random errors do not occur often. However, unanticipated changes can and do occur as a result of malfunction, media degradation, human error, and malicious intent. Therefore, any digital repository must routinely monitor checksums through some form of manual or automated process—once every six months to two years.

Refreshing

If you have digital materials on old media, you need to "refresh" them periodically. You refresh them by "playing" them—that is, putting them into the electronic environment that created them and in which their creators intended them to work. Refreshing will preserve digital materials for a while, but as we discussed in chapter 2, eventually both the hardware and the storage media die. Before that happens, you must migrate the materials to a new environment.

Migration

Migration is a commonly recommended method for preserving digital materials by copying them from an old storage medium to a new one. Migration means copying—that is, moving documents from one system to another while maintaining their authenticity, integrity, reliability, and usability. The new storage media will be either of the same type as before, for example, hard drive to hard drive, or of a different type, such as floppy to flash drive. You may already have had the experience of migrating the content of 5.25-inch floppy disks to 3.5-inch floppy disks and then to CDs.

Migration causes change. The Cornell University Library did some testing to find out whether we can know and measure and thus plan for the changes caused by migration. The tests showed that we can. We can measure the changes that migration will cause, thus preparing for them to happen.[9] As I've indicated, other techniques do exist, but for now migration seems the best temporary solution.

Reformatting

Reformatting provides another way to move documents from one format to another. In the paper world, long-term retention techniques like preservation photocopying come to mind as a form of reformatting.[10] Reformatting digital materials causes many known changes, and some unknown changes. Think about the time you reformatted a document from one word processor to another. You could see some changes, and some you couldn't. Reformatting produces another version of the document; it does not re-create the original.

Normalization

The National Archives of Australia (NAA) developed the normalization strategy to preserve reformatted digital materials, because they distrust the migration process and the unpredictable changes it introduces.[11] Normalization calls for converting all document types, especially those created by proprietary software, to standard file formats. The NAA developed XENA, a conversion program to do that for them. They have made XENA available as an open-source program anyone can download from an NAA site called SourceForge.[12]

Normalization has gained many followers. In general, they recommend that you normalize digital materials to an open-source format to preserve both your documents and the metadata that applies to them. Open-source systems do not depend on any particular software system or hardware. Ideally, you will choose a format defined by a formal international or national standard. ASCII files will retain the content of text files, but will not retain the look and feel of the document. XML or HTML can retain both the content and the look and feel of original documents done in a proprietary format. Today most word processing software has the power to convert a document from the proprietary format of the program to an XML or HTML file. Adobe software's PDF format has become ubiquitous as a method for creating digital images of a wide variety of documents. However, Adobe's proprietary PDF format's algorithms use the reader program's fonts and other resources outside the saved document itself; it does not create a self-contained file. Adobe recognized the problem these practices caused for archival storage needs and developed PDF/A, which does create a self-contained and self-described file. Adobe has made PDF/A available as a formal standard.[13]

Using any of the protocols above—ASCII, XML, HTML, or PDF—will ensure that you don't have to depend on any one supplier of hardware or software to provide continued access to the documents. Many software suppliers support such standards, so even if you reach a stage where no commercially available software exists that can process your preserved files, the existence of the standards documentation means that someone can create new software to read, render, process, and reformat the files. If the standard comes from a recognized standards body, you can trust that the standards body will provide copies of the standard from copyright libraries and similar bodies in perpetuity. If the standard comes from a less formal body, you may want to retain and preserve a copy of the standards documentation with the digital materials.

The ICA recommends that you look for these characteristics in the format you choose as your normalization format:[14]

1. it should represent all information and relationships between information in the original record that we regard as significant;
2. it should comply with an international, national, or publicly available standard;
3. it should have a proven record in terms of longevity or widespread adoption;
4. it should allow you to access the records or you should have a way to transform [the data] into formats that you can use that way;
5. it should not rely on any particular software or hardware environment;
6. it should have a capacity to automatically convert from original formats to long-term retention formats, with automated detection and reporting of conversion problems or errors where applicable; and
7. (optionally) to automatically convert from our long-term retention format to the format used in the original or current record-creating systems.

Why do we need the requirements listed above? They assure some flexibility in what we store and how we store it. The ICA recognizes that files, as they exist on your donors' systems, may have some properties you don't need and that a long-term retention format which cannot preserve all those properties may still allow you to preserve the essential content and context of the document. For example, in a text document such as this book, the words and the order in which they appear matter significantly. In addition, matters such as pagination and section numbering also carry meaning, particularly if internal or external cross-references specify sections or pages of the document. While the exact font or type size used does not usually matter, stylistic variation such as the use of bold, italic, or underlined text often do. Exactly which properties matter usually depends on the type of document and the information within it. You want to show that your conversion process preserves all significant properties, or that it will warn you if it encounters a document that it cannot preserve.

Requirement (6) ensures that we can take documents from your donors' original systems into archival custody with the minimum of manual effort. It calls for a reporting system that alerts you to any problems that require human intervention to resolve. Having an automated system, or at least a well-defined process and workflow, improves the auditability of the long-term retention process and helps to demonstrate the integrity of the end result. Easy auditability allows you to focus your efforts on acquiring digital documents and the tools you will use for the work, rather than on proving the qualities of each preserved object.

The ICA made requirement (7) optional, since you need it only if you foresee a need to move documents back and forth between long-term retention in archival custody and use in the original document-creating system. That's not very likely in a collecting repository. If the donor continues to work with files, you can receive the newer versions without having to return the older ones.

After you have saved and normalized the bitstreams, you must find a place to store them. A strategy of keeping multiple copies scattered among a wide variety of repositories—the Lots of Copies Keep Stuff Safe (LOCKSS)[15] strategy—works on the assumption that disaster won't hit all copies at any one time. LOCKSS thinking starts by assuming that you will store your materials in areas that do not have the same exposure to the same natural disasters your area does. Repositories in Louisiana should seek a partner in an area not subject to hurricanes; repositories in Oklahoma should find a partner in an area not known for tornados; repositories in California should look to areas not subject to earthquakes. Obviously natural disasters don't pose the only threat to digital materials, but they represent the biggest and least controllable threat, so your thinking should start there and move down through a whole list of needs in partner repositories. In addition to geographical location, consider corruption of the storage media, human errors in the administrative process, and the potential for malicious destruction.

Most computer storage media can be counted on to last for about five years—some types last longer under ideal conditions. All types will last less long if stored in conditions that do not meet known specifications for temperature, humidity, or light levels. The LOCKSS strategy of creating multiple copies in multiple locations helps to protect information, to some degree, especially in analog format. The protection you gain through the use of multiple copies can mean that you can reduce the frequency of some of the other tests and processes referred to in this section. If you preserve material in digital formats and do all your copying at one time, you should assume that all the copies have a life expectancy of more or less the same length, depending on storage and use conditions.

Emulation

Emulation refers to building computer systems that can mimic (i.e., emulate) older hardware or software systems. Using emulation, a modern and presumably relatively inexpensive and easily maintainable computer can make old software applications appear and behave as they did in their original environment. In practice, emulation programs may not strictly maintain the look and feel of the original, but users may not insist on this.[16]

People who favor emulation over various "copy and move" techniques remind us that you can't copy something without changing it. If you change it, you no longer have the original document. They argue that we should use new technology to create an environment that exactly emulates the look and feel of the original. A few years ago, emulation did not have much of a following. But as digital materials have become more complex, emulation has begun to attract greater interest. If we think back to Lynch's hierarchy of complexity of digital media, it seems that emulation could solve the problems encountered in levels two, three, and four.

Metadata: The Key to Long-Term Retention and Integration

Just like content, we must capture and preserve metadata. Successful long-term retention and management of digital materials depends on metadata. Metadata forms the hub through which disparate modules and functions integrate and share content. In the context of an archival setting, a trustworthy digital repository with fully integrated metadata achieves functionality that can meet both repository and researcher needs.

Metadata serves many purposes; consequently many different types and standards have developed over the past two decades. Every step in the life of a digital object has metadata associated with it: technical metadata that describes the equipment and time of its creation; use metadata that tracks the various hands (figuratively speaking) the object passed through; administrative metadata that informs the system and IT people about how to manage it; and preservation metadata that may document actions such as migration or emulation or record the effects of strategies and thereby assert the authenticity of the digital object over time. There's also discovery metadata that allows a user to find and retrieve information from a digital archive. John Roberts of the Archives of New Zealand and Andrew Wilson of the National Archives of Australia have done a good job of explaining metadata varieties.[17] They have their own agenda in presenting the information they present, but you can ignore the agenda and just absorb the concepts.

During his SAA workshop on *Basic Electronic Records*, Geoffrey Huth emphasizes that you should check metadata as soon as you receive new materials. When the materials are fresh in your hands, they may be fresh in the mind of the creator; if key metadata is missing, maybe you can successfully go back and get the metadata that you need.

Who Will Do It?

Noncustodial Responsibility versus Custodial Control

In the world of paper documents, we all assume we will store and manage our collections under our own roofs, so to speak. During the late 1980s and into the 1990s, leaders in the digital materials world debated whether it might be better if digital materials should be moved to a repository or whether they should stay with their creators, under the authority of the archivist. Corporate and governmental shenanigans at the turn of the twenty-first century discredited the "leave the documents in the hands of the creator but under archival supervision" school of thought. We have come to recognize that creators may have reason to destroy archival documents, and that the archivist may not have enough authority to protect those documents adequately. Storage has become relatively cheap; I think it's best to move physical materials to an archives and digital materials to a trustworthy digital repository (TDR).

Skills for Doing It

The skills and knowledge required to ensure effective long-term retention of digital materials will likely come from a variety of people. Someone in your repository must understand the donors and the technical context of their collections: applications, file formats, and how people use(d) them. The knowledge rarely needs to be very technical, but it must be there, and it will vary from donor to donor. Most donors will have used a small number of common file formats. In time, you can expect to develop or find guidelines on managing the most common file formats as well as the file-conversion software to do the job. I go into this more deeply in chapter 5. Thereafter, if you have someone who can assess which guidelines apply to which donors, and how to apply them, you're in good shape.

If you must deal with unique or obscure file formats for which no guidelines exist, or for which existing guidelines do not provide sufficient practical advice, you may need to have a greater level of technical skills available to develop the necessary tools to preserve the documents and test and validate those tools. Perhaps you could work with another archival institution in situations like this.

Relationship to the Access System

"Access" to digital materials can mean many things. It can mean providing a way to print them; it can mean providing copies using a portable medium; it can mean providing interactive access via the World Wide Web; or providing access to users with a mobile telephone or other handheld devices. Whatever "access" might mean now or in the future, a properly designed long-term retention system will permit access while it protects the material from any changes to the mechanisms or formats used to retain the documents.

The OAIS model calls for one system for long-term retention of digital materials (a dark archive that no users have access to), and another for providing access to them. This separation of access from long-term retention will allow you to choose long-lived file formats and software systems for long-term retention while accommodating short-term requirements of the user community. For instance, since the 1990s, the preservation community has recommended the Tagged Image File Format (TIFF) as the ideal choice for the long-term retention of digital still images, and we can expect that recommendation to continue for at least the next ten years.[18] However, TIFFs tend to be very large and load slowly, transfer over network links slowly, and fill a lot of storage space. Many users lack software that enables them to work with TIFF images easily. Further, other formats do a better job than TIFF at allowing copyright holders to exercise control over what the end user can do with the images. So, while TIFFs may provide the best long-term retention format for the foreseeable future, they do not serve the researcher well. Instead, most researchers prefer smaller, more easily controlled derivative files in a less sophisticated format, like a Joint Photographic Experts Group (JPEG) file. In the OAIS model, the archival storage module would hold the TIFF images, while the public module would hold JPEG files. Only rarely would a specialized researcher need access to the larger TIFF file.

While we will probably change how we present our materials to the public, if we use a normalized stable archival format we will not need to worry that we have compromised our copy of the materials made for long-term retention. Further, separating the systems divides the risks. If we have problems on one or the other server, we can address them without fear that we might destroy everything. With a separate long-term retention system in place, we can then think about how to create derivative materials for users to access, or separate systems that have one or more interfaces for users.

We can keep documents accessible even if we no longer have the hardware or software initially used to produce them if we have something that makes them available to researchers. Our long-term retention systems do not need all the functions of the system that created the documents. For example, we don't want anyone to have the ability to alter them. For most flat documents, viewing suffices. Databases and database-like materials get trickier. If the creating system allowed users to locate and/or sort documents by specific properties such as date, title, and author, we will need to replicate something of that access mechanism.

Handling Common Types of Storage Media

Magnetic Technology

Magnetic media—tape and floppy disks—consist of a flexible base of plastic, an inert binding material, and magnetically charged metal filings. The plastic can become relatively rigid and break. The binding media can lose its ability to bind. It will flake off and take the magnetic media with it. The magnetic medium can lose its charge and with it the information the charge represents. You may not know exactly what combination of problems will confront you, so you cannot count on any guidelines as firm and fixed. As a general rule, however, store magnetic media in temperatures ranging from 40° to 68° F (5° to 20° C) with 20 to 45 percent relative humidity.

Unfortunately, the best storage conditions will only make the best of a bad situation. Magnetic media do not have a long life expectancy. Figure on a maximum of ten years under optimal conditions. If you get longer than that you have, as they say in Louisiana, *lagniappe*—a little something extra.

Because researchers will want to use the magnetic media in an environment that does not provide optimum conditions, good practice calls for having an archival copy stored in optimal conditions, and a user copy that you will replace occasionally. You'll find a very useful chart on storage and life expectancy of magnetic media in Alan A. Andolsen's article in the May/June 2006 issue of *The Information Management Journal.*[19]

Optical Technology

Optical technology—CDs and DVDs—lasts longer than magnetic technology. Created by encasing the recording material in a sandwich of plastic, the recording process uses light to encode the recording medium by changing its physical properties, not magnetic ones. So long as the recording medium holds up, the information remains accessible. Therefore, you need to provide the physical medium optimal conditions for its long-term retention. As with magnetic media, consistency in the environment is a big factor. Keep temperatures between 59° and

68° F (15° to 20° C) with relative humidity of 25 percent to 45 percent. Under those conditions, you can expect an optical disk to last from twenty-five to two hundred years, depending on its structure and the recording process used to create it.

Again, because researchers will want to use the disks in an environment that does not provide optimum conditions, good practice calls for having an archival copy stored in optimal conditions, and a user copy that you can replace as needed. Andolsen's article also includes disk technology.

Digital Images

Beginning around the year 2000, the standard domestic camera took digital images. Some people transferred the images to their computers or a variety of digital storage devices. Even people who used older film-based cameras could receive their images from the developer on a CD instead of printed photographs. In addition, home scanners helped people convert older photographs and negatives to a digital format. All of these will show up in your collections.

Digital images bring some advantages to your repository, the most obvious being that you can duplicate them for the researcher with no loss of quality. Further, scholars can access them with no concern about any degradation of the original. Finally, digital images can be output to a variety of formats, again with no degradation of the original. Digital images carry some disadvantages as well. First, their digital format makes them vulnerable; second, we can manipulate them so easily, neither you nor your researchers can fully trust that what they show represents an unaltered image of the picture as first taken.

Donors may have scanned lots of "born analog" text documents in a variety of ways for a variety of purposes. In no case, as they scanned, did they have you in mind. You must assume that quality will vary, both the quality of reproduction, the quality of the content, or the amount and quality of the metadata collected or applied. When confronted with digital material created that way, you will start by appraising whether they are worth keeping, considering their content, their technical quality, and their provenance.

Only you can determine if the scans have good enough technical quality[20] to serve your institutional needs. To help that process, consider adopting Anne Kenney and Stephen Chapman's suggested minimums for scanned images for access purposes.[21] They call for a minimum resolution of 300 to 600 dots per inch. With such guidelines (if not absolute rules), you have an objective standard for deciding whether the quality of the scans you have received makes them worth keeping.

If the digital images and digital materials started as analog documents, you might find no compelling reason to keep them. You could note in your description of materials that digital images once existed, but choose the analogs to store in your repository. Alternatively, you could use the digital version as an "access copy" for posting and copying as needed. Put the analog copy away so it will receive as little handling as possible. Also store the original digital image out of harm's way, using a copy for public purposes. As you decide, consider the commitment of resources in both personnel and technical infrastructure you must make to retain them; are they worth it?

E-mail

One observer suggested that "e-mail is probably the painpoint that is most likely to result in a longer-term resolution for electronic preservation. After all, there isn't an analog storage alternative for databases. . . . Same thing for video and audio, and Flash-based animation, and the volume of Web page snapshots that organizations need to store (and just don't realize it yet). We have to come up with a better mechanism for digital preservation (or better media and hardware), and email is the catalyst because of the importance of the information, the importance of the underlying functionality and metadata, and the volumes that are prohibitive to convert to analog."[22]

For many people, e-mail has become the preferred way of communicating, and e-mail types now parallel all types of physical mail: personal correspondence, business correspondence, commercial offers, and even junk mail. Further, like regular mail, most people "throw out" most e-mail they get by deleting it. Or, it may just disappear when the storage system that houses it ceases to function after a "crash" or replacement. When e-mail comes to your repository, treat it as you would paper mail. That means appraise it, process it, describe it, and hang on to it.

While we haven't solved all the issues surrounding e-mail, a great deal of work has occurred. I'm particularly impressed by Maureen Pennock's work on "Curating E-mails: A Life-cycle Approach to the Management and Preservation of E-mail Messages." It's an installment of the evolving *DCC Digital Curation Manual* from the Digital Curation Center; as intended it provides a good place to start by addressing the issues clearly and offering lots of recommendations and practical approaches.[23] After thoroughly discussing the issue of standard file formats for storing e-mail, Pennock advises using a standard format, but does not recommend a particular one. She does advise that you avoid image-producing formats.[24]

A report entitled *From Digital Volatility to Digital Permanence: Preserving Email* by the Digital Preservation Testbed, an initiative of the Dutch National Archives and the Dutch Ministry of the Interior and Kingdom Relations, reads well and explains the technical issues clearly.[25] In the end, the authors recommend conversion of all e-mail formats to XML and explain how to do that.

Web Pages

You have probably noticed the growing number of web pages, "zines," and other sorts of newsletters. When you look at them, you will start with appraisal in mind: if this information were on paper, would you keep it? If you answer, "Yes, probably," you need to look at what you've gotten yourself into.

Individual web pages have analogues in the paper world, but complete websites don't. Further, websites change rapidly and have explicit linkage and relationships that may or may not reflect a paper system but which you must maintain. Web pages with interactive elements move beyond their paper analogues, making websites into something more like databases.

There are three ways commonly used for creating web pages. As with all other documents, knowing the creation process informs the long-term retention process. First, the creator can produce one long flat page and create links from one part to another on that one page. Second, the creator can make a relatively small home page and connect all other information to it through a series of links. In both cases, the sites the page links to have other links to other sites for an unknown depth—it's a web of relationships. Third, the creator sets up a database of information and presents it as requested by the user. All these methods may appear on a single site. All three present different capture and long-term retention problems.

Method 1: when the owner replaces text, the old text likely disappears completely. It's gone. If you want to capture it, you should plan to monitor the site regularly, capturing it every time it changes so you have a history of its evolution. Since the page is self-contained, capturing it in some analog form doesn't present the problem of vital links being rendered useless. It does mean that any animation will be stilled. Depending on how central animation might be, you may need to describe the animation and its contribution to the message of the site.

Method 2: much of what I've said above applies here as well. However, since this type consists of a variety of files linked in a variety of ways, you cannot simply capture it to analog; you must decide what to do about the links. The first layer of links undoubtedly has real meaning to the home page, and the second layer may also. But what about the third and fourth—and can you expect consistency of importance across layers? Probably not. You'll have to answer these questions as you appraise your donors' websites.

Method 3: the database presents the most problems. Like all databases, it has no permanent presentation form, and the context of its use changes with each user. Websites can pull data and content from both databases and Web environments, and then convert and export the content for viewing on a web page. In organizations, communications, publishing, and public relations, people—and sometimes librarians—create and manage websites while IT personnel provide the technical skills to maintain the content. At home, anyone with a few technical skills can make a web page. Frequently, large website owners have good policies in place governing webmasters and web content, but as Terry Cook points out,

> few in this community recognize the relevance of recordkeeping approaches for the website, issues of authenticity and accountability for its content, or require-ments for retention, disposal, and long-term retention, even though web content

has rapidly evolved from publicity and image to include business transactions and operational guidelines. As with the systems world . . . records managers are rarely consulted or involved as part of the normal business practices of the web world, and so again, archivists are also left out of the loop.[26]

Fortunately, since web pages are presented in an open-source format (HTML) used all over the world, creating a server on which you preserve web pages related to your collections isn't as daunting a task as creating a server for idiosyncratic proprietary software. A partnership among the University of Illinois; the Online Computer Library Center (OCLC); the National Center for Supercomputing Applications (NCSA); Tufts University's Perseus Project; the Michigan State University Library; and an alliance of state libraries from Arizona, Connecticut, Illinois, North Carolina, and Wisconsin has created a project called Exploring Collaborations to Harness Objects in a Digital Environment for Preservation (ECHO DEPository)[27] "to address the issues of how we collect, manage, preserve, and make useful the enormous amount of digital information our culture is now producing."[28] They include websites in their mission. They have adopted an appraisal strategy based on a model developed at the Arizona State Library. The strategy encourages archivists to appraise a website as a collection, not as a series of individual items.[29]

The Web-at-Risk project is another large effort to test issues in archiving the Web. It is one of eight collaborative projects funded by the Library of Congress as part of the National Digital Information Infrastructure Preservation Program (NDIIPP) and includes the California Digital Library, the University of North Texas, and New York University. The California Digital Library has chosen to build a prototype Web Archiving Service (WAS).[30] Like the ECHO DEPository above, this bears watching.

Alternatively, you could contract with the growing number of website archiving services that have begun to appear.[31] Doing so will require some homework to determine the trustworthiness of the various services.

The community of repositories attempting to preserve websites has become large enough that in May 2008, the International Internet Preservation Consortium (IIPC) established a listserv for archivists interested in web-harvesting issues, associated quality review, and archival issues as they relate to archiving websites. The list discusses tools for harvesting web material, using web archives, working with archived material, and accessing harvested material, with a focus on practical advice and solutions that apply to a wide range of tools and situations.[32]

Web 2.0

The Web has evolved. Yesterday it held electronic "papers" and databases that gave information to us, but which we could not respond to. Today, it acts like a village: Web users use Google Maps, GMail, Blogger, Flickr, Delicious, and Wikipedia regularly. These new services all exist on a decentralized infrastructure that provides a dynamic architecture for participation, capitalizes on collective intelligence and trust, scales up or down effectively and economically to allow users to loosely connect and share everything they want. This interactivity has reset expectations of and about user participation and community services in the online world.

A number of web-based services and applications demonstrate the foundations of the Web 2.0 concept.[33] They include blogs, wikis, multimedia-sharing services, content syndication, podcasting, and content-tagging services, discussed in chapter 3. These services (or user processes) are not real "technologies." Instead, Web 2.0 sites use building blocks of technologies and open standards that underpin the Internet and the Web.

Web 2.0 challenges archivists in two ways: 1) appraisal and acquisitions of Web 2.0 generated digital materials, and 2) joining the village by adding Web 2.0 services to our online repositories. Below I'll examine the first issue here and the second in chapter 8.

The Web 2.0 services have provided the tools for creating new cultural documentation based on both networking and collaboration. Leaving behind the traditional idea of authorship, these digital creations grow organically, constantly evolving as the author(s) add to the content—both original work and content copied from others. These services will offer future researchers invaluable information about the construction and functioning of our society. The evolution of the text over time, the thematic tags, and the patterns of links themselves constitute socially valuable data. Users will also manipulate the content in these services by cutting, pasting, copying, and editing within a personal digital space and carrying out a process of blending, mixing, mashing up one with another.[34] Any facet of the information acquires additional meaning because of other facets. Since this information derives much of its meaning from the conceptual relationships represented by the links, archivists must find a way to capture the links. However, capturing the links in any complete and authentic form raises huge issues.

Most of what fits under the umbrella of the Web 2.0 label lacks any comparable documentation among traditional archival objects. It falls almost completely outside the familiar expression of our cultural habits and expectations. Yet, the archivist should consider such collections as manifestations of a creator's persona that she or he may have shared and exchanged for similar works.[35] The resulting collections could represent a form of *personal archive* of a lifetime. They may well contain content from a person's educational experience and have direct links with "personal learning environments."[36] As the amount of available online information grows and network effects increase, a person's path through the virtual world will become archivally important. The history of this path might include a record of interaction with people or information sources, the setting up and continual modification of personal filtering mechanisms, records of group interactions with an information source and the interactions with other people's filters and knowledge. Besides this trend of tracking information paths, digital objects such as word processed documents or personal photographs may become history-enriched with the digital equivalents of scrawled marginalia, dog-earedness, etc.[37] In addressing this collaborative dynamism behind the new social media, an archivist must wonder how to evaluate the content and when to freeze it for capture. That's the appraisal issue I cover in chapters 6 through 8. It's also a technical issue for which we have no answer at the moment.

Summary

You will find many different ways to preserve digital materials, but all must preserve the core characteristics of authenticity, completeness, accessibility and understandability, processability, and potential reusability. Tools change over time, and I cannot advocate any one technique as the solution everyone should adopt. One of your principal considerations in planning for long-term retention will address how you can best accommodate future change. But you must act. The best way to learn how to preserve electronic materials is to get into the game. Sitting to the side and watching others will get you only so far.

Notes

1. Records managers and institutional archivists may cooperate to have series of inactive records, both electronic and paper, stored in the archives until their retention schedule runs out. But the collecting repository, by accepting a collection, deems it as having enduring value not ended by a records retention schedule.

2. *Evidence*, as used here, establishes that an action or event did or did not take place, decisions were or were not made, etc. Here it does not relate to formal legal processes alone.

3. David M. Levy, "Where's Waldo? Reflections on Copies and Authenticity in a Digital Environment," in *Authenticity in a Digital Environment: May 2000*, ed. Charles T. Cullen (Washington, D.C.: Council on Library and Information Resources, 2000), www.clir.org/pubs/reports/pub92/levy.html (accessed April 17, 2008).

4. HD-ROM (storage) and HD-Rosetta (human readability) from Norsam Corporation of Los Alamos, New Mexico. Based on work done at the Los Alamos National Laboratory in New Mexico, Norsam Technologies has developed a nonmagnetic, nonoptical data storage medium impervious to deterioration over time. On that medium, they use nanotechnology to engrave data and images that are eyeball readable with the help of a 500x microscope. See www.norsam.com (accessed Feb. 3, 2008).

5. David O. Stephens, *Records Management: Making the Transition from Paper to Electronic* (Lenexa, Kans.: ARMA International, 2007): 237–38.

6. Bill Roach, e-mail to the ERECS-L listserv December 12, 2004, subject line:

"email records," archived at http://listserv.albany.edu:8080/cgi-bin/wa?S1=ERECS-L/ Item #001693 (accessed July 23, 2008).

7. Sharon Gavitt, *Computer Output Microfilm (COM)*, New York State Archives Publication, no. 52 ([Albany, N.Y.]: New York State Archives and Records Administration, 2000), reprinted online March 14, 2002, www.archives.nysed.gov/a/records/mr_pub52.pdf (accessed June 25, 2008).

8. Checksums can be created by simple mathematical calculations, but those algorithms lack robustness as a security measure.

9. For more information, see Gregory W. Lawrence, et al., *Risk Management of Digital Information: A File Format Investigation* (Washington, D.C.: Council on Library and Information Resources, 2000), www.clir.org/pubs/abstract/pub93abst.html (accessed April 27, 2008). "The report includes a workbook that will help library staff identify potential risks associated with migrating digital information. Each section of the workbook opens with a brief issue summary; this is followed by questions that will guide users in completing a risk assessment. The appendixes also include two case studies for migration: one for image files and the other for numeric files." Maggie Jones and Neil Beagrie, *Preservation Management of Digital Materials: A Handbook* (London: British Library, 2001), http://www.www.dpconline.org/graphics/intro/definitions.html (accessed July 23, 2008).

10. Converting to analog is a form of reformatting.

11. Adrian Cunningham, "Digital Creation/Digital Archiving: A View from the National Archives of Australia" (paper presented at DigCCurr2007: An International Symposium in Digital Curation at the School of Information and Library Science at the University of North Carolina at Chapel Hill, April 20, 2007), www.ils.unc.edu/digccurr2007/papers/cunningham_paper_7.pdf (accessed July 12, 2008). Accompanying slides available at www.ils.unc.edu/digccurr2007/slides/cunningham_slides_7.pdf.

12. National Archives of Australia, "Xena Digital Preservation Software," http://xena.sourceforge.net/ (accessed April 25, 2008).

13. AIIM, "Frequently Asked Questions (FAQS): ISO 19005-1:2005 (PDF/A-1)," July 10, 2006, http://www.aiim.org/documents/standards/19005-1_FAQ.pdf (accessed July 23, 2008).

14. ICA Committee on Current Records in an Electronic Environment, *Electronic Records: A Workbook for Archivists*, ICA Study 16 (Paris: ICA, April 2005), 41, http://www.ica.org/en/node/30273 (accessed April 17, 2008).

15. Victoria A. Reich, "Lots of Copies Keep Stuff Safe as a Cooperative Archiving Solution for E-journals," *Issues in Science and Technology Librarianship* 36 (Fall 2002), www.istl.org/02-fall/article1.html (accessed June 25, 2008).

16. Margaret Hedstrom, et al., "'The Old Version Flickers More': Digital Preservation from the User's Perspective," *American Archives* 69, no. 1 (Spring/Summer 2006): 159–87.

17. John Roberts and Andrew Wilson, *International Recordkeeping/Records Management Metadata Initiatives: Report and Recommendations for DC Advisory Board*, http://dublincore.org/groups/government/dcmi_resource_management.pdf (accessed June 5, 2008).

18. ICA Committee on Current Records in an Electronic Environment, *Electronic Records: A Workbook for Archivists*, ICA Study 16 (Paris: ICA, April 2005), 38, www.ica.org/en/node/30273 (accessed April 17, 2008).

19. Alan A. Andolsen, "Will Your Records Be There When You Need Them?" *The Information Management Journal* 40, no. 3 (May/June 2006): 56–61.

20. Meaning do they accurately and legibly portray the original image—the image has not been substantially altered from the original thus raising the issue of authenticity and reliability—contain a useful level of detail, etc.

21. Anne R. Kenney and Stephen Chapman, *Digital Imaging for Libraries and Archives* (Ithaca, N.Y.: Department of Preservation and Conservation, Cornell University Library, 1996), 33.

22. Jesse Wilkins, "Email Records" to ERECS-L Listserv, December 21, 2004, http://listserv.albany.edu:8080/archives/erecs-l.html (accessed July 23, 2008).

23. Maureen Pennock. *DCC Digital Curation Manual Instalment on Curating E-mails: A Life-cycle Approach to the Management and Preservation of E-mail Messages* (Bath, England: Digital Curation Center, 2006), www.dcc.ac.uk/resource/curation-manual/chapters/curating-e-mails/ (accessed April 17, 2008).

24. Pennock, *DCC Digital Curation Manual Instalment on Curating E-Mails*, 33, www.dcc.ac.uk/resource/curation-manual/chapters/curating-e-mails/ (accessed April 17, 2008).

25. Testbed Digitale Bewaring, *From Digital Volatility to Digital Permanence: Preserving Email* (The Hague: Digital Preservation Testbed, 2003), www.digitaleduurzaam-heid.nl/bibliotheek/docs/volatility-permanence-email-en.pdf (accessed June 13, 2008).

26. Terry Cook, "Byte-ing Off What You Can Chew: Electronic Records Strategies for Small Archival Institutions," *Archifacts* (April 2004): 1–20, www.aranz.org.nz/Site/publications/ papers_online/terry_cook_paper.aspx (accessed June 13, 2008).

27. ECHO DEPository, www.ndiipp.uiuc.edu/index.php?option=com_frontpage& Itemid=1 (accessed April 17, 2008).

28. Judith Cobb, Richard Pearce-Moses, and Taylor Surface, "ECHO DEPository Project," http://www.ndiipp.uiuc.edu/pdfs/IST2005paper_final.pdf (accessed April 17, 2008).

29. ECHO DEPository, www.ndiipp.uiuc.edu/index.php?option=com_content&task=view&id=18&Itemid=44 (accessed April 17, 2008).

30. Kathleen Murray and Mark Phillips, "Collaborations, Best Practices, and Collection Development for Born-Digital and Digitized Materials" (paper presented at DigC-Curr2007: An International Symposium in Digital Curation at the School of Information and Library Science at the University of North Carolina at Chapel Hill, April 20, 2007), www.ils.unc.edu/digccurr2007/papers/murrayPhillips_paper_9-3.pdf (accessed June 17, 2008). Accompanying slides at www.ils.unc.edu/digccurr2007/slides/murrayPhillips_slides_9–3.pdf.

31. Wikipedia contributors, "'Web Archiving,' subsection on 'External Links,'" *Wikipedia: The Free Encyclopedia*, http://en.wikipedia.org/wiki/Web_archiving#External_links (accessed June 25, 2008).

32. "International Internet Preservation Consortium Announces New Mailing List for Web Curators," *Netpreserve.org*: International Internet Preservation Consortium, http://www.netpreserve.org/press/pr20080519.php (accessed June 25, 2008).

33. Paul Anderson, "What Is Web 2.0? Ideas, Technologies and Implications for Education," *JISC Technology and Standards Watch* (February 2007), www.jisc.ac.uk/media/documents/techwatch/tsw0701b.pdf (accessed April 17, 2008).

34. Christine Borgman, "Personal Digital Libraries: Creating Individual Spaces for Innovation" (paper presented at the NSF/JISC Post Digital Library Futures Workshop, June 15–17, 2003, Cape Cod, Massachusetts), http://www.sis.pitt.edu/~dlwkshop/paper_borgman.html, in Anderson, "What Is Web 2.0?" (accessed June 25, 2008).

35. Neil Beagrie, "Plenty of Room at the Bottom? Personal Digital Libraries and Collections," *D-Lib Magazine* 11, no. 6 (June 2005), www.dlib.org/dlib/june05/beagrie/06beagrie.html; Borgman, "Personal Digital Libraries" in Anderson, "What Is Web 2.0?" (accessed June 25, 2008).

36. Wikipedia contributors, "History of Personal Learning Environments," *Wikipedia: The Free Encyclopedia*, http://en.wikipedia.org/wiki/History_of_personal_learning_environments (accessed June 25, 2008).

37. Peter Morville, *Ambient Findability* (Farnham: O'Reilly, 2005), 150, in Anderson, "What Is Web 2.0?" (accessed June 25, 2008).

Chapter 5

TDR or Dark Archive?

To TDR or Not to TDR?

"Digital curation and preservation is a risk management activity at all stages of the longevity pathway," argue Ross and McHugh.[1] "Preservation is an outcome," says Clay Shirky. "You don't know if it is working until afterward. All you can do is reduce the risk of loss. Making digital durable is a 'wicked' problem, meaning it can't actually be solved. It will be an endless process of negotiation."[2] Nobody thinks that every archival repository will find a way, in-house, to retain its own digital materials, and many people have committed to the idea of defining and creating a *trustworthy digital repository* (TDR). The real question comes down to this: Will you become a TDR yourself or will you hire space in one?

While no official definition of a TDR exists, over the past twenty years, our profession's understanding of what a digital archive must provide has broadened from an initial focus on software systems to an overall commitment to the stewardship of digital materials. A sustainable, trustworthy, well-supported, and well-managed digital repository needs hardware, software, policies, processes, services, and people to assure long-term retention and, perhaps, access to its content and metadata. It needs the ability to integrate a significant number of document and file types created through word processors, spreadsheets, e-mail systems, database management systems, website systems, imaging systems, computer-assisted design/computer-assisted publishing systems, and a host of other media, known and unknown, creating both structured and unstructured data. As I mentioned in chapter 3, the OAIS reference model provides the best high-level scheme to date. I'll repeat part of what I said there.

According to the OAIS model, a digital repository must have six major units: 1) ingest, 2) archival storage, 3) data management, 4) administration, 5) planning for long-term retention (called preservation planning in the model), and 6) access.

Ingest: the repository must have a defined routine for moving digital materials from the system of creation to the repository's storage devices—a process with hardware and software to make it happen. The model assumes that the repository will set certain parameters for the materials it can accept and that the creator will meet those requirements before submitting its Submission Information Package (SIP).

Archival storage: the repository must have the facilities—hardware, software, and peripherals—to store authentic materials across time The model assumes that the archived materials will have certain characteristics that protect its integrity, making it an Archival Information Package (AIP).

Access: the repository must have a facility—hardware, software, and peripherals—that will allow anyone with the necessary authority to retrieve the contents. The model assumes that researchers will not work with "original" documents or systems. Instead they will work through a system that provides them with "use copies," called the Dissemination Information Package (DIP). The access system will not allow users to alter the archived data in any way.

Planning for long-term retention: the repository must have people and policies that stay current with technological development and routinely question the long-term retention facilities and policies in use.

Data management: the repository must have people and policies to manage the archival storage in a way that protects the integrity of the materials in its care. That will undoubtedly mean periodic migration and could mean the use of emulation systems. Regardless, only with rigorous management of the data and its related metadata can the repository fulfill its mission.

Administration: the repository will need an administrative structure to manage personnel, policies, facilities, and finances.

The OAIS reference model provides a graphic scheme for visualizing a repository, but it provides no specific details beyond defining and describing processes and basic requirements for the various information packages. Any repository can adopt the whole system or parts of it as seems needed to improve its own operation.

TDR Guidelines

The OAIS model provides the de facto standard for TDR architecture; the experts agree that it defines what an archives must feature to provide indefinite long-term retention of digital materials. With the OAIS as the accepted conceptual model, a number of large research consortia and archival institutions have created checklists to define in greater detail the functionality needed to ensure that a repository is "trustworthy."

One of the first sets of guidelines came from the State Archives Department of the Minnesota Historical Society that grew out of a grant to the Minnesota State Archives from the National Historical Publications and Records Commission to establish an electronic records program in March 1998. In 1999, the project published its first section of what would become the *Trustworthy Information Systems Handbook*. It published its most recent version in 2002.[3] The *Handbook* reads well. Because it came early, it did not assume that its audience had deep knowledge of either the technology or the issues involved and explains them well. It does, however, focus on government information in Minnesota. Appendix G's tool called "Legal Risk Analysis Tool" provides a very nice format for documenting your issues. When you look at it, look for general principles rather than the answer to specific questions.

The Digital Preservation Testbed project also published a very readable report, *Functional Requirements for a Preservation System*, for the Dutch government. It uses the OAIS model and clearly explains, at a somewhat more technical level than I have here, what an archives' program will need to retain digital materials over time. It has some very clear diagrams and explanations that other materials rather assume you've already picked up on.[4]

A certification task force assembled by the Research Libraries Group (RLG) and the U.S. National Archives and Records Administration (NARA) completed their Trustworthy Repository Audit and Certification (TRAC) criteria in 2003 and subsequently released a checklist that provides a series of objective characteristics or functions that a trustworthy repository must have.[5] The checklist includes all aspects of the repository, including policies it should enforce, personnel it should hire, and characteristics of physical storage facilities it should have.

Others have developed requirement or specification documents for electronic records management systems (ERMS) that have interested the archival community. Australia, for instance, has developed its Functional Specifications for Electronic Records Management Systems Software;[6] the European Union has developed the Model Requirements for Electronic Records Management, now in its second iteration (MoReq2);[7] Germany has developed its Network of Expertise in Long-Term Storage of Digital Resources (NESTOR);[8] New Zealand has developed its Standard for Electronic Recordkeeping Systems;[9] the United States Department of Defense has developed DoD 5015.02-STD (2007)[10]—to name a few.

While each standard has slight variations, they all agree that a trustworthy digital repository must start with "a mission to provide reliable, long-term access to managed digital resources to its designated community, now and into the future."[11] The German NESTOR working group says a trusted, "long-term digital repository is a complex and interrelated system" (NESTOR 2006).[12] While it starts with a "digital preservation system," it must have an organization-wide commitment to the goal. That includes the organization's governance, organizational structure and staffing, policies and procedures, financial fitness and sustainability, the contracts, licenses, and liabilities under which it must operate, and inheritors of data.

Core Requirements

In a meeting at the Digital Curation Centre (U.K.) in 2007, DigitalPreservationEurope, NESTOR (Germany), and the Center for Research Libraries (North America) developed a list of ten "core requirements " for a digital repository:[13]
The repository

1. Commits to continuing maintenance of digital objects for identified community/communities;
2. Demonstrates organizational fitness (including financial, staffing structure, and processes) to fulfill its commitment;
3. Acquires and maintains requisite contractual and legal rights and fulfills responsibilities;
4. Maintains an effective and efficient policy framework;
5. Acquires and ingests digital objects based upon stated criteria that correspond to its commitments and capabilities;
6. Maintains/ensures the integrity, authenticity and usability of digital objects it holds over time;
7. Creates and maintains requisite metadata about actions taken on digital objects during preservation as well as about the relevant production, access support, and usage process contexts before preservation;
8. Fulfills requisite dissemination requirements;
9. Maintains a strategic program for preservation planning and action;
10. Maintains a technical infrastructure adequate to continuing maintenance and security of its digital objects.

The key premise underlying the core requirements is that for repositories of all types and sizes, preservation activities must be scaled to the needs and means of the defined community or communities. I'll come back to this point later.

Framework for Evaluating a Digital Repository

Kenneth Thibodeau of the National Archives has also put together a framework for evaluating a digital repository.[14] He takes issue with RLG/OCLC's insistence on the complete OAIS model as the only acceptable level by which to judge repositories, and provides points of evaluation and a rationale for several levels that he regards as successful within the mission of the repository. He argues that you should look at:

1. Services: do they meet the needs of the depositors; do they provide their services in a way that works for depositors, and do they provide them well?
2. Orientation: are they accepting "old stuff"? Do they provide access to it or just hold and protect it?
3. Coverage: are they large or small? Will material deposited in their repository affiliate it with similar material in terms of both coverage and technical needs? Will the repository work with depositors to meet their needs?

4. Collaboration: does the repository perform all the OAIS functions on its own, or does it collaborate with others so that among them they do everything depositors need?
5. State: what state of development has the repository reached?

When he wrote this, Thibodeau didn't have the small repository in mind, but you can see yourself in his logic and narrative.

Thibodeau asks the general questions, while Seamus Ross and Andrew McHugh get more detailed by defining the type of evidence you will want to gather to do an actual evaluation of a TDR.[15] They include lists of documents you could use, such as 1) mission statement, 2) deposit agreements, 3) job descriptions, 4) organizational charts, 5) staff profiles and work histories, 6) annual financial reports, 7) business plan, 8) risk management plans and a registry of individual risks, actions taken to avoid its occurring, and response in case it does occur, 9) policy statements, 10) procedure manuals, 11) workflow models, 12) schemes of the technical architecture, 13) maintenance reports, and 14) results of previous audits. Ross and McHugh recognize that documents may not tell you everything. They encourage you to observe the repository in action and/or talk with those who have. They also recommend that you talk with administrators at the repository and officers responsible for various operations. Then talk with other depositors and users of the data.

Ross and McHugh readily acknowledge that you also need measures to apply to the information you find to define when a repository has reached a level of competence you can trust. Such measures exist in other contexts, but have not yet come into the TDR world. Watch for them.

Beginning in about 2005, giants in the dot.com technology world started to offer services that allowed customers to store data on their servers. By the middle of 2007, those services had begun to specialize, with companies focusing on specific types of customers.[16] None of these firms, however, currently indicates that it could qualify as a TDR. Perhaps some of your donors will use them to store digital materials you will want to acquire. So, while they do not now offer a solution to your archival need, you should keep an eye on developments in this area, because they might have an impact on you.

Will Your Repository Become a TDR?

You shouldn't make a decision right now. If you immediately want to say "NO!," at least scan through the "yes" section below to get a better sense of what "yes" really means.

If "Yes," What Will It Take?

It will take a lot. To get a sense of how prepared you are, I recommend a

DRAMBORA audit. The Digital Repository Audit Method Based on Risk Assessment (DRAMBORA), developed jointly by the Digital Curation Centre (DCC) and DigitalPreservationEurope (DPE), allows you to assess your capabilities, recognize your strengths, and discover your weaknesses. It guides you in 1) developing an organizational profile that describes and documents your mission, objectives, activities, and assets; 2) identifying current and potential risks in each of those areas; 3) determining the likelihood/probability and potential impact of each identified risk; and 4) determining appropriate risk management responses. It then prioritizes your responses, giving the highest rank to areas with the greatest shortcomings or the greatest potential for disruption. The first step requires an extensive review of policies and procedures and interviews with staff. The rest rely more on observation and analysis of workflow procedures and policies.[17] It's not a trivial process, but thorough—and comforting when finished.

By the time you read this, some or all of what I say in this section may have changed a little or a lot. You need a place to go to find the latest thinking and technology, and I heartily recommend the Digital Curation Centre (DCC). Located in the United Kingdom, the DCC has an expansive vision and a number of worthy goals. The vision that benefits you most has the DCC becoming an "authoritative source of advocacy and expert advice and guidance."[18] With that in mind, the DCC addresses a wide variety of issues, but here I want to point you to its catalog of digital curation tools, which presents

> an overview of existing non-commercial tools and technologies, which could be implemented by creators, curators and re-users of digital information. The list is not limited to technical tools, but also incorporates any relevant technical manuals, methodologies and papers. Each tool requires a certain level of expertise; this is indicated after each tool description.[19]

Below I describe the general type of tool you'll need; go to the DCC for an update on and broadening of what I describe.

Tools

First you will need an overall "system" for holding and managing your historically significant bits and bytes. Given your budget, most of you will have no choice but to go with an open-source system. Open-source systems appear very attractive when we focus on the cost, but they come with some real drawbacks to take into account. In the first place, any system's capabilities and design will reflect the design philosophy and local requirements of the developing institution(s). Therefore, it will have definite strengths and weaknesses you should know about. It may be that you don't need functions the system has, and that you can't do without features and functions it lacks. The Open Society Institute (OSI) conducted a comparative assessment of institutional repository (IR) systems, including the two described below, and it offers an excellent table that spells out each system's functionality and design.[20] When making a decision regarding which system best suits your needs, do consult such guides.

As I mentioned in chapter 3, the Repository66 project indicates that several IR systems have proved very popular, including DSpace and Fedora. I discuss them below as a way of showing how differences appear. I want to indicate why, when you make any decision, you should know as exactly as possible what you need before you buy.

Between 2000 and 2002, Hewlett-Packard and the Massachusetts Institute of Technology (MIT) developed DSpace as a digital repository to capture the intellectual output of multidisciplinary research organizations.[21] Because DSpace structures its system to reflect a user community's organization chart, it supports the participation of the schools, departments, research centers, and other units typical of a large research institution. In this way, DSpace's architecture can preserve the provenance of materials submitted from many different donors. For "departments," you could read "collections."

DSpace comes with an interface for the public, for contributors to the repository, and for administrators. The public interface allows browsing and searching, and the repository can customize the look of the Web user interface. In 2004, DSpace joined in collaboration with Google to enable searching across DSpace repositories.

The Fedora digital object repository management system comes out of the Flexible Extensible Digital Object and Repository Architecture (FEDORA) developed by the University of Virginia and Cornell University. From the beginning, the Fedora project sought to develop a protocol from which to build full-featured institutional repositories and interoperable web-based digital libraries.[22] The Paradigm project chose Fedora over DSpace, primarily because Fedora can "support complex objects and their hierarchical relationships,"[23] a highly desired feature for an archival repository.

While Fedora does not have the user interface modules that DSpace has, Fedora users have begun to develop them and release them to the Fedora world. Fez,[24] developed by the University of Queensland Library, works as a front-end and administration tool. Anyone can download it from SourceForge,[25] which hosts a number of other Fedora add-on utilities. Each object in Fedora has layers of associated metadata—structural, rights, preservation—which ensures that all objects in the repository remain usable over time.

Lee, Clifton, and Langley explored the functionality of the various open-source systems for use in an Australian project, and they compared DSpace and Fedora specifically.[26] You should review as many of those reports as you can get before you choose. Others exist, but these two have generated the most interest. Do check out what the DCC offers, however.

As you look for a system, be aware that you will need a variety of tools to use with it. I include the examples below to give you an idea of the types of tools available and the issues they address; I'm not recommending anything.

File Identification and Validation Tools

Moving digital materials into your repository starts with giving the system a way to recognize the data types and file formats you want it to ingest. Over the past few years, a number of tools for identifying the format of a digital object has appeared. Other tools determine the level at which a digital object complies with the specification for its identified format. I'll describe some here so you have an idea of what these tools actually do. I do not mean to endorse one over another. As I've said, you'll want to find out what the current market has to offer.

PRONOM provides information about data file formats and their supporting software products. The National Archives (U.K.) developed PRONOM to support the accession and long-term retention of its own electronic records; it has now made PRONOM publicly available. PRONOM holds information about which software products can process (read, write, identify, etc.) which file formats. It also holds information related to the file formats themselves, such as their compression types, character-encoding schemes, and intellectual property rights. The developers intend PRONOM to offer a range of tools and services to support ingest functions such as risk assessment, migration pathway planning, object identification and validation, and metadata extraction.[27]

JHOVE (JSTOR/Harvard Object Validation Environment) came out of Harvard University as a tool for both format identification and validation. JHOVE also captures technical metadata including file pathname or URI, last modification date, byte size, format, format version, MIME type, format profiles, and, optionally, checksums derived a variety of ways. JHOVE2 can generate Submission Information Packages (SIPs) from digital materials as well as perform preingest validation of objects submitted as an SIP. This conformance to the OAIS model allows JHOVE to integrate easily into a repository that is based on that model.[28]

DROID (Digital Record Object Identification), developed by the National Archives (U.K.), performs automated batch identification of file formats. JHOVE handles a smaller set of formats than DROID. While DROID does better at identifying the format of files than JHOVE, it does not perform format validation. In light of their complementary features, the RLG has suggested using JHOVE in conjunction with DROID, to validate file formats based on what DROID initially identifies them to be.[29]

Metadata Extractors and Harvesters

As you collect materials, you will need a way to identify each uniquely. The OAI-Protocol for Metadata Harvesting (OAI-PMH) defines a mechanism to harvest metadata records from digital materials.[30] OAI-PMH supports only data aggregation—it does not provide linking to the resources or searching of the data gathered. Limited as that may seem, harvesting metadata into a single location for further processing opens up possibilities for union databases and federated searches of disparate materials. Further, as a standard protocol, the OAI-PMH helps ensure your archival system can have shared search capabilities with other repositories.

The National Library of New Zealand (NLNZ) metadata extractor is a Java-based tool used to extract preservation metadata from the headers of numerous types of formats, to convert them into a standard XML format systematically, and to output the data in XML.[31] While the tool extracts a fairly limited set of metadata, its strength lies in its ability to detect complex relationships, such as you will find in website files, and define the relationships between them.

File Conversion/Normalization Tools

The National Archives of Australia's (NAA) approach to digital long-term retention involves conversion of electronic records into open file formats. To that end, the NAA has open-source software tools, such as Xena, which work in conjunction with a number of other related open-source tools to convert numerous formats to XML. Xena, which stands for XML Electronic Normalizing of Archives, determines file formats and converts files into open formats for long-term retention.[32] For instance, Xena uses OpenOffice to convert Word files to Open Document Format. A similar open-source software tool called DAITSS (Dark Archive in the Sunshine State), written in Java and created by the University of Florida, uses Linux tools to perform file conversions. Unlike Xena, which converts all file formats to XML, DAITSS can handle conversions such as converting PDF to TIFF images or JPEG to the more long-term retention conscious JPEG2000.[33]

Web Harvesting Tools

The Web Curator Tool (WCT), developed as a collaborative effort by the National Library of New Zealand and the British Library, manages selective web harvesting.[34] Designed for use in libraries and other collecting organizations, it supports web harvesting by nontechnical users while allowing them complete control of the web harvesting process: a partial website, a group (or collection) of websites, or any combination of these.[35]

Ingest Tools

These tools manage the capture, classification, and identification of records. The process, if done well, ensures the content, structure, and context of creation of the records will not change over time. Digital materials, regardless how complicated, all need an orderly and safe process for entering an electronic repository. The ingest process must provide that to ensure that they survive unaltered and accessible. Therefore, an ingest system should *automatically* create a Metadata Encoding Transmission Standard (METS) Archival Information Package (AIP) with all the metadata needed to preserve each object; creating a METS file by hand invites human error.

The Cairo project seeks to develop a software package that provides an interface to bring together ingest functions, especially metadata creation tools, into a single coherent, usable, and documented tool, suitable for use by professional archivists and curators with limited technical skills. With Cairo, the curator can process formats commonly found in personal digital archives and add the metadata they need. Cairo will output digital archives properly processed for ingest and repository-independent metadata packages in the form of METS files. The METS files document the workflow the files went through and record metadata needed for long-term life-cycle management.[36]

Producer-Archive Workflow Network (PAWN) software, developed by the Institute for Advanced Computer Studies at the University of Maryland, supports the OAIS ingest function. PAWN allows the user to define his or her own domain and the policies that control it; the program then enforces those policies. Creators or holders of digital materials negotiate with a TDR that uses PAWN to move data into a secure environment. PAWN focuses on the process of moving the data into the TDR, but it assumes that the TDR will also manage user access to any given set of records based on terms negotiated between the depositing repository and the TDR.[37]

Migration Tools

Migration tools enforce migration policy by evaluating the quality of conversion tools or services and recommending migration strategies based on those evaluations. The recommendations produced by the system take into account the specific long-term retention requirements of each client institution.[38]

CRiB (Conversion and Recommendation of Digital Object Formats)[39] supports the implementation of migration-based long-term retention by 1) recommending optimal migration alternatives that take into consideration the long-term retention requirements of the institution, 2) converting digital materials to up-to-date encodings that most users can use, 3) evaluating the outcome of migration by comparing the original digital object with its converted version, 4) identifying improperly preserved properties, and 5) generating migration reports for inclusion in the preservation metadata of migrated objects.[40]

I have just touched the surface here; if you become a TDR, you will need to know a great deal more. However, I remind you of the final point of the ten core components of a TDR: the key premise underlying the core requirements is that for repositories of all types and sizes, preservation activities must be scaled to the needs and means of the defined community or communities.

Having read through that, you may now be firmly committed to "NO!," and no one doubts that "no" makes a lot of sense for most small collecting repositories.

However, "no" doesn't take you off the hook completely; you will still have to do something with all those electrons coming through the door until you move them into a TDR.

If "No," Halfway Measures

At this point, the concept of TDR has been driven by the need for storage for huge collections of governmental, business, and scientific materials. But, none of the principles precludes its use by smaller repositories, and the RLG guidelines provide the small repository an understanding of what it should do if it sees itself being pushed into functioning as a TDR—even if only temporarily.

Everyone accepts that digital repositories need some clearly defined basic functionality to maintain and preserve digital content. Even if you choose not to become a full-blown TDR, your donors will use electronic devices to do their work, and you will need to develop a system of software, hardware, policies, and processes to assure safe retention of electronic donations in anticipation of the day you can transfer them to a TDR. In this halfway state, you have a choice of becoming a light or dark archives. If a repository only stores content but does not allow user access to it, we call it a dark archives; if such a repository provides access to its holdings, we refer to it as a light archives. If you choose to become a dark archives, the storage options don't change and the migration issues don't change; it's access issues that change, as Priscilla Caplan explains.[41]

If you decide to become a light archives, you know by now that you should not provide access to original digital materials out of fear of compromising authenticity. You may decide to make "use copies," in which case you should make two: one for further copying and one for actual use. Since you can't assure authenticity after someone has used the "use copy," you should probably create a new one every time a researcher asks to see something and destroy the files when she or he has finished. Rather than go back to the "original" that came through the door to create a copy for the next researcher, have a copy to copy on hand.

TDRs for Hire

I include this section with the very strong caveat that it will quickly become dated, but having laid out what becoming a TDR requires, I want to suggest some services already available to you as TDRs. As you decide how to proceed, find out all you can about each of these services and what using each of them will entail. I present them in alphabetical order, lest I seem to favor one over another.

OCLC's Digital Archive[42] promises "a secure storage environment for you to easily manage and monitor the health of your master files and digital originals. . . . It stores master files and digital originals in a secure, managed and separate environment whether you've built your digital collections using CONTENTdm or another local access repository." The Digital Archive will provide a dark archive while you maintain an access system.

The Internet Archive[43] "is building a digital library of Internet sites and other cultural artifacts in digital form. Like a paper library, [they] provide free access to researchers, historians, scholars, and the general public." I approached the management at a conference in June of 2007 and they agreed "in principle" that they could be a TDR. I don't know that they've actually taken anything in as yet, however.

Summary

The archives community has a high-level model, the OAIS, for creating a TDR. While the model has received general acceptance, there's some debate about the implementation of it: must all modules reside in one institution, or can institutions collaborate to create the full model? If you decide to become a TDR, you'll need to work out an answer to that question, and if you decide on the collaborative effort, you'll need partners. But everyone knows you'll need partners anyway. If you decide to hire space in a TDR, the model provides you with an understanding of what you must do to create a safe halfway holding tank for the digital materials you now have or will acquire before you get everything lined up with a TDR.

Notes

1. Seamus Ross and Andrew McHugh, "Role of Evidence in Establishing Trust in Repositories," *D-Lib Magazine* 12, no. 7/8 (July/August, 2006), www.dlib.org/dlib/july06/ross/07ross.html (accessed April 18, 2008).

2. Clay Shirky, "Making Digital Durable: What Time Does to Categories." Summarized by Stewart Brand (November 14, 2005), blog.longnow.org/?p=51&akst_action=share-this (accessed April 18, 2008).

3. State Archives Department, Minnesota Historical Society, *Trustworthy Information Systems Handbook, Version 4* (July 2002), www.mnhs.org/preserve/records/tis/tis.html (accessed April 18, 2008).

4. Testbed Digitale Bewaring, *Functional Requirements for a Preservation System* (The Hague: Digital Preservation Testbed, January 2005), www.digitaleduurzaamheid.nl/bibliotheek/docs/Technical_and_Functional_Requirements.pdf (accessed April 18, 2008).

5. Center for Research Libraries and OCLC, *Trustworthy Repository Audit and Certification (TRAC): Criteria and Checklist*, Version 1.0 (Chicago and Dublin, Ohio: Center for Research Libraries and OCLC, 2007), www.crl.edu/content.asp?l1=13&l2=58&l3=162&l4=91 (accessed April 18, 2008).

6. National Archives of Australia, *Guidelines for Implementing the Functional Speci-*

fications for Electronic Records Management Systems Software, February 2006, www.naa. gov.au/Images/ERMSguidelinesupdated_tcm2-1019.rtf (accessed April 18, 2008) or www. naa.gov.au/Images/ERMSguidelines_tcm2-1018.pdf (accessed April 18, 2008).

7. Serco Consulting, *MoReq2*, www.moreq2.eu/ (accessed April 18, 2008).

8. Susanne Dobratz, et al., *Catalogue of Criteria for Trusted Digital Repository Version 1 (Draft for Public Comment)*, Nestor-Materials 8 (Frankfurt am Main: Nestor Working Group on Trusted Repositories—Certification, 2006), edoc.hu-berlin.de/series/nestor-materialien/8/PDF/8.pdf (accessed April 18, 2008).

9. Archives New Zealand, *Electronic Recordkeeping Systems Standards* (Wellington, N.Z.: Archives New Zealand, June 2005), www.archives.govt.nz/continuum/documents/publications/s5.pdf (accessed April 18, 2008).

10. United States Department of Defense, *Electronic Records Management Software Applications Design Criteria Standard* (DoD 5015.02-STD) (Washington, D.C.: Department of Defense, April 25, 2007), www.dtic.mil/whs/directives/corres/pdf/501502std.pdf. For context and application, see the Joint Interoperability Test Command (JITC), "Records Management Application (RMA)," jitc.fhu.disa.mil/recmgt/ (accessed April 18, 2008).

11. Center for Research Libraries and OCLC, *Trustworthy Repository Audit and Certification.*

12. Dobratz, et al., "The NESTOR Catalog."

13. Center for Research Libraries, "Core Requirements for Digital Archives," www. crl.edu/content.asp?l1=13&l2=58&l3=162&l4=92 (accessed April 18, 2008). In a related effort, the International Council on Archives announced a set of internationally agreed-upon principles and functional requirements for electronic records management systems. International Council on Archives, *Principles and Functional Requirements for Records in Electronic Office Environments*, www.ica.org/ (accessed August 14, 2008).

14. Kenneth Thibodeau, "If You Build It, Will It Fly? Criteria for Success in a Digital Repository," *Journal of Digital Information* 8, no. 2 (2007), journals.tdl.org/jodi/article/view/197/174 (accessed April 18, 2008); Thibodeau also addresses this issue in "What Constitutes Success in a Digital Repository?" (paper presented at the Joint Conference on Digital Libraries Opening Information Horizons Workshop: Digital Curation & Trusted Repositories, Seeking Success, June 15, 2006, Chapel Hill, North Carolina), sils.unc.edu/events/2006jcdl/digitalcuration/Thibodeau-JCDLWorkshop2006.pdf (accessed April 18, 2008).

15. Ross and McHugh, "Role of Evidence in Establishing Trust in Repositories."

16. Michelle Kessler, "Stash Stuff Online with Us, Tech Firms Say," *USA Today*, June 5, 2007, www.usatoday.com/tech/products/services/2007-06-05-online-storage_N.htm (accessed April 18, 2008).

17. Digital Curation Centre and DigitalPreservationEurope, DRAMBORA: Digital Repository Audit Method Based on Risk Assessment, www.repositoryaudit.eu/ (accessed April 18, 2008).

18. Digital Curation Centre, "About the DCC: Vision," www.dcc.ac.uk/about/ (accessed April 18, 2008).

19. "Digital Curation Tools," Digital Curation Centre, www.dcc.ac.uk/tools/digital-curation-tools/ (accessed April 18, 2008).

20. Ryan Crow, "Open Society Institute: A Guide to Institutional Repository Software," 3rd ed. (New York: Chain Bridge Group, 2004), www.soros.org/openaccess/pdf/OSI_Guide_to_IR_Software_v3.pdf (accessed April 18, 2008).

21. Maron Prudlo, "E-Archiving: An Overview of Some Repository Management Software Tools," *Ariadne* 43 (April 2005), www.ariadne.ac.uk/issue43/prudlo/ (accessed April 18, 2008).

22. Fedora Commons, "History of the 'Fedora Project' and 'Fedora Commons'™ Names," www.fedora-commons.org/about/history.php (accessed April 18, 2008).

23. Susan Thomas, *Paradigm: A Practical Approach to the Preservation of Personal Digital Archives*, Version 1.0 (Oxford: Bodleian Library, 2007), 3. www.paradigm.ac.uk/projectdocs/jiscreports/ParadigmFinalReportv1.pdf (accessed April 18, 2008).

24. FezWiki. dev-repo.library.uq.edu.au/wiki/index.php/Main_Page (accessed April 18, 2008).

25. SourceForge.net, sourceforge.net/projects/fez/ (accessed April 18, 2008).

26. Bronwyn Lee, Gerard Clifton, and Somaya Langley, *Australian Partnership for Sustainable Repositories PREMIS Requirement Statement Project Report* (Canberra: National Library of Australia, 2006), Appendix 4, www.apsr.edu.au/publications/presta.pdf (accessed April 18, 2008).

27. National Archives, U.K. Government Records and Information Management, "PRONOM: The Technical Registry," *Digital Preservation Department*, www.nationalarchives.gov.uk/prono (accessed April 18, 2008).

28. Harvard University Library, "JHOVE2: A Next-Generation Architecture for Format-Aware Digital Object Preservation Processing," rev. 2006-06-01, hul.harvard.edu/jhove/JHOVE2-proposal.doc (accessed April 18, 2008).

29. Brian Franklin, "Trial by File: Five Tools for Managing Formats," *RLG DigiNews* 10, no. 5 (October 15, 2006). Available at: worldcat.org/arcviewer/1/OCC/2007/07/10/0000068996/viewer/file1.html#article3 (accessed April 18, 2008).

30. Open Archives Forum, "OAI for Beginners—the Open Archives Forum Online Tutorial," www.oaforum.org/tutorial/ (accessed April 18, 2008).

31. National Library of New Zealand, *Metadata Extraction Tool,* www.natlib.govt.nz/about-us/current-initiatives/past-initiatives/metadata-extraction-tool/?searchterm=metadata%20extract (accessed April 18, 2008).

32. National Archives of Australia, "Xena Digital Preservation Software," www.xena.sourceforge.net (accessed April 18, 2008).

33. Priscilla Caplan, "How to Build Your Own Dark Archive (In Your Spare Time): A Talk for the Cornell Digital Preservation Management Workshop" (lecture at the Cornell Digital Preservation Management Workshop, Cornell University Library, November 2004), www.fcla.edu/digitalArchive/pdfs/Howtobuildyourowndarkarchive.pdf (accessed April 18, 2008).

34. National Library of New Zealand, *The Web Curator Tool*, webcurator.sf.net/ (accessed April 18, 2008). See also Gordon Paynter, et al., "A Year of Selective Web Archiving with the Web Curator at the National Library of New Zealand," *D-Lib Magazine* 14, no. 5/6 (May/June 2008), www.dlib.org/dlib/may08/paynter/05paynter.html (accessed July 29, 2008).

35. As described in the DCC study of repository tools, "Web Archiving Tools," www.dcc.ac.uk/tools/digital-curation-tools/#122 (accessed July 29, 2008).

36. Oxford University Library Services, *Complex Archive Ingest for Repository Objects* (October 2006), cairo.paradigm.ac.uk/about/index.html (accessed July 29, 2008).

37. Mike Smorul, Mike McGann, and Joseph JaJa, "PAWN: AQ Policy-driven Software Environment for Implementing Producer-Archive Interactions in Support of Long

Term Digital Preservation," *ADAPT—A Digital Approach to Preservation Technology*, adaptwiki.umiacs.umd.edu/twiki/pub/Lab/Papers/pawn-archiving07-uploaded.pdf (accessed April 18, 2008); Mike Smorul, Mike McGann, and Joseph JaJa, "The Use of Producer-Archive Workflow Network (PAWN) in Support of Customized Archival Practice" (paper presented at DigCCurr2007: An International Symposium in Digital Curation at the School of Information and Library Science at the University of North Carolina at Chapel Hill, April 19, 2007), www.ils.unc.edu/digccurr2007/papers/smorul_paper_6-3.pdf (accessed April 18, 2008); the accompanying slide presentation is available at adaptwiki.umiacs.umd.edu/twiki/pub/Lab/Papers/digccurr07-v1.ppt.

38. As described in the DCC study of repository tools, "Preservation," www.dcc.ac.uk/tools/digital-curation-tools/#113 (accessed April 18, 2008).

39. University of Minho [Portugal], Department of Information Systems, *Conversion and Recommendation of Digital Objects Format (CriB)*, 2007, crib.dsi.uminho.pt/ (accessed April 18, 2008).

40. Digital Curation Centre, "Web Archiving Tools," www.dcc.ac.uk/tools/digital-curation-tools/#122 (accessed April 18, 2008).

41. Caplan, "How to Build Your Own Dark Archive."

42. OCLC, Digital Archive, www.oclc.org/digitalarchive/ (accessed April 18, 2008).

43. Internet Archive, www.archive.org/index.php (accessed April 18, 2008).

Chapter 6

Solving the Problems: Implementing the Tools

At the Digital Preservation Coalition's workshop on cost models for preserving digital assets in 2005, Anne Kenney closed her presentation with a quote from Casey Stengel, manager of the New York Yankees, 1949–1960, and the New York Mets, 1962–1965. Stengel used the English language in such a way that the listener understood the message, even if the words didn't quite make sense as spoken: "They say you can't do it, but remember, that doesn't always work."[1] The Stengel entry in Wikiquote has the same sentiment as: "They say you can't do it, but sometimes that doesn't always work."[2] Regardless of the exact wording, the meaning comes through. Take it to heart. If you've come this far in the book, you may have serious plans to take on long-term retention of digital materials. Good for you. Add Casey's observation to your collection of inspirational quotes.

Making the Case

Obviously you will not wait until you know everything before you start implementing changes in policies and practices in relation to digital materials. Very early into your learning you can start to plan—planning could give you a sense of what's feasible. Further, it can give you a sense of purpose and direction, and what you *really* need to learn. Finally, it can give you a framework as you address the issues you will face from staff and upper management about staffing, finances, and services. You could start by articulating why it is important and the benefits you want to reap for your repository. Don't make arguments based just on good rational analysis. Make those, but add some vision to them, something to catch the readers' emotions and provide inspiration.[3] For example:

1. Long-term retention of archival materials is the essence of the archival function; it's the right thing to do;
2. Enhanced systems and services will apply to other projects;
3. Increased user satisfaction leads to an enhanced reputation;
4. Improved collaboration with similar repositories contributes to greater influence in the field;
5. An enhanced confidence and professionalism will resonate throughout the repository.

With general goals in mind, you can look at resources—who, what, and how much do you have or must you find? Obviously:

1. Project funding and staffing;
2. Technical expertise for system design and support;
3. Changes in working procedures or job duties.

Next think about what you want your system to do in a nontechnical way:

1. Support the research needs of users, both known and potential or future users;[4]
2. Support the archival functions of preserving and managing materials of enduring value.

With those understandings, map a strategy for success:

1. Learn how others did it. The resource sections at the back of the book contain lots of role models and places that offer strategies and ideas to adopt or adapt;
2. Find organizations to collaborate with for technical, political, and moral support;
3. Explore a number of choices for systems or tools. Find out what various tools and systems do and don't do and how other repositories use them;
4. Investigate various off-site digital repositories;
5. Determine how much you want your digital materials' long-term retention system to integrate with other system components you work with.

Voices of Experience

It does seem a little daunting, doesn't it? But take heart. As you start the implementation process, consider the decisions, insights, and strategies, which others have suggested. To start with, Gregory Hunter points out some decisions you will need to consider:[5]

Go It Alone versus Work Cooperatively

You almost do not have a choice about this when you think about long-term retention and access issues. Earlier in this book I discussed the need to collaborate with IT people. Hunter recommends that if the system you decide to work with is big enough, you should work closely with an assigned liaison whom you can educate about your mission, circumstances, and needs.

With your donors you do have a choice. I think it's safe to assume that everyone whose papers you might want to collect has some digital materials in the collection. The argument against approaching donors about their digital materials management practices rests on a fear of interrupting the unself-conscious flow of materials by giving the donor a heightened awareness of his or her records and record-keeping habits that could lead to a potential "rigging" of the collection. It's not an unfounded fear, for sure. But I hold that we should risk that. I think it naive to pretend that if you have already identified some living person whose papers you want to collect that you will catch that person totally off guard with your acknowledgment of his or her obvious importance in the world. She or he may be surprised at having generated *that* much importance, but nobody doing important work does so with no awareness of it, and most recognize that their papers may have some historical value.

Think Small versus Think Big

Where do you start? With an overall plan, or a few "pilot" projects? The savvy archivist or curator will work at his or her level of proficiency, which probably means starting small, developing skills and strategies. With experience you can both increase the size of the projects you tackle and the amount of profile you show to your repository and donor community. Hunter reminds us that "long-term plans don't sell."[6] While you can't afford to ignore the long game, you should pitch your vision in increments to both your management and your donors. Technology changes rapidly, so you must stay aware of what's happening in the preservation of electronic records world while you establish facilities and procedures that accommodate the less than perfect now. Jeanne Young presents three very practical case studies about how imaginative people set up an electronic records management system on a shoestring. While records management and archival appraisal aren't synonymous, the strategies she describes could work for you.[7]

System Design versus Legacy Systems

Like so much of what you must juggle, you have this problem in two arenas: your internal system and your donors' systems. As you work with donors, you will want to encourage them to use software that produces well-known and widely used results, preferably the least proprietary platform they will accept. Undoubtedly that means open-source software, addressed below.

In the meantime, you should also start deciding how much time and energy you will put into "old stuff" you already have or that will come along over time. If you have WordStar, VisiCalc, Javelin, or other old formats, can you realistically plan to migrate the data from them at all? If so, the sooner the better. If not, why have them taking up space you could use for viable materials?

Proprietary Systems versus Open Systems

You have no choice but to take in materials created with proprietary software, but when at all possible, promote open-source software.

Identify the Valuable versus Destroy the Worthless

With known donors, you can suggest guidelines about what's especially important or you can suggest what's not worth keeping. Be careful here, however, lest your donor take offense. Working with donors on the type of software they use and the way they organize their documents has fewer social dangers. Of course, when donations come to you after the death of the creator, you will simply take what you can get and be grateful.

Custodial Archives versus Noncustodial Archives

Your place or an off-site repository? Chapter 5 addresses this in some detail. By now, you may have decided to find a trustworthy digital repository (TDR), but you don't have to jump at the first chance that comes along. Get to know the guidelines for what a TDR must have and do to really qualify as trustworthy; there are several sets. Bear in mind, however, that in 2006–2007 the Center for Research Libraries (CRL) systematically evaluated some respected TDRs. They found most doing a credible job of fulfilling their charge, but none lived up completely to the RLG specifications.[8] The CRL research indicates that a TDR doesn't have to be perfect before you can put your trust in it. Nor do you as you create a dark archives holding tank. Geoffrey Huth, in his "Basic Electronic Records" workshop, admonishes his audience that doing nothing guarantees 100 percent failure; doing anything else raises the probability of less failure.

Media Preservation versus Content Preservation

The paradox of digital documents and digital materials is that you must destroy the media in order to preserve the content.[9] Peter Van Garderen[10] quotes Kenneth Thibodeau as observing that the essence of retaining an electronic record for the long term is maintaining the ability to reproduce an authentic copy of it. We cannot preserve the "originals." In the digital world, metadata for long-term retention assures both media long-term retention and content long-term retention.

Keep Digital versus Transfer to Analog

Transfer to analog means transferring content to some medium that a human can read without mechanical interpretation: typically a paper format or computer output microforms. This issue most clearly differentiates the choices a collecting repository has compared to the choices an institutional archives has. If you had to maintain materials in a condition that will allow them to stand up in court—as an institutional archives must—you would have to keep born-digital materials in a digital format. However, unless you have included that assurance in a deed of gift, you don't have that obligation, so you have choices.

Lucia Paquet and others argue that printing e-mail or correspondence to paper destroys unique information about the creation of the document, because it does not print out with the content. They also argue that researchers will find paper more difficult to work with than an electronic collection because researchers will not have the search tools to find information in the paper collection that they could have in an electronic collection.[11] That's true: transferring digital materials to analog transfers the content and some creation metadata, but does not transfer all the metadata. Further, the researcher *will* have to sort through the paper or microform. However, given your particular constraints and resources, you need to do what is most expedient, least experimental, and known to have the longest life—today—so the researcher has something to sort through ten years from now. In time, you may be able to keep the digital in a digital format, but for now, transferring to analog when possible makes a lot of sense. As David Stephens puts it,

> For a given set of archival data, the expense and technical complexity associated with the long-term preservation of electronic records are such that preservation in a digital format should be selected only after careful consideration of which particular solution—paper or digital—can best meet the organization's needs. . . . Microfilm, in particular, is an ideal preservation medium in many fixed-content situations.[12]

Audit Compliance versus Don't Audit

You can't audit your donors' actions on a regular basis without making a nuisance of yourself, but you can roll this concept into your donor education efforts. I'll address this more fully in chapter 7.

Donor Education versus Leave Them Alone

As you will see in chapter 7, I advocate educating your known donors. Obviously, you can't do anything about the creators of the materials that show up at your door unexpectedly, or that you acquire from the estates and family members of deceased creators. Where possible, however, educate, emphasizing your specific requirements for long-term retention.

Lessons Learned—from Cal Lee

In 2002, Christopher (Cal) Lee published a list of "lessons learned" during his work on an electronic records program in Kansas.[13] In it he raises further issues.

Research Does Matter

See step 4 in chapter 1. There are no magic bullets. Lee points out that research "can yield a variety of results: propositions, hypotheses, theories, concepts, terminology, frameworks, models, recommendations, exemplars, explanations, and persuasive stories."[14] You're looking for the models, recommendations, exemplars, explanations, and persuasive stories—information you can actually adopt into your own situation. Therefore it makes sense for you to stay aware of research projects and to scan reports for adoptable models, etc. By 2007, conferences all over the world began to have speakers talk about how they developed their repository. A conference called DigCCurr2007, for instance, had a number of such presentations. Read through the papers for "propositions, hypotheses, theories, concepts, terminology, frameworks, models, recommendations, exemplars, explanations, and persuasive stories."[15] The conference website has most of the papers and slide presentations for you to look through. I decided not to cull a "how to do it" model from them, because, as you will see, there's no one way to do it; everyone has different circumstances to work with. Planning has begun for DigCCurr2009; keep an eye on it.[16]

DigCCurr isn't the only conference, however. The Digital Curation Centre (DCC) regularly has conferences and makes the presentations, and documentation from other events, available online.[17] The DCC tends to focus on scientific digital data, but that doesn't mean you can't find something useful in what happens there.

Another conference called iPRES tends to float around the world. Its website says that

> iPRES is a series of conferences on digital preservation. Since 2004, iPRES conferences have been held on three continents. The iPRES series embraces a variety of topics in digital preservation—from strategy to implementation, and from

international and regional initiatives to small organisations. Within this broad topic area, each conference defines a slightly different focus. . . . Each iPRES conference has a different focus and convenes different participants. The local host shapes and organises the event with the assistance of a group of international experts.[18]

Much that you find on the iPRES website after a conference will not relate to you, but some will.

YMMV (Your Mileage May Vary)

As you become familiar with the models, etc., that research produces and you start to apply them to your own situation, you may find that you don't get the exact results that the researchers did. Nor should you expect to apply the whole body of methods and protocols you may want to try. Pick what you can do and determine how well it works for you. Doing something beats doing nothing.

Everyone Can Do Applied Research

As you look for answers, you undoubtedly will identify a number of specific problems you will want to address. As you apply a method or create a system based on your integration of others' models, recommendations, exemplars, explanations, and persuasive stories, make notes on how well it does or does not work. Note things as specifically as possible. When you find a consistent pattern that does or does not work, tell someone—at least your colleagues at a local gathering of people like you. Consider publishing it, if only locally. We're all in this together; share what you know. Ask others what they have learned.

Resources Are Limited, Meaning Is Expensive

To have any meaning, digital materials need far more explicit metadata and contextual information around them than analog materials. Capturing and retaining that metadata can become costly, and you have limited resources. Therefore, you must figure out fairly precisely what content and metadata you will and will not capture and keep. You don't want to waste time capturing a lot of isolated content that has no context and therefore no confirmable meaning.

Ask for Help

Nobody knows everything about anything. While your knowledge will grow, acknowledge your questions and seek help. Ask your local colleagues, join a listserv, go to a professional meeting, make a phone call, go to a workshop, and ask your question.

Look for Help

Search the Internet. Search the archives of listservs. Search the literature, and don't feel constrained to read only the archival literature.

You Get Extra Points for Copying off Your Neighbors

Others have the same problems you have. If your neighbor has invented a wheel, see if it fits on your cart. When you follow the research, you do so looking for techniques and strategies that will work in your repository.

Everyone Can Be a "Techie"

You need to learn what you need to know, but do not expect to learn everything. Nobody does.

Open Systems Are Your Friends

Lee has written a very good piece explaining how open systems work,[19] and he advocates that we all adopt them as much as possible. Encourage your donors to use them. As he points out, if your materials conform to a standard, you need only understand the standard to understand the care and feeding of the materials. The open-system approach is far simpler than trying to keep track of idiosyncratic proprietary systems that change regularly.

We Have to Pick Our Battles

Building alliances and moving people to change processes, perspectives, and priorities may take a lot of time; we succeed through a lot of little victories. You will run into roadblocks, and you must decide how to spend your time, energy, money, and influence. Spend wisely. Be charitable. Focus on your successes. You undoubtedly work in a relatively small organization: tomorrow is another day. Stay in touch with your stakeholders and their concerns; they will come around to your position when they see an advantage for themselves, at which point you've finally won. You won't win them all; choose wisely.

Remain Flexible

Things will not all go as you plan; be prepared to shift the plan to respond to new circumstances. Flexibility in the face of uncertainty takes courage; rigidity, however, will always slow you down, and it may shut you down.

We Must Learn and Then Address the Concerns of Our Stakeholders

When we ask people to change, we usually do it because of something we need or want. If we want them to genuinely address our needs, we need to know and incorporate theirs. We have the repository, but the donors have the goods. We have the idea, but the board has the money. We're all in this together, and everyone has to feel like a winner.

Explore Multiple Modalities

Lots of forces shape the digital materials world and our attempt to archive the product of it. Lee focused on four: technological change, market forces, legal environment, and popular norms about history, accountability, and cultural heritage—all of which we use as reasons to maintain archives. We need to keep a feeler out for significant changes in any of these four, because a shift in one undoubtedly causes shifts in all of them. When something shifts, we need to adjust our perspective on what we're doing, and perhaps on how we're doing it.

It Will Only Break If You Don't Play with It

If you do not act to save the digital materials you have and will surely get, they will undoubtedly slip out of reach. Only by playing with them can you keep them from breaking.

Try not to feel overwhelmed. Focus on those steps everyone agrees on—find partners, start small, watch new developments. You can come back to the others when you have developed some comfort with your initial steps, or when you feel a need.

Creating a Repository

Learning the Steps

Cornell University Library has kept itself on the cutting edge of digital repository research and implementation for several decades, and it has produced a lot of publications worth reading—most of them for free. Two seem most useful here: CLIR Report 141: *Preservation in the Age of Large-Scale Digitization*, by Oya Y. Rieger, and the *Cornell University Library Digital Preservation Policy Framework*.[20] Both these documents come out of Cornell's work in the digitization of library holdings, and that's not your focus. But what applies to their work does apply to yours. On page 27 of the CLIR Report, you'll find a list of "Key Organizational-Infrastructure Requirements for Preservation Programs" that inspired what I have below. I do not include all of Rieger's points, however, as several don't address your situation at all.

1. Update your organizational mission statement and other supporting documents to accept digital materials to your repository. By now you know that this initiative will take a lot of resources to accomplish. Once you get it up and running, you don't want someone to pull the plug on it because it's not in your guiding documents. Lock it in as soon as you can.

2. Identify the scope and extent of your long-term retention activities and priorities. You can't save everything; be really clear about what you intend to try to save.

3. Make sure that you have the money you will need to carry out your mandate and priorities. That means you'll need to have some cost projections.

4. Know your technical requirements and choose the "best practice guidelines" and standards you will adhere to. Nobody will expect you to invent anything, but they will expect you to follow what experienced programs recommend. In doing so you can make a stronger argument for the resources this effort will take.

5. Know who will do what and what skills (read: training) each responsibility will require.

6. Create policies based on a framework that describes your mandate. The Cornell policy framework mentioned above does a very good job of defining and organizing the issues, but also look at others.

7. Create emergency-preparedness and disaster-recovery plans. You will put too much of yourself and your repository's resources into this to have it wiped out by some disaster.

8. Start noticing technological developments and keep an eye open for projects designed to cope with the changes. It appears that text messaging may replace a great amount of e-mail. Who's doing what to test that issue from an archival perspective?

Management Issues

In late spring of 2006, the National Archives and Records Administration (NARA), the Arizona State Library, and the Society of American Archivists (SAA) hosted "a colloquium exploring the skills librarians, archivists, and records managers need to flourish in the digital era" called *New Skills for the Digital Era Conference.*[21] The core work of the colloquium occurred in small-group discussions that addressed a series of case studies about the basic functions of libraries and archives. In all the case studies,[22] the conference attendees emphasized the need for two sets of skills—archival and technical. They made it very clear that archival skills play as much a role in managing digital materials as do technical skills, and that archivists' technical decisions must adhere to established institutional policies.

Costs

Research projects have just begun to address effectively the cost an organization like yours can expect to bear to retain digital materials and keep them usable. The work shows that the complexity of calculating the true cost requires that key decision makers support both calculating the costs of developing a digital program and then proceeding with the work of collecting and preserving digital materials understanding those costs.[23] The costs include the initial cost of selecting and acquiring the material and the ongoing cost of keeping it "alive" and usable by researchers.

A number of models now exist using a variety of approaches to determine the cost of archiving digital materials. No one cost model suits every situation. Some include the costs of archiving paper materials that we then convert to a digital format, and commit to maintaining as digital materials forevermore. Others calculate the capture, management, and long-term retention of materials that were born digital. For all their various perspectives, however, all include the cost of acquisition, either capturing born-digital objects or converting analog materials, labor needed to acquire, process, and manage the digital materials, costs of technology needed for the process, and institutional overhead costs such as facilities and space, insurance, legal advice, etc. Calculating costs also includes the costs or savings of collaboration with other repositories, or departments within your own institution, any services you contract out, any training you seek or provide, and any additional work that adherence to particular standards may engender. You'll find a fairly concentrated collection of discussions of various models in the papers presented at a conference hosted in 2005 by the Digital Curation Centre and Digital Preservation Coalition on the topic of cost models.[24] Several presenters provide formulas for calculating costs.

We do understand a few constants: the ingest process costs more than any other step in the OAIS model and is linked primarily to the complexity of the transfer, not the volume of materials; preservation planning costs come in second. Emulation has a large up-front cost to develop or buy a system—after that costs may fall off; migration costs recur every time, though the implementation of a migration system may not cost much. With both emulation and migration, the cost per unit goes down as the number of units goes up. The complexity of the files you collect will have an impact on the cost of keeping them across time. For example, preserving proprietary formats will cost more over time than preserving those created with open-source software on an open-source platform. For this reason, audiovisual files incur more costs than text files: their highly complex, largely proprietary formats change often.

All the above makes the "normalization" strategy very attractive where possible. With this in mind, repositories have to develop charts that evaluate the long-term stability of various file formats. Based on those charts, they advise their donors what they can and cannot promise to support for the long term. The guidelines developed by the State Archives Department of the Minnesota Historical Society[25] provide a good place to start. A set of guidelines from the Kentucky Department for Libraries and Archives, based on the Minnesota guidelines, also seems worth considering.[26] As always, the Paradigm Project has good advice to offer on the issue of the costs of acquiring and retaining materials as part of your appraisal activity.[27]

Calculating the cost of providing access to digital materials differs substantially from calculating the cost of providing access to paper materials. Because digital materials need more extensive metadata to describe them than paper documents, the initial cost of description of digital materials runs higher than the typical cost of describing paper documents. Over time, however, these costs could go down as users become self-sufficient in use of the materials. Staff will always have to retrieve paper materials for researchers; that's not the case with electronic materials.

In 2000, the Dutch government established a unit to research different strategies for preserving digital documents for the long term. In 2005 they published a highly readable report[28] that analyzes factors contributing to the costs of maintaining digital material and that details how handling each variable in a variety of ways changes costs. For instance, their research shows that "the creation of records in an appropriate manner is a quicker, cheaper, and less risky manner of obtaining suitable durable records, compared to the 'repair' of those records at a later date."[29] As an example, they reported that they could create a good preservable set of a thousand records for €333. The same set of records, poorly created, would cost €10,000 to repair for long-term retention.

On the same website that links to their report, they have a link to a decision model for choosing a format in which to preserve various types of documents. As technology changes, undoubtedly various solutions will change, but the decision model[30] provides an instructive guide down that path. Below I lay out the categories of costs you will need to factor into your plans.

1. The initial work to develop your rationale for moving in this direction, including developing a statement of requirements and the research to support your choices of hardware and software. You, or someone in your organization, may do this, or you may decide to hire a consultant. Just deciding which way to go will cost time.
2. If you decide on commercial software, you will face licensing fees. If you decide on open-source software, you will face development fees.
3. If you choose commercial software, you will face annual support fees. Open-source software will need periodic maintenance, which may mean the cost of technical support, or it may mean the time of someone in your organization.
4. Regardless of the hardware and software you choose, you will face training costs.[31]

Obviously you and everyone in your organization understand that creating a responsible program for managing digital materials represents a long-term investment, just like the institution's commitment to its paper documents. Start-up costs can run high, but your institution's commitment to providing stewardship of, and perhaps access to, the digital materials it has and collects in the future makes meeting the costs imperative. Once into it, you will have no choice but to continue managing the technology as systems and services evolve. Undoubtedly, the constant change in a work environment that has been relatively stable will take a toll on staff and require additional time for training on a regular basis. The decision to archive electronic materials in-house is not unlike deciding to adopt quintuplets. You can manage it, but not without a lot of adjusting.

Policies

The first line in managing historical documents, paper or otherwise, resides in the policies that set the tone and process for the work. That means that you should start your work by developing your policies, however broad, based on a clear understanding of your repository's mission and researcher base. The more clearly you can define them, the better you can focus your policies on your purpose. Charles M. Dollar's book[32] offers a wealth of advice on policies, being very precise about exactly what you should have policies on. Further, in 1998, Cornell University received a grant from the NHPRC to address the issue of managing their electronic student records.[33] The project focused on management aspects and includes eighteen recommendations still relevant to any historical repository that wants to manage digital materials. The report reads easily because of its lack of technical jargon.

Expertise

Someone in your institution must know how to implement the policies it develops, whatever they are. If the policy requires migrating everything to analog, someone must know how to do that and have the time in his or her day to perform that task. "Know how to do" implies some form of education, either through some self-teaching process or attending workshops or courses. It comes down to this: training costs time and money. So as you develop your understanding of the cost of your digital materials program, consider the trade-offs between educating someone in-house and contracting with experts outside your institution.

Organizational Structure

As expertise shifts, so might the structure and power distribution in your institution. If you, in fact, do everything yourself, you'll find yourself shifting priorities. If you work with other people, whether paid or volunteer, you will undoubtedly find that you will work with them differently around digital documents compared to the way you work with them around paper documents. For instance, long-term retention issues will assume a much higher priority as you consider whether to acquire or retain digital documents than typically applies to paper documents. You'll find that you'll need to note more data elements for describing digital documents/collections than for paper documents/collections.

If you hire someone to oversee your digital holdings, you obviously have changed the organization. In reality, the organizational structure and priorities *will* change. Don't just let it happen; plan it and manage it as professionally as you can.

Roles of Personnel

As expertise shifts, so will the roles people play within the institution. If you decide to put all your digital documents in an external TDR, your role will shift from the keeper of the materials to the negotiator with the keeper of the materials. If you decide to retain them in your own shop, you will need to take on additional duties or personnel. Like organizational structure, roles and priorities within the organization will change. Don't just let it happen; plan it and manage it as professionally as you can.

A Development Strategy for Information Architecture and Metadata

Start your project by defining your information architecture, and establishing the metadata needs. Both will define your requirements for software. Neither can be developed in isolation from your overall objectives. Follow this sequence:

1. Define your objectives to meet the information requirements of your repository;
2. Specify how users (both researchers and management) will want to find and use information, understanding that you could create a dark archives that does not allow researcher access—knowing that will help to define descriptive and administrative metadata needs;
3. When you know your descriptive and administrative metadata needs, you can choose the thesauri and classification schemes you'll use to develop subject-level metadata;
4. Define your workflow pattern to ensure that good metadata will accompany all content in the system. That will probably mean designing templates for entering any metadata the system can't capture automatically.

Although this looks like a linear process, in the real world there will be continuous adjusting among the various processes listed above until all points come together.[34]

Site Design

Whether you decide to become a TDR or a dark archives until you find a

TDR you can affiliate with, you will need an interface to perform various tasks on the digital materials in your repository. So, as you plan all other aspects of your repository, you will want to develop at least an outline of the interface you will use to access your electronic holdings.

If you intend to make your holdings available to the public, you will probably do so through a website. In thinking about that design, consider these key issues: graphic design of the user interface, amount of information on any particular page, organization of the information, types of metadata it will require, types of media needed to use it, and general accessibility issues. You will then need to add more detail as you develop your requirements for software. Don't wait until the software actually arrives; developing user interfaces calls for a lot of consultation and testing. The design also has an impact on the way you develop your metadata.

You will find you can make some changes after you have launched the site, but only to a very limited extent; it's best to plan early and thoroughly, and document your process and decisions.

System Design Documentation[35]

After you have the system designed, you will want to collect the following documentation to support the implementation process:

1. Diaries kept during the design phase that detail original design decisions and rationale—remember to document changes made to the design over time;
2. Initial test plans;
3. Policies and procedures to support the implementation of the software you choose;
4. A system implementation plan;
5. Plans for change management, training, and communication, and
6. Plans for system integration, detailing how the software will integrate with existing systems and processes.

System Assessments, Audits, and Certification

At all times, you need to have a firm grasp on your repository's IT infrastructure and understand the strengths and weaknesses of the underlying foundation that supports the electronic repository. You'll find a number of audit and requirements checklists available to outline the characteristics of a secure, well-constructed repository as compared to standard or model requirements. They assess repositories' capabilities, identify their weaknesses, and recognize their strengths in such areas as: 1) ease of use and intuitiveness of user interface, 2) consistency of content and finding aids, 3) security and access controls, 4) help features and training, 5) system design documentation, and 6) download times and search efficiency.

Help Now

A few projects have made public some specifics about their operations. They don't tell you all the details, but they go into enough detail to give you an idea of what's involved. Oya Rieger of Cornell University Library presented at the DigCCurr2007 conference on the topic of "Key Principles in Assessing Repository Models."[36] She points out that you need to know what you want the system to do, but that's just the beginning. After that you have several political and financial processes to go through, including getting buy-in from your users.

Another presentation at DigCCurr2007 will interest you. Leslie Johnston, head of Digital Access Services at the University of Virginia Library, explained the large steps her institution took to develop a digital repository and its services. First they started by developing Fedora. To do that, they needed to develop their assumption about what their repository would do and how its various parts would relate. Then they developed their assumptions about the services it would provide. Only after that had happened could they start envisioning Fedora.[37]

In yet another presentation at that conference, Randy Fischer, a programmer for the Dark Archive in the Sunshine State (DAITSS) project, presented a step-by-step description of the ingest and dissemination process from the technical perspective. He also identified what group, within the Florida context, has responsibility for what.[38] For instance, he defines the ingest process: 1) check for viruses, 2) identify format, validate and record anomalies, 3) extract technical metadata, 4) identify and record external references, 5) create normalized and migrated versions.

Geoffrey Huth, who leads the SAA's "Basic Electronic Records" workshop, emphasizes in that workshop that when you acquire new digital materials, you should load them onto what he calls a *quarantined computer*, by which he means a computer that stands by itself, not connected to any network. On it, you make sure the new materials bring no worms, bugs, viruses, or serious deficiencies of any form—including arrangement—before you expose the rest of your system to them.

Summary

Remember:

> "They say you can't do it, but sometimes that doesn't always work."
>
> "Flexibility in the face of uncertainty requires courage."
>
> "Listen, sonny, you rush a miracle man, you get rotten miracles."
>
> "It is not up to you to complete the work, nor are you free to desist from it."

Notes

1. Anne R. Kenney, " The Cornell Experience: arXiv.org" (presentation at the Digital Curation Centre/Digital Preservation Coalition [DCC/DPC] Workshop on Cost Models for Preserving Digital Assets, British Library Conference Centre, July 26, 2005), www.dpconline.org/docs/events/050726kenney.pdf (accessed April 22, 2008).

2. Wikiquote contributors,"Casey Stengel," *Wikiquote,* http://en.wikiquote.org/wiki/Casey_Stengel (accessed April 22, 2008).

3. Robert J. Marshak, *Covert Processes at Work: Managing the Five Hidden Dimensions of Organizational Change* (San Francisco: Berrett-Koehler, 2006), 1–18.

4. Do you know what those needs are? Consider creating (or finding on the Internet) a very low-tech survey of questions about your users and collections. Your survey doesn't have to meet the rigors of an academic study to provide you with valuable insight.

5. Gregory S. Hunter, *Preserving Digital Information: A How-To-Do-It Manual* (New York: Neal-Schuman, 2000), 118.

6. Hunter, *Preserving Digital Information,* 116.

7. Jeanne Young, "Electronic Records Management on a Shoestring: Three Case Studies," *Information Management Journal* 39, no. 1 (January/February 2005): 58–60.

8. Bernard Reilly, "Certification of Digital Repositories: A Status Report on International Consensus-Building" (*Session 705: Measuring Digital Preservation Readiness: Digital Site Surveys and Certification of Trusted Digital Repositories,* paper presented at the Society of American Archivists 71st Annual Meeting, Chicago, September 1, 2007).

9. Su-Shing Chen, "Paradox of Digital Preservation," *Computer* 34, no. 3 (March 2001): 24–28.

10. Peter Van Garderen, *Digital Preservation: An Overview,* Managing Information Assets in the Public Sector, Edmonton, Alberta, October 12–13, 2006. http://archivemati.ca/wp-content/shockwave-flash/digital_preservation_overview.html.

11. Lucia Paquet, "Appraisal, Acquisition and Control of Personal Electronic Records: From Myth to Reality," *Archives and Manuscripts: The Journal of the Archives Section, the Library Association of Australia* 28, no. 2 (November 2000): 79.

12. David O. Stephens, *Records Management: Making the Transition from Paper to Electronic* (Lenexa, Kans.: ARMA International, 2007), 237.

13. Christopher A. Lee, "Guerilla Electronic Records Management: Records Management Lessons Learned," *Records and Information Management Report* 18, no. 5 (May 2002): 1–14.

14. Lee, "Guerilla Electronic Records Management," 3.

15. DigCCurr2007: An International Symposium on Digital Curation at the School of Information and Library Science at the University of North Carolina at Chapel Hill, April 18–20, 2007, www.ils.unc.edu/digccurr2007 (accessed April 18, 2008).

16. DigCCurr2009: Digital Curation Practice, Promise and Prospects, Chapel Hill, N.C., April 1–3, 2009, www.ils.unc.edu/digccurr2009/ (accessed April 18, 2008).

17. Digital Curation Centre, "DCC Events," www.dcc.ac.uk/events (accessed April 18, 2008).

18. International Conference on Digital Preservation: iPRES 2007, Beijing, China: October 11–12, 2007, http://rdd.sub.uni-goettingen.de/conferences/ipres/ipres-en.html (accessed April 18, 2008).

19. Cal Lee, "Open-source Software: A Promising Piece of the Digital Preservation Puzzle," www.ils.unc.edu/callee/oss_preservation.htm (accessed April 22, 2008).

20. Oya Y. Rieger, *Preservation in the Age of Large-Scale Digitization*, CLIR Report 141 (Washington, D.C.: Council on Library and Information Resources, 2008), www.clir.org/pubs/abstract/pub141abst.html (accessed April 22, 2008); Cornell University, *Cornell University Library Digital Preservation Policy Framework*, December 2004, http://commondepository.library.cornell.edu/cul-dp-framework.pdf (accessed April 22, 2008).

21. National Archives and Records Administration, Arizona State Library, and the Society of American Archivists, New Skills for the Digital Era Conference (Washington, D.C., National Archives, May 31–June 2, 2006), http://rpm.lib.az.us/newskills/ (accessed July 27, 2008).

22. National Archives and Records Administration, Arizona State Library, and the Society of American Archivists, "New Skills for a Digital Era: Case Studies" (paper presented at the New Skills for the Digital Era Conference, Washington, D.C., National Archives, May 31–June 2, 2006), http://rpm.lib.az.us/newskills/CaseStudies.asp (accessed April 22, 2008).

23. Deborah Woodyard-Robinson, "Section 3.7 Costs and Business Modelling," in *Digital Preservation Coalition Online Handbook*, added March 17, 2006, www.dpconline.org/graphics/inststrat/costs.html (accessed April 22, 2008).

24. Digital Preservation Coalition, "Report for the Digital Curation Centre/Digital Preservation Coalition (DCC/DPC) Workshop on Cost Models for Preserving Digital Assets: British Library Conference Centre, July 26, 2005," www.dpconline.org/graphics/events/050726workshop.html (accessed April 22, 2008).

25. State Archives Department, Minnesota Historical Society, *File Formats, Version 4* (March 2004), www.mnhs.org/preserve/records/electronicrecords/docs_pdfs/erfformats.pdf (accessed April 22, 2008).

26. Kentucky Department for Libraries and Archives, "Electronic Records Management Guidelines—File Formats," www.kdla.ky.gov/recmanagement/tutorial/fileformats.htm (accessed April 22, 2008).

27. Paradigm Project, "Appraisal and Disposal: Issues to Consider When Making Appraisal Decisions," in *Workbook on Digital Private Papers, 2005–2007*, www.paradigm.ac.uk/workbook/appraisal/appraisal-issues.html (accessed April 22, 2008).

28. Testbed Digitale Bewaring, *Costs of Digital Preservation* (The Hague: Digital Preservation Testbed, May 2005), www.digitaleduurzaamheid.nl/bibliotheek/docs/CoD-Pv1.pdf (accessed April 22, 2008).

29. Testbed, *Costs of Digital Preservation*, 15.

30. Testbed Digitale Bewaring, "Decision Model," in *Digital Longevity* (The Hague: Digital Preservation Testbed), www.digitaleduurzaamheid.nl/bibliotheek/docs/Decision_model.pdf (accessed April 22, 2008).

31. Research Libraries Group, *RLG Worksheet for Estimating Digital Reformatting Costs* (May 1998), www.oclc.org/programs/ourwork/past/digimgtools/RLGWorksheet.pdf (accessed April 22, 2008).

32. Charles M. Dollar, *Authentic Electronic Records: Strategies for Long-Term Access* (Chicago: Cohasset Associates, 2002).

33. Nancy McGovern, *Cornell University Electronic Student Records System Project Report* (Ithaca: Cornell University, 2000), http//rms.library.cornell.edu/online/studentRecords/default.htm (accessed April 22, 2008).

34. Martin White, *The Content Management Handbook* (London: Facet, 2005), 41.

35. National Archives of Australia, Guidelines for Implementing the Functional Specifications for Electronic Records Management Systems Software, February 2006, www.naa.gov.au/Images/ERMSguidelinesupdated_tcm2–1019.rtf (accessed April 22, 2008).

36. Oya Y. Rieger, "Select for Success: Key Principles in Assessing Repository Models" (paper presented at DigCCurr2007: An International Symposium in Digital Curation at the School of Information and Library Science at the University of North Carolina at Chapel Hill, April 20, 2007), www.ils.unc.edu/digccurr2007/slides/rieger_slides_8-3.pdf (accessed April 22, 2008).

37. Leslie Johnston, "Development of Repository Architecture and Services at the University of Virginia Library" (paper presented at DigCCurr2007: An International Symposium in Digital Curation at the School of Information and Library Science at the University of North Carolina at Chapel Hill, April 20, 2007), www.ils.unc.edu/digccurr2007/papers/johnston_paper_8-1.pdf (accessed April 22, 2008); accompanying slides available at www.ils.unc.edu/digccurr2007/slides/johnston_slides_8-1.pdf.

38. Randy Fischer, "Florida Digital Archive: Ingest and Dissemination with DAITSS" (paper presented at DigCCurr2007: An International Symposium in Digital Curation at the School of Information and Library Science at the University of North Carolina at Chapel Hill, April 20, 2007), www.ils.unc.edu/digccurr2007/slides/fischer_slides_84.pdf (accessed April 22, 2008).

Chapter 7

Working with Your Donors

It seems to me that savvy curators, when they recognize someone whose papers they want eventually to collect, will start gently encouraging that person to send his or her digital materials as soon as possible or to adopt good record-keeping practices. I have in mind a writer whose papers I worked with at the University of Vermont (UVM). When we started to collect them, he was in his mid-fifties. At one point he asked me about his e-mail. He observed that whereas he had always written a lot of letters, he now wrote most of them electronically. I suggested that he print out the ones he wanted to keep. He declined, and we quietly dropped the subject. I shouldn't have done that. In fifty years, researchers will have a rich and full view of his life and development as a young man, but his records will thin away to very little but business records and published works unless 1) someone puts all that electronic stuff onto paper, or 2) UVM's Special Collections Department initiates a program of systematic migration of electronic records in its holdings. In my classes, I refer to these issues as management decisions. Both options cost dearly, but to choose neither and just let the matter slide subverts the archival function.

I can imagine objections to that perspective. The objectors would suggest that the records will no longer have the unself-conscious quality that they have when we just let the creator carry on, uncontaminated by thoughts of archival immortality. However, a lively conversation on the Archives and Archivists listserv in February 2008 revealed that many donors already "construct" their donation by consciously saving or destroying certain documents to put a particular spin on their place in history.[1] While I cannot deny that making specific and ongoing arrangements for managing donors' digital materials may increase that practice, I wonder how well the objections stand up against the possibility of your receiving, twenty years from now, a wide variety of electronic storage gadgets from which you cannot remove the information.

Throughout this book, I have referred to your known donors in the context of the topic at hand, but never with much detail nor with a developed framework for your working relationship with donors; in this chapter, I do. Whether you see yourself becoming the TDR or contracting with an external TDR, you *must* work with your known donors—however you define them. Here's why: eventually the day will come when their current equipment will not read the documents created on an earlier system, and those documents could disappear. Unless the donor has a felt need to migrate older documents to the newer system, the older documents could slip slowly and silently beyond the range of easy migration to modern formats.

Below, I have compiled advice and wisdom on this topic from those who have gone before.

Voices of Experience

Gregory Hunter reminds us that if donors do a poor job managing paper, we should expect the same with digital materials.[2] Even if they do a good job with paper, digital documents may not receive the same kind of attention. Although you can suggest and coach all along the way, in the end they have control.

In chapter 6, I described the implementation decisions that Hunter says you will face. He supports teamwork, open systems, and standards, ongoing education at all levels, and incremental solutions. He also offers a seven-step process for making and implementing your decisions.[3] Hunter's process suggested a corporate environment, so I've modified his suggestions for the context of the small collecting repository.

Hunter's Seven-Step Process

Identify Partners

Begin by working with receptive donors—perhaps people whose materials you've already begun to collect. Learn their concerns and address them. Encourage them to talk to colleagues about your work (positive gossip).

Understand Your Donor's Context in Its Entirety

This differs for each donor, and you must go to the donor's environment to understand it. You start educating your donor by speaking about his or her reality. Not only does the trip educate you, it clearly demonstrates your commitment to this issue.

Determine Your Role

To get a donor to buy in to your requests/needs, advocate for historical concerns, demonstrate your competence as the custodian of his or her legacy, suggest your role as a consultant to ensure they get the best results. Ask to be involved in "new system" discussions. Emphasize that if the donor's "papers," regardless of format, are all in one place, both their descendants and scholars will find them easily.

Define Issues and Concerns That Matter Most

Those issues will differ depending on the donor, whether that means control of e-mail, long-term retention of a website, managing old computer technology, or something else. Present your ideas on paper, summarizing the issues in a language free of technical jargon and acronyms.

Design a Pilot Project or Two

Start small. Work with a receptive donor. Don't overcommit. Know your objectives. Figure out how to do it. Set a time frame. Figure out who's responsible for what.

Get Your Program Going

Start small, be careful. Note problems. Adjust as necessary. Summarize the findings and generate policies and procedures. Be willing to find and admit problems and mistakes—that's how you learn to do it right. Separate what doesn't work from what does.

Announce Your Program to the Public

Explain your capabilities to both potential donors and your network of professional colleagues.

McDonald's "Lessons Learned"

In the early 1990s, the National Archives of Canada started coming to grips with digital materials and conducted a project to identify and develop methods of controlling the digital materials being created as a matter of daily business in the Canadian government. In the summary publication found in the *American Archivist*,[4] John McDonald, the project director, outlined "Lessons Learned," which I've reworded to apply to the collecting repository and your work with donors.

Someone, Probably You, Must Be the Point Person in the Repository

You'll start by taking responsibility for the digital materials, staying abreast of technological developments and the growing sophistication in the archives world about best practices in relation to digital materials. In the collecting repository, this is the person who works with the identified donors about how they should handle their digital materials. This person not only needs to have enough technical knowledge, but must also have masterful skills in human communication. The project discovered, to nobody's surprise, that records creators and users resist being told how they should handle "their" records and files. In an institutional setting, the archivist must show creators that "their" records aren't their records: they belong to the institution. In the case of private donors, the materials are in fact theirs, so the curator works with them only as a consultant, armed with knowledge but no actual power. Therefore, the curator must find ways to make sure the donor turns materials over in a timely fashion or takes responsibility for their care. The curator must find a motivator, such as a desire to make digital materials available to researchers of the future, a recognition that keeping them in a way that works for the repository actually makes them easier to work with generally. You may find that as donors become increasingly reliant on digital materials, they will welcome guidance in meeting a felt need.

Donors Will Need Guidance

They'll ask about the specifics of file management, but you should also be prepared to offer advice on broader issues of what software can do, and how the researcher can use it to his or her best advantage. Also, be really clear about how much and what kind of contextual information the archives needs with any given document, how best to store materials, how long to keep them before migrating or refreshing, what to document through the migration process, and so on. Be as specific as possible.

Help the Donor to Know When to Capture a Record

Thinking more broadly than just the creation of particular records, work with donors on their whole system. Help them recognize when records from various software systems relate to each other—a spreadsheet calculation that leads to a letter, a physical picture that inspires a poem, etc. Help him or her develop processes that make these connections, even as the systems he or she uses evolve. With that understanding, the donor will grow in knowing when to "capture" a record for his or her collection and when to let it go.

Get Involved with Professional Groups

Support the effort to promote the development of software that offers what you need to build appropriate technological solutions.

Know What Software to Recommend

To make records creation and collection as complete and easy as possible, don't be afraid to suggest reliable software to your donors. Phil Bantin's book on the records-creating power of various systems could give you some ideas of what to look for.[5]

Keep an Eye on the Standards and Best-Practice Guidelines

Figure out how to pass them along to potential donors in ways they can comprehend and apply them.

The McDonald article offers a model for sorting out what to tell your donors as you work with them. It all begins, of course, with your understanding of just what your repository needs to have so you can preserve, at least for the short term, the materials your donor gives you. Ultimately you must start with a self-analysis. McDonald provides a tool that will help you in that process.[6] So, too, does an audit using Digital Repository Audit Method Based on Risk Assessment (DRAMBORA), discussed in chapter 6.

Stephens and Wallace's Principles for Records Managers

In 1997, ARMA International published a guide to electronic records retention by David O. Stephens and Roderick Wallace. In it, the authors provide a list of fourteen basic principles for records managers who must develop rules and timelines for their employing institutions. I have adapted them for use by a small collecting repository as it works with its donors.[7]

Understand Electronic Records Retention

Stephens and Wallace stress that the term *retention* implies appraisal for long-term retention or systematic destruction. Develop a schedule or system that your donor can refer to and use to determine what to save and what to destroy; it will bring comfort to you both.

Collect Appropriate Data That Describe Existing Computer Applications

If you are to collect a donor's electronic files and preserve them over time, you must know about the hardware and software system that created them. You can get that information only from the donor.

Apply the Series Concept to Electronic Records

Don't think of digital materials as a series separate from their paper counterparts. If an author switches from typewriter to word processor for creating and editing manuscripts, both media fit into his or her manuscripts series and should be identified as part of it, regardless of where the actual data live.

Conduct Interviews with Donors

By interviewing the people who create the materials you want to collect, you will develop an understanding of the provenance of the files you will ultimately receive. An interview will also help your appraisal decisions as you learn where particular materials fit into the overall collection.

Solicit Information from Donors through Questionnaires

Developing a questionnaire, even if you fill it out yourself during the interviews recommended above, will ensure that you get uniform information. If the donor fills it out before you have the interview, it will give you a basic overview of his or her materials that you can sharpen and refine through the interviewing process. Further, the act of developing the questionnaire will help you focus on what you need to know. Stephens and Wallace include a general questionnaire on page 41 of their book. While clearly designed for the institutional and corporate environment, it will give you a glimpse of the sort of information you might consider. The SAA/ARMA International book of forms also offers models to work with.[8]

Use Fundamental Principles to Make Appraisal Decisions

After you have learned what the donor has, use fundamental archival appraisal concepts to guide your decisions about what to collect. Given the nature of the electronic materials, you should pay particular attention to a few additional details related to the realistic probability of your being able to retain some formats across time. It's best to acknowledge up front that you may not be able to promise immortality to everything. In the end you want to develop a consensus with your donor and repository as to what digital materials you can honestly acquire and assure their long-term retention.

Construct Total Life-Cycle Retention Periods

When you've sorted out what you want and what you can reasonably acquire and retain, help your donor develop a system that will provide everyone with confidence about the safety of the materials from the moment of creation to the moment of transfer to your institution. ISO 15489 and the accompanying Designing Information and Recordkeeping Systems (DIRKS) protocol defines what makes an effective records management system and how to develop one that will take into account the long-term concerns of archivists. It covers how digital materials are managed over time, and also how the systems in which they are created and kept can be designed for optimal performance from *all* perspectives. Again, I've adapted this process for your environment; by now much of it will look familiar.

1. Preliminary investigation: the information gathered during this step provides a useful overview of the total environment of the donor's materials and their creation. Collecting background information provides an overview of a donor's activities and major stakeholders. It also serves as the basis for the development of a retention schedule that will appear in a later phase. Finally, it will help define the problem areas and assess the feasibility and risks of possible solutions.

2. Functional analysis of activity: this step develops a model or map of what a donor does and how records relate to his or her processes and activities. Building a bird's-eye view of his or her life by mapping the donor's papers and information flow will illuminate the relationships between the papers and the activities that generate them; that is, it will firmly connect the papers to the *context* of their creation. Information gathered through this data analysis and interview process will help you make decisions about what papers you must capture.

3. Identification of record requirements: DIRKS, originally developed for records management programs, includes this step for checking legal requirements for records retention. You probably don't need to address that issue unless you're looking at your own institution's records or you've accepted that responsibility for a business whose records you have collected.

4. Assess existing systems: this step surveys your donor's existing systems, including those that work with paper, to assess actual practice in the way she or he "manages" her or his "papers." The information you collected earlier becomes vital to this analysis. This analysis also determines if the donor's system can maintain records over the long term.

5. Strategy identification: here you define strategies to help your donor establish good records management practices and habits. In it, you determine what policies, procedures, standards, and tools to recommend to your donor. Obviously you can't *require* anything, but once you have defined the possible strategies and their potential risks and benefits, your donor can decide on the mix that works for him or her.

6. System design: this step involves converting the strategies you developed earlier to a plan for processes and systems. Effective communication with your donor and his or her associates is key to success here, and you must include feedback as part of an ongoing effort to develop your donor's sense of responsibility for his or her system. You want to create a system that meets the donor's document-creating needs and your archival capture or long-term retention needs.

7. Implementation: DIRKS provides guidance in how to develop a detailed plan, how to implement your policies and procedures, etc. Paramount to the process is good communication and user training.

8. System/process review: after you have a system in place, DIRKS recommends regular reviews of the effectiveness of the system and its continuous

development, being prepared to remedy any deficiencies. We all know that our donors' document-creation processes and systems change regularly. The feedback loops built into the systems you set up provide you with a heads-up on changes.

Determine the Total Retention Period Based on Access Requirements

This addresses the question of when the donor should send materials to your repository. Essentially, it suggests that you should receive materials at the point that the donor has no foreseeable need to access and manipulate them. For instance, after the book is published, the author no longer needs the drafts; those files could reasonably move to your hands. Traditionally, literary archives have collected drafts and versions that illustrate the evolution of a piece. That form of scholarship won't be possible unless creators consciously copy various versions of a work to protect it from being overwritten on the computer, so you'll want to encourage the keeping of more than just the final draft.

The Paradigm Project's *Workbook on Digital Private Papers* discusses six different approaches to accessioning digital materials:

1. Periodically taking snapshots, in the form of exact copies, of the creator's digital materials you've already appraised as valuable and adding those copies to your digital repository;
2. Working with donors on long-term retention issues and allowing them to hold the materials on their own system;
3. Combining the two approaches described above;
4. Approaching donors, as we have traditionally done, at the end of their careers, or waiting for the approach to come from the donor;
5. Periodically transferring "old" materials on the hardware and media that created them;
6. Providing donors with all the tools they need to work digitally and harvesting archival materials from those tools.[9]

The *Workbook* describes the advantages and disadvantages of each method in some detail. Clearly one way will not suit every repository or even every donor. You'll have to make decisions on what works best for you after really analyzing your capabilities and revisiting that analysis on a regular basis.

Determine If Migration and Deletion Occur Automatically

For instance, if an author ships you files that reflect the development of his or her most recent work, should you expect him or her to delete the files on the home computer? Probably not—there may be a revised version developed from the first. What about certain correspondence or financial records? Leaving old files in the hands of the creator raises the issue of accidental alteration or corruption and the duplication of files.

Determine the Disposition of Materials That Exist in Several Forms

Do you want both the electronic version and the print version of a donor's photograph collection or manuscript for a published work? Probably. If you accept both, you have a stable hard copy to store. You may find that the electronic works have undergone some editing, which makes them different images from the hard copy. If they haven't been altered, you can at least use the digital copy for access purposes.

Be Highly Selective about Appraising Electronic Records as "Permanent"

This issue has some debate around it. One camp holds that adding a sophisticated search software application to a digital archive precludes the need to appraise anything. Storage is cheap, the argument goes. Throw everything in and let the search engine discover the valuable; it will ignore the worthless.[10] Opponents resist the notion on the basis that the cost per byte of storage has dropped dramatically, but the number of bytes has risen alarmingly. In the end, sufficient space to store everything puts a substantial crunch on the budget. Further, search success requires good metadata, some of which humans must apply. Do we want to spend labor costs on junk?

Use COM or COLD Solutions for Lengthy Retention Requirements

In 1997, computer-output microfilm (COM) and computer-output laser discs (COLD) provided the most reliable long-term storage potential. A decade later, the principle has changed: use the most reliable long-term storage media you can identify when you need it, understanding that it will change and you will need to move the data from it to something else.

Retain E-mail under Stringent Records Management Control

E-mail contains a lot of historically worthless messages among which a researcher will find some genuine jewels. E-mail systems tend to be volatile; you want to find a way to collect e-mail as frequently as possible. Chapter 7 of Stephens and Wallace's *Electronic Records Retention: An Introduction* has good concrete advice on this issue.[11]

Because e-mail systems shape the character of the messages they carry and possibly their long-term retention, get as much data as you can about the hardware and software used, file-naming conventions used (if any), backup procedures, and other security procedures. Unlike the institutional archivist, you will probably not get to work with the system that produces the files, but merely the end results that the donor has chosen to save. You may want to coach the donor about how and what to file to create a logical order to them, if the system allows it.

Maureen Pennock has written a manual on curating e-mail that includes a list of specific issues to discuss with donors about the way they create and treat e-mails. Pennock emphasizes the need for appropriate creation practices. Although she has written for a business setting, the points that relate to your donors include 1) enter a meaningful subject line, so related e-mails stand out, 2) think carefully about the message threads created by the reuse of subject lines, and change subject lines when the subject changes, 3) think carefully about blind-copying people, since systems generally strip out information about blind copies, 4) think carefully about attaching information as opposed to embedding it into the body of the e-mail, because embedded material is easier to capture, 5) keep copies of significant sent messages as well as received, 6) delete insignificant messages in both the inbox and outbox.[12] Pennock promotes the notion that your donor should manage attachments according to file types while keeping track of their origins as e-mail attachments.[13]

A Collaborative Electronic Records Project (CERP) between the Smithsonian Institution Archives (SIA) and the Rockefeller Archives Center (RAC) has also put out an excellent set of guidelines that they developed for use with their own managers and employees.[14] CERP makes very clear on the title page that "This document may be used freely and modified by any non-profit organization," so feel free to borrow liberally. The RAC receives papers from sixteen Rockefeller-affiliated institutions and the Smithsonian Institution receives materials from its many branches. The two archives collaborated to "develop management guidance and technical preservation methods that will enable archives to make electronic information accessible and usable for future researchers." They acknowledge that they may need much more time to actually collect the digital materials, but they wanted to make sure that donors had the materials when that time came. Therefore, they set out to create materials that will "assist organizations in planning for the transfer of electronic records, whether to the RAC or another archive."[15] The core nine pages (pages 10–19) pull together gobs of good advice, both for you and for your donors. Again, the book was written for an institutional setting, so you must translate the concept "records manager" to your position and the concept of "employee" to donor. Once you get through that translation, you'll find lots of "do now" advice for donors. For instance, establish/encourage subject headings and inbox file folder naming standards,[16] and establish/encourage backup procedures and frequent storage routines, and offer off-site storage.[17] The same project has also provided a records retention schedule with enough details to give you some ideas, but not so detailed it will overwhelm you.[18] Do look at both the documents.

Because these documents have come from institutional settings where legal issues may arise, they do not advocate "converting to analog." But, for the reasons given in chapter 4, you may also want to suggest your donor create a paper or microform version. While the conversion will destroy the "search" function that storing materials electronically would provide as well as a fair amount of transmission and reception information, it will preserve the content, which is what the users two generations from now will most likely want. Along with the content, the analog version should contain the basic transmission metadata: the name of the sender, the names of all recipients, for outgoing messages the date and time sent, for incoming messages the date and time received and the subject line.[19]

E-mail attachments present other problems. E-mail software does not handle attachments the way it handles the main content. Some systems store the attachments with the file, others separate them on receipt. A conceptual link between attachments and the original message must exist, especially if you plan to migrate to analog. So, you need to know what system(s) the donor used along the way.

Retain PC-based Electronic Records Based on Official Record Status

This meant more in the corporate/institutional world than it does here. In 1997, most "official" records within institutions were created on some institution-wide mainframe or networked system, and staff's desk computers held few "official" records. That may or may not be true today, especially of those businesses whose records you may acquire. Since you have no legal responsibility beyond the acquisition documentation, you have far more discretion to save what you think most useful as either evidence or information.

The Paradigm Project: Advice on Working with Donors

In its final report, the project leaders of the Paradigm Project generated a list of fifty recommendations about working with donors around digital materials; only some apply to you, and I paraphrase them below.[20]

- Recommendation 5: lest you overlook something important, be aware of the "range of potential locations and mediums" your donor might use for storing materials. Ask about them all.
- Recommendation 6: use record-surveying techniques when working with donors; "screenshots and directory trees can be very helpful" for appraising the contents of any storage medium.
- Recommendation 12: identify critical moments in the life of every donor's materials and aim to acquire material before disaster strikes. David Bearman identifies the point of creation and any point at which a file gets moved from one system to another as generally critical.[21] While the content of the file may travel across systems in good shape, the real danger lies in its loss of metadata and, in the case of e-mail, loss of attachments.
- Recommendation 19: encourage your donors to deposit their materials as soon as possible after creation. This issue makes adopting an institutional repository (IR) model very attractive; IRs assume that creators will input their own materials. You may want to impose some controls on the process, but to make this a real option takes a lot of work out of your hands.

- Recommendation 20: depending on the donor's need, offer generic or specific advice about the technology he or she uses, and stay in touch so you can monitor that technology.
- Recommendation 22: generally raise an awareness in your institution and community about the issues around long-term retention of digital materials.
- Recommendation 23: keep up with developments in web-archiving initiatives and technologies.
- Recommendation 24: if you think it is possible that your institution will ever move your digital material holdings to an external TDR, rewrite your deed of gift form to include permission to move digital materials to a TDR.
- Recommendation 25: prepare or find "how to" sheets for the extraction and migration of common old media and formats.
- Recommendation 31: be aware of incidental copies of digital materials already in your holdings that may exist in other places and see to their permanent destruction.
- Recommendation 32: create rules for handling data types and formats so they all receive the same treatment.

Appraising the holdings of a donor with whom you can expect to work for some years to come can become a very sensitive task and calls for tact and diplomacy. Everyone has hot buttons you'll want to avoid. Indeed, Hyry and Onuf express concern about the difficulty of dealing with donors over the course of years.[22] Nevertheless, with each donor you probably should start with a general appraisal of what has enduring value and what doesn't. The appraisal process will give you the opportunity to assure donors that they need not pay much attention to those materials you're not interested in. From that point you can work with them to establish a schedule of transfers for the archival materials from their hands to yours. In effect, you will create a records retention schedule for each donor you work with. You will find samples of these useful documents in Stephens and Wallace[23] as well as the Paradigm Project's *Workbook*.[24]

Jones and Beagrie devote a section to rights management issues.[25] Your donors may have some concern about their intellectual property rights and how you or they will manage them. Jones and Beagrie have very specific provisions you should include in licensing and deposit agreements. They present issues as issues, but do not claim they have the answers. The answers, they suggest, depend on local circumstances.

Educating Your Donors

Virtually everyone mentions educating your donors, and the Paradigm Project gets very specific about what you should cover. They put together a small publication called *Guidance for Creators of Personal Papers* meant as a largish pamphlet for potential donors.[26] While the guide frequently goes into very specific detail—"Use the format yyyymmdd (e.g., 10 June 2005 = 20050610) for recording dates: that way your file will be presented chronologically in the file management tools"[27]—I will list only the topics that it covers—that is, the topics you should address as you work with your donors:

1. How to name files and folders;
2. How to set up a file system that documents itself as much as possible;
3. What and when to delete materials;
4. How to manage e-mail;
5. What file to look for in software and file formats for text documents, images, e-mail, websites and Web 2.0 technology, and operating systems;
6. How and when to back up data;
7. How to maintain hardware and software;
8. How to administer a personal computing system;
9. Considerations around passwords and encryption;
10. Considerations around intellectual property rights and privacy;
11. Why and how to keep up to date with technological change;
12. How to handle legacy files.

The guide ends with an eleven-step chart of tips for preserving personal data. Do read it carefully.

If your donors come out of academia, you'll find two guides that speak directly to that culture. The first one comes from the University of North Carolina (UNC) at Chapel Hill. Between 2003 and 2006, Helen Tibbo headed a research project there called "Managing the Digital University Desktop" (MDUD), which developed a comprehensive list of questions and responses, guidelines, and recommended best practices on managing e-mails and electronic materials for the faculty at Duke University and UNC.[28] The documentation focuses very much on the needs and practices of those two universities, but much of what the project put together can be generalized to any institution whose materials you'd like to have. This seems like a good time to point out that while we tend to think of the holdings of collecting repositories as personal and family papers, in fact they hold a substantial number of business papers. Further, every person has an aspect of a business about them as they manage their lives; institutional practices translate very well to those aspects of personal life.

It will come as no surprise that the MDUD study found that people manage their information for present use, with little or no thought to the future. As a result, they tend not to describe their files well, and do not keep them well organized. They know where they put things and that's all they need to know. MDUD guidelines strongly support the notion of educating donors to "carefully maintain the most important evidential/historical/mission critical materials."[29] The project's website has made all its documentation available, including survey forms and questionnaires: it's a good place to find ideas to adapt to your own needs.[30]

Second, Harvard University's *Guidelines for Managing Faculty Files*,[31] written for faculty's use, may also prove useful. Different university, different specifics, but similar generalizations.

What's Missing

For all the good advice offered above, a few issues do not appear as explicitly as they might have. I'll cover them here.

Timing Counts

The degree of difficulty in capturing digital materials for long-term retention usually depends on how much warning we have about major changes a donor plans for his or her systems and how much we know about what the change involves. If we have sufficient ingenuity and technical knowledge, we can overcome many of the problems discussed in this book, but doing so costs a lot of money and time. In the perfect world, we would avoid the heroic rescue efforts needed to recover information from twenty-year-old recording media.

You want to predict, and perhaps control, the timing for moving documents off the original system. Typically, donors will plan to change their record-creating system some time in advance. If you participate in the overall planning for the new system, you could have sufficient time for an orderly transfer of documents to the new system or to your system for long-term retention.

On the other hand, a sudden problem in the donor's system can necessitate sudden, unplanned transfers. In the perfect world, we would all monitor our systems carefully and detect circumstances that indicate a need to copy or remove information from it. But we do not live in a perfect world. Even so, we should all strive to avoid sudden transfers. Sudden transfers can lead to loss of information, loss of contextual metadata, or loss of authenticity. It can also prove very difficult for you as the receiving organization to handle large volumes of documents you had not planned for.

Three Critical Issues

If you want the digital materials your donors have, work with them on three things.

First, emphasize that donors must actively manage their digital materials themselves until they hand them over to you: individual documents, e-mail messages, images, etc. You will have made some appraisal decisions by this point, and you might assure them that materials you don't think have archival value don't need any special care beyond what they think important.

Second, emphasize the importance of preserving the contextual information that accompanies documents—that is, the record-keeping metadata. The metadata will range from indices of the documents through code lists and fixity information such as checksums or mechanisms for verifying digital signatures within the documents.

Finally, demonstrate how they can preserve the relationship between the metadata and the documents (or other digital materials). That may include lists of dates, titles, and authors, which the system should link to the list of electronic objects to which it refers.

Metadata

Unless you and the donor put some effort into defining the relationship between metadata and the documents, it may not appear at all. Databases, for instance, commonly employ coding systems for some elements of information. Over the life of the database, the creator may alter the codes. For the relationship between the original code and the altered code to appear knowable to future researchers, a donor must document exactly what changes she or he made, when, and why.

If donors preserve the original objects in a form that current computer users can use and in a way that ensures the authenticity of each individual object, and if they preserve the metadata that lists and describes each object, they have met your need for authenticity, completeness, accessibility, and understandability. If the new system can process the metadata and documents together, then we have processability and, potentially, reusability for the future.

Collecting Specific Technologies

The Desktop

Stephens and Wallace[32] use this term to refer to the content of a PC. They strongly suggest that you find or develop a guide outlining fairly simple but crucial steps to good desktop management. Your guide should include basic instructions on how to organize files (directories/folders organized by project or subject and perhaps further by file type, etc.), your expectations of what files you would like the donor to pass along to you, and when (in terms of the life of the file) the transfer should take place. Stephens and Wallace, as well as the Paradigm Project, provide models to work with,[33] but obviously you can individualize parts of the guide to specific donors.

E-mail

Stephens and Wallace promote two strategies that seem useful in your relationship with your donors: 1) ask them to print out messages for long-term retention, and 2) ask them to move messages and any attachments off the e-mail system and onto another program, such as a word processor or textual database.[34]

Websites

Initially websites functioned as a form of one-way communication, rather like newspapers or brochures in the paper world. Soon they allowed the user to send feedback of many different sorts, but the owner always controlled the page. Now we have begun to use websites and advanced web services as a replacement for a wide variety of paper document forms and to merge them in their functions—the whole Web 2.0 world.

Even when the Web was simply a hyperlinked brochure, it was unstable. Owners could add and remove links at will, and neither the server software that contained it nor the client software that read and displayed it had any way to determine the version currently being made available (and certainly wasn't programmed to care). Now that Web 2.0 has emerged, that instability has been networked and made several orders of magnitude more complicated while remaining unstable. Nobody thinks this problem is trivial for the historical record, but the whole arena is so new that little research has been applied to it. As electronic documents blogs, wikis, and the like have all the vulnerability that others do for the archivist. The difficulty lies in maintaining the links and sequencing that reflect their use as interactive communication—an electronic conference call. The solution will lie in harvesting and metadata issues.

In the meantime, Stephens and Wallace make some suggestions that you could use: encourage your donors to date anything they include on their websites, any time they revise anything, and when they review anything. For example, many companies, arts organizations, and individual artists use a web page as a way to disseminate information about their latest products or services. Unfortunately, once the information has been altered, the previous information disappears. Encourage your donors to capture copies of versions before they change them. If the Web replicates information that's available in another form, it will undoubtedly have a different presentation form. While capturing the content may not be as urgent as it would if the information did not exist in another form, periodic capturing of the "look and feel" of the presentation mode still matters.[35]

If your donor has active involvement with Web 2.0 technologies, you will want to work out a protocol for archiving that participation; Web 2.0 participation constitutes a form of documentation similar to letters, diaries, and journals.[36]

In 2001, the Smithsonian Institution Archives published a report by the Dollar Consulting firm on handling the web pages created for them.[37] While old by Web 2.0 standards, the fact that SIA focused on strategies and policies makes their guidelines still useful for you as a model for developing a policy framework before you approach your donors about "archiving" their websites. It identifies areas your policy should address, although it includes a lot of issues you may ignore. Most of what follows I have adapted from section 5 of that report.

Given the hyperlinking that the Web depends on, you should first ask what your donors consider their website. Adapting the Dollar Consulting report, you might define "theirs" as any website your donors control and use to provide information, services, or products to a defined audience. Having defined their websites, you should then go on to suggest best practices for constructing websites that make them archivable: 1) using nonproprietary technology for coding the site, and 2) using a search engine that the webmaster controls, not a third-party proprietary search engine controlled by that third party.

You should then suggest practices that you and your donor can cooperate on to ensure full documentation. For instance, develop a site map and identify the areas with particular archival value. Schedule periodic captures of those areas, depending on the scope and frequency of change you and the donor can anticipate. Repeat this process for any new pages. Establish a history log of the changes to the website.

Dollar Consulting recommends that donors transfer websites and their content pages to an archival repository as early as possible, along with the documentation that provides the history and context of the materials being transferred.

The Smithsonian Institution Archives set up a project to implement the Dollar Consulting recommendations and has posted the report of that activity on the Web.[38] Though now out of date in its specifics, the SIA project provides a good view of how to go from a general recommendation to a specific implementation.

Legacy Materials

So far we have spent a lot of energy thinking about known donors, but I think it's fair to say that most of our collections come through the door long after the creator has stopped creating—sometimes very long after. Today those collections may contain old storage media encoded with files from old systems, and the only way to get at them for appraisal and acquisitions takes digital archeology, also called data forensics, computer forensics, and data archeology. As you might imagine, this area holds great interest for the legal and commercial sectors of the economy, and a substantial industry has developed to serve the need. However, the process costs a lot. In 1999, Seamus Ross and Ann Gow conducted a research project to "examine the approaches to accessing digital materials where the media has become damaged (through disaster or age) or where the hardware and software are either no longer available or unknown."[39] Their final report does an outstanding job of explaining the issues involved, and the price. They report that "the National Security Association (Washington DC) estimated that the 'cost of rebuilding just 20 megabytes of data in a US engineering firm is $64,400.'"[40] Another site reports that the costs of digital discovery in legal cases can run into hundreds of thousands of dollars.[41] Clearly it's a service you will want to use sparingly, if at all.

So what should you do with those floppies and CDs and flash drives? I'd suggest you start with policies. If you can read the floppies and CDs and flash drives, appraise them. If they're worth keeping, put them into your process for digital materials. If not, discard them. If you can't read them, you have much more difficult issues. Have you buddied up with someone who has capabilities you don't? Might the CDs and floppies belong in a repository that can rescue them? If you have contracted with a TDR, can they help you? Are the contents potentially valuable enough to make a pitch to your "Friends" organization to support a heroic rescue effort with a data forensics expert? Whatever you decide, act on it immediately. Like leaky plumbing, the passage of time will only make the problem more difficult.

Summary

The world of the small repository revolves around donors. From my own experience, I can attest that most donors do not realize the fragility of their computer-based life's work. Once over the initial shock of the bad news, they will welcome you. Reach out to them.

Notes

1. "Intentional Archives." Archives&Archivists listserv, February 18–22, 2008.

2. Gregory S. Hunter, *Preserving Digital Information: A How-To-Do-It Manual* (New York: Neal-Schuman, 2000), 115.

3. Hunter, *Preserving Digital Information*, 125–32.

4. John McDonald, "Managing Information in an Office Systems Environment: The IMOSA Project," *American Archivist* 58, no. 2 (Spring 1995): 142–53.

5. Philip C. Bantin, *Understanding Data and Information Systems for Recordkeeping* (New York: Neal-Schuman, 2008).

6. John McDonald, "Managing Information in an Office Systems Environment," 152–53.

7. David O. Stephens and Roderick C. Wallace, *Electronic Records Retention: An Introduction* (Prairie Village, Kans.: ARMA International, 1997), 11–20.

8. Mary L. Ginn, *Sample Forms for Archival and Records Management Programs* (Lenexa, Kans.: ARMA International; Chicago: Society of American Archivists, 2002).

9. Paradigm Project, "Accessioning," *Workbook on Digital Private Papers, 2005–2007*, www.paradigm.ac.uk/workbook/accessioning/ (accessed April 22, 2008).

10. Clifford Lynch, "Authenticity and Integrity in the Digital Environment: An Exploratory Analysis of the Central Role of Trust," *Authenticity in a Digital Environment: May 2000*, ed. Charles T. Cullen (Washington, D.C.: Council on Library and Informa-

tion Resources, 2000), 44, www.clir.org/pubs/reports/pub92/lynch.html (accessed April 18, 2008).

11. Stephens and Wallace, *Electronic Records Retention: An Introduction.*

12. Maureen Pennock, *DCC Digital Curation Manual Instalment on Curating E-Mails: A Life-cycle Approach to the Management and Preservation of E-mail Messages* (Bath, England: Digital Curation Centre, 2006), 31–32, www.dcc.ac.uk/resource/curation-manual/chapters/curating-e-mails/ (accessed April 18, 2008).

13. Pennock, *DCC Digital Curation Manual Instalment on Curating E-Mails*, 27–28.

14. Collaborative Electronic Records Project, *E-Mail Guidelines for Managers and Employees*, (Sleepy Hollow, N.Y.: Rockefeller Archive Center, 2006), archive.rockefeller. edu/CERP/pdf/emailguidelines.pdf (accessed July 15, 2008).

15. Collaborative Electronic Records Project, *E-Mail Guidelines for Managers and Employees*, 11.

16. Collaborative Electronic Records Project, *E-Mail Guidelines for Managers and Employees*, 3.

17. Collaborative Electronic Records Project, *E-Mail Guidelines for Managers and Employees*, 13.

18. Collaborative Electronic Records Project, *Records Retention and Disposition Guidelines* (Sleepy Hollow, N.Y.: Rockefeller Archive Center, 2007), http://siarchives. si.edu/cerp/RECORDS_RETENTION_SCHEDULE_rev2.pdf (accessed July 15, 2008).

19. Pennock, *DCC Digital Curation Manual Instalment on Curating E-Mails*, 15–16.

20. Susan Thomas, *Paradigm: A Practical Approach to the Preservation of Personal Digital Archives*, version 1.0 (2007), 5–8, www.paradigm.ac.uk/projectdocs/jiscreports/ ParadigmFinalReportv1.pdf (accessed April 18, 2008).

21. David Bearman, "Moments of Risk: Identifying Threats to Electronic Records," *Archivaria* 62 (Fall 2006): 15–24.

22. Tom Hyry and Rachel Onuf, "The Personality of Electronic Records: The Impact of New Information Technology on Personal Papers," *Archival Issues: Journal of the Midwest Archives Conference* 22, no. 1 (1997): 43.

23. David O. Stephens and Roderick C. Wallace, *Electronic Records Retention: New Strategies for Data Life Cycle Management* (Lenexa, Kans.: ARMA International, 2003), 5–8.

24. Paradigm Project, *Workbook on Digital Private Papers, 2005–2007*, www.paradigm.ac.uk/workbook/accessioning/ (accessed April 18, 2008).

25. Maggie Jones and Neil Beagrie, *Preservation Management of Digital Materials: A Handbook* (London: The British Library, 2001), Section 3.4, Rights Management, www. dpconline.org/graphics/inststrat/rights.html (accessed April 18, 2008).

26. Paradigm Project, *Guidance for Creators of Personal Papers* (2007). www.paradigm.ac.uk/guidanceforcreators/guidance-for-creators-of-personal-digital-archives.pdf (accessed April 18, 2008).

27. Paradigm Project, *Guidance for Creators of Personal Papers* (2007), 3.

28. University of North Carolina at Chapel Hill, School of Library and Information Science, *Managing the Digital University Desktop*, www.ils.unc.edu/digitaldesktop/ (accessed July 6, 2008).

29. Helen Tibbo, "Researching the Researchers: Finding Out How University Em-

ployees Manage Their Digital Materials" (paper presented at the NHPRC ERR Fellowship Symposium, Wilson Library, University of North Carolina at Chapel Hill, November 19, 2004), ils.unc.edu/nhprcfellows/tibbo.ppt (accessed July 6, 2008).

30. University of North Carolina at Chapel Hill, School of Library and Information Science, "Timeline & Results," *Managing the Digital University Desktop*, www.ils.unc.edu/digitaldesktop/ (accessed July 6, 2008).

31. Harvard University Library, *Guidelines for Managing Faculty Files,* August 2006, http://hul.harvard.edu/rmo/downloads/FacultyGuidelines.pdf (accessed July 6, 2008).

32. Stephens and Wallace, *Electronic Records Retention: New Strategies for Data Life Cycle Management*, 42–45.

33. Paradigm Project, *Workbook on Digital Private Papers.*

34. Stephens and Wallace, *Electronic Records Retention: New Strategies for Data Life Cycle Management*, 48–49.

35. Stephens and Wallace, *Electronic Records Retention: New Strategies for Data Life Cycle Management*, 61–63. One should note that this book appeared before much of the Web 2.0 technology became popular. While the strategies they suggest still have a great amount of merit, they don't cover all the issues that you will face. They provide a place to start, however.

36. Catherine O'Sullivan, "Diaries, On-line Diaries, and the Future Loss to Archives: Or Blogs and the Blogging Bloggers Who Blog Them," *American Archivist* 68, no. 1 (Spring/Summer 2005): 53–73.

37. Dollar Consulting, *Archival Preservation of Smithsonian Web Resources: Principles and Best Practices*, Smithsonian Institution Archives (July 2001), http://siarchives.si.edu/pdf/dollar_report.pdf (accessed July 6, 2008).

38. Smithsonian Institution Archives, *Archiving Smithsonian Websites: An Evaluation and Recommendation for a Smithsonian Institution Archives Pilot Project* (May 2003), http://siarchives.si.edu/pdf/websitepilot.pdf (accessed July 7, 2008).

39. Seamus Ross and Ann Gow, *Digital Archaeology: Rescuing Neglected and Damaged Data Resources, A JISC/NPO Study within the Electronic Libraries (eLib) Programme on the Preservation of Electronic Materials* (London: Library Information Technology Centre, South Bank University, 1999), 2, www.hatii.arts.gla.ac.uk/research/BrLibrary/rosgowrt.pdf (accessed April 22, 2008).

40. Ross and Gow, *Digital Archaeology*, 2.

41. CyberControls, LLC, "Basics of Computer Forensics," www.cybercontrols.net/forensics/attorneyforensicbasics.asp (accessed July 6, 2008).

Chapter 8

The Future of Curators, Archivists, and Digital Collections

Digital Archivist and Curator—The New Norm

In chapter 1, I reviewed the various components of the archival function. Here I'll go back through them again, pointing out how those functions might look in future repositories where every archivist is part digital archivist.

Appraisal will include digital materials. Your criteria may not change, but your process may. You'll find yourself heavily reliant on sets of series and system metadata that provide most of the provenance information.

Acquisition will pick up very much where appraisal left off. You'll find yourself using clearly defined procedures that you have established with your donor to make sure the digital materials come to you in good order. That process will involve more detailed agreements that spell out the relationship between you and the donor across time—donor procedures, checklists, acknowledgments, etc.—than you need today. You'll probably want to keep stricter records about the materials you don't keep, so you can say with certainty what you discarded and what just seems to have gone missing.

Arrangement and description will probably include something like the general inventories we now make (essential information doesn't change with the format of the materials), but it will undoubtedly include a fair amount of metadata from the materials that will facilitate the access process. There will be no boxing, foldering, and labeling of digital materials.

Providing access and reference services will mean making the materials available to users and probably educating them how to use the access system—just like now. You'll need a new range of policies that parallel your current access policies. For instance, must researchers register electronically to get into the access system? Will you allow patrons to copy materials? If so, in what format? Print only or download onto a storage device of some sort? How much may they have? How will you enforce your limits? What data will you collect about the collections they touch? Eventually the questions will end, but not until you have created a substantial body of policies.

Long-term retention will remain an ongoing concern. Like preservation of paper-based materials now, long-term retention of digital materials starts with good policies, an adequate budget, and diligent compliance. The policies and methods of monitoring compliance will change, but the basics won't.

Since about 2005, leaders in the profession have begun to focus quite intently on the issue of what the digital curator will need to know: what theory and what skills. Richard Pearce-Moses, an innovative leader in the proactive approach to digital records and archives management, outlined similar lists of essential technical skills that call for knowledge of a given area and also *practical experience* with both digital objects and the tools and systems used to create and manage them. In 2006, while president of the Society of American Archivists (SAA), Pearce-Moses convened the New Skills Conference.[1] While the details from that conference differ from Adrian Cunningham's list below, the basic thrust does not. The digital archivist and curator must have a solid understanding of archival principles and activities, a solid understanding of the variety of processes that create the materials sought by his or her repository, a solid understanding of the political forces that affect his or her repository, and a solid understanding of the systems that create digital materials, transmit them from one form of storage to another, and store them safely. Further, before the rest of the repository's stakeholders fully understand the issues digital materials raise, the digital curator must have the skills of a diplomat and the savvy of a businessperson.

The DigCCurr2007 program stated that its goal was "to develop an openly accessible graduate-level curriculum to prepare students to work in the field of digital curation, [and] bring the issues of digital curation and this curriculum to the broader library, archives, and museum communities as well as the public."[2] One of the DigCCurr2007 papers came from Adrian Cunningham, a long-time proponent of a proactive approach toward digital materials. Using a long list of the skills required of a modern-day archivist, he argued that archivists will need to understand and accept the impact of digital materials and archivists need to gain knowledge in the following areas—many new to most in the archival profession:

1. Communication, records creation, and information management environments, including the way modern "culture creators" work;
2. Modeling and analytical ability (including functional and workflow analysis);
3. Communication, influencing and change management skills;
4. Awareness of systems design and implementation skills;
5. Knowledge of metadata regimes for discovery, record keeping, data management, etc.;

6. Extensible Markup Language (XML) and types of markup languages, and eventually Extensible Stylesheet Language Transformations (XSLT) skills;
7. Knowledge of approaches to quality control, including approaches to auditing and compliance assessment;
8. Disaster preparedness and business continuity skills including security management regimes and encryption and authentication;
9. Knowledge of broader digital curation communities and initiatives;
10. Knowledge of storage options and technologies, including provenance and context management in archival systems.[3]

While the task of acquiring all these skills may at first seem daunting, many of us will take heart to see that "programming skills" do not rank very high, although both Cunningham and the New Skills proceedings do encourage basic programming skills for those who wish to truly master the digital landscape. Undoubtedly archivists should have skills beyond those of the average document creator. At a minimum we need to understand basic system structure and how to manage file formats for conversion or description purposes. We also need to understand the underlying architecture or purpose of web services. At a more advanced level the digital curator will find it useful to understand how to write simple scripts to do batch conversions and other time-saving procedures; this may blur into programming. But trial and error through practical test applications of tools, technologies, and services—that is, getting your hands dirty—is the only way to tackle the issues successfully.

Potential for Seamless System Integration

Collection Management and Storage

While we have genuine trouble predicting some futures, others rather lay themselves out fairly clearly in front of us. It seems that's the case with this topic. Given the legal issues that have arisen around digital materials, institutional archivists have no choice but to address some of the system integration gaps that exist and to develop solutions and tools with which to address them. I have mentioned various implementation projects that have addressed the use of open-source repositories and related tools to implement digital object long-term retention and access. However, we still have a gap between these "collection side" tools (such as Fedora or Xena) and any "management side" tools for routine archival management functions. While it's true that with some ingenuity we can integrate both types of tools with other similar tools to form a comprehensive solution for collection management, few examples of knitting together the functionality of the two sides exist today.

Federated Access

From the very beginning of archivists' involvement with the Web, visionaries' ultimate goal has involved developing the capacity for the researcher to sit at a search engine and find any and all materials that might relate to his or her research,[4] and the concept has become known as *federated access*, employing federated searching across federated systems. There still exists the need for an enormous amount of work in the area of federated access to multiple repositories, as well as in learning the potential of social networking tools and proper handling of emerging media such as blogs, wikis, and the like. Not only do we need to learn how to integrate such emerging tools and objects into our systems' architectures, but we also need to imagine inventive ways of integrating and using these new tools and media to bring added value to collections of digital material. In the following sections we will briefly explore the issues surrounding these topics and explore a number of projects tackling them.

Integrating a Repository's Archives Management Records and Collections

While much of the discussion in this book regarding systems has focused on collection management tools (primarily related to the creation and maintenance of digital repositories), you should know about projects that focus on the archival management side. Some of these projects, such as Archon[5] and the Archivists' Toolkit[6] support *only* historical collection management and description; others, such as the University of Hull's REMAP project, seek to integrate the administrative management content with collection content. The power that comes from that perspective lies in the use of these tools as access systems to support both repository management functions and researchers. Below I'll briefly describe some of the work in this area of the past few years.

RepoMMan, a project at the University of Hull in the United Kingdom, developed a way to extract descriptive metadata from digital materials and contextual metadata from sources already within the repository's files and then apply the metadata to digital materials.[7] Further, it analyzed repository requirements for space and any digital rights management issues. From there, it adapted a generic workflow framework to the specific requirements of common repository tasks and produced a tool for interacting with a Fedora digital repository.

Based on the success of the RepoMMan project, the university's REMAP project seeks to further integrate the metadata automation tools with the workflow framework. The project will also test how the Fedora digital repository system could be used to support records management and the long-term retention of digital as an integrated part of workflow. If it succeeds it will show one way to provide seamless integration of archival management record-keeping functionality with a repository of digital materials. For example, REMAP could link donor and accession records directly to the digital material in the repository so that both the digital material and all related management metadata are accessed via a single search interface.[8]

Collaborative and Networked Repositories

If we imagine a future digital collection documenting any aspect of the war in Iraq, we can easily imagine a researcher finding related content housed in multiple repositories located worldwide.[9] In the world of analog materials we could not establish a centralized collection of all relevant materials. In the digital world, we could reasonably expect to link the self-contained silos that repositories now represent to create virtual collections through the use of federated metadata models. These models create aggregations of metadata describing collections and their management needs while the content remains in the custody of parent organizations. OAIster provides a prototype to study. Other models pull digital materials from many collections to a single server, much as a "light archive" access module at a TDR might do.

The Networked Infrastructure for Nineteenth-century Electronic Scholarship (NINES)[10] is a scholarly organization in British and American nineteenth-century studies supported by a software development group assembling a suite of critical and editorial tools for digital scholarship. The NINES database includes various kinds of content: traditional texts and documents—editions, bibliographic entries, and critical works of all kinds—as well as born-digital materials relating to all aspects of nineteenth-century culture. The NINES project provides a model and working example for scholarship that takes advantage of digital resources and Internet connectivity. It provides scholars with access to a federated digital environment and a suite of computerized analytic and interpretive tools. NINES strives to go beyond presenting static images or transcriptions of manuscripts onscreen. Software tools that aid collation and comparative analysis and enable pedagogical application of scholarly electronic resources demonstrate the richness of the electronic environment.

The collective nature of NINES, and its clear appeal to large numbers of scholarly users, also implies a strong potential for social-software applications within this matrix. Once basic elements of the project were in place, the project leaders turned to develop an open-source tool set that would combine the best elements of social bookmarking or collecting systems like Delicious, and of specialized online curation and exhibit services. Below is a brief description of each of the core tools designed for NINES that allows the social networking aspect of this project to work.[11]

Juxta is an open-source collation and bibliographic visualization tool[12] for comparing and collating multiple versions to a single textual work. The implementations of Juxta include:

- Damozel—a collation of seven versions of the poem "The Blessed Damozel" by Dante Gabriel Rossetti. Damozel demonstrates the use of Juxta XML files to associate images and milestones with text;
- Hamlet—a collation of three early texts of William Shakespeare's *Hamlet*, which demonstrates using Juxta on large texts with highly variant spellings;
- Renaissance—a collation of two versions of Walter Pater's *Studies in the History of the Renaissance*, which demonstrates the collation of prose texts.[13]

Collex, the collecting/exhibiting tool that powers NINES,[14] provides a set of tools designed to aid students and scholars working in networked archives and federated repositories of humanities materials with a mechanism to collect, annotate, and tag online objects and to repurpose them in illustrated, interlinked essays or exhibits.

The China Digital Museum Project (CDMP)[15] is a collaborative project involving the Chinese Ministry of Education, Hewlett-Packard Company, and several Chinese universities, with Beihang University as the main technical partner. The CDMP provides an example of a federated, collaborative repository that routinely collects the university archives' digital collections, using the OAIS model, into the "mega-repository" with a current goal of incorporating over a hundred identified repositories.

CDMP wants to develop a way for participating universities to use DSpace to store, manage, preserve, and disseminate the digitized versions of their artifacts. Each university museum runs a local DSpace repository. Two mega-repositories, one in the north and one in the south of China, replicate the contents of all of those university museums. The mega-repositories can then focus on various long-term retention activities, freeing each university museum from the need for local expertise and resources for that purpose.

The Digital Repository Infrastructure Vision for European Research (DRIVER) project responds to the vision that any form of scientific-content resource, including scientific/technical reports, research articles, experimental or observational data, rich media, and other digital objects, should be freely accessible through simple Internet-based infrastructures. The project initially brought together ten international partners to create a knowledge base of European research by establishing a testbed across Europe to support the development of a knowledge infrastructure for the European Research Area. It aimed for one large-scale virtual content resource that would access and integrate individual repositories.[16]

These mega-repositories have begun to exploit the benefits of a federated system. Such arrangements will clearly benefit long-term retention and disaster recovery needs of digital materials as linked repositories agree to replicate each other's content. They also provide multirepository search capacity and form a repository network with individual institutions or collections acting as nodes.

In addition to the benefits inherent in having your repository's content mirrored on multiple offsite locations that update their holdings automatically, collaborative and federated repositories can:

1. Enable metadata integration for the creation of virtual collections that could only exist in digital form;
2. Collaborate to share resources and skill sets across repositories; and
3. Ensure uniform normalization of file formats and metadata use through standard ingest requirements or conversion tools.

I can imagine a day when smaller institutions partner with larger institutions or federated repositories to the benefit of both. Most small repositories have some significant holdings that would enhance the prominent digital collections of the larger institution. Large institutions can provide the infrastructure small repositories probably cannot.

The preceding examples demonstrate how large institutions have managed some significant successes in the integration of various types of systems, services, and repositories. However, technology shows no signs of slowing in its evolution. Just as our profession has begun to come to terms with many of the initial issues (such as long-term retention of digital materials or format normalization) surrounding twentieth-century digital materials, the new century has brought new challenges. Social media, including blogs, wikis, massive multiplayer role-playing games, and various online social spaces, are not stable and fixed like photographs or films or books. They fall outside of the familiar limits of our cultural habits and expectations, but they will appear in our archives—and they should.

Getting In on the Act

Whether or not you seek a full education in digital curation, you'll need to start behaving like a digital curator for the digital material you have now and will receive in the future. In light of the work we have reviewed above, I have no doubt that researchers will work toward solutions and tools to address Web 2.0 problems. You don't have to build the solutions, but you need to keep abreast of the issues surrounding the new technologies and examples of how others in our profession are addressing them.

Given this rapidly changing digital landscape, learning to use and adapt the success of others has become one of the most important skills required for success. Remember those signs you put somewhere: "It's not up to you to complete the work, nor are you free to desist from it" and "Listen, sonny, you rush a miracle man, you get rotten miracles." Here's another to put beside them: "Flexibility in the face of uncertainty requires courage." You have the courage, or you wouldn't have committed yourself to a small repository. Stay flexible, but stick to the work. Take your time. Remember you are creating a miracle.

Notes

1. National Archives and Records Administration, the Arizona State Library Archives, and the Society of American Archivists, New Skills for the Digital Era Conference (Washington, D.C.: The National Archives, May 31–June 2, 2006), http://rpm.lib.az.us/newskills/ (accessed July 7, 2008); Richard Pearce-Moses and Susan E. Davis, eds., *"New Skills for a Digital Era"* (preprint of conference proceedings sponsored by National Archives and Records Administration, Society of American Archivists, Arizona State Library Archives and Public Records, Washington, D.C., The National Archives, May 31–June 2, 2006). Proceedings edited by the Society of American Archivists and the Arizona State Library Archives and Public Records, August 28, 2007.

2. DigCCurr2007: An International Symposium in Digital Curation at the School of Information and Library Science at the University of North Carolina at Chapel Hill, April 19, 2007, www.ils.unc.edu/digccurr2007/ (accessed April 19, 2008).

3. Adrian Cunningham, "Digital Curation/Digital Archiving: A View from the National Archives of Australia" (paper presented at DigCCurr2007: An International Symposium in Digital Curation at the School of Information and Library Science at the University of North Carolina at Chapel Hill, April 20, 2007), www.ils.unc.edu/digccurr2007/papers/cunningham_paper_7.pdf (accessed April 18, 2008). Accompanying slides available at www.ils.unc.edu/digccurr2007/slides/cunningham_slides_7.pdf.

4. Daniel V. Pitti and Wendy Duff, eds., *Encoded Archival Description on the Internet* (Binghamton, N.Y.: Haworth Information Press, 2002).

5. University of Illinois at Urbana-Champaign, *Archon™: The Simple Archival Information System*, www.archon.org/ (accessed April 22, 2008).

6. Archivists' Toolkit http://archiviststoolkit.org/ (accessed July 29, 2008).

7. Joint Information Systems (JIS) Committee, "Digital Repositories" Programme, *Repository Metadata and Management Project (RepoMMan)*, www.hull.ac.uk/esig/repomman/project_aims/index.html (accessed April 22, 2008).

8. REMAP allows for security controls and user authentication tools in this scenario.

9. Helen Willa Samuels, "Who Controls the Past," in *American Archival Studies: Readings in Theory and Practice*, ed. Randall C. Jimerson (Chicago: The Society of American Archivists, 2000), 193–210.

10. NINES: A Networked Infrastructure for Nineteenth-century Electronic Scholarship, www.nines.org/ (accessed April 22, 2008).

11. More information about NINES is available on the project website at www.nines.org/about/index.html (accessed April 22, 2008).

12. Juxta, *User's Manual for Juxta 1.0* (February 1, 2006) is available on the project website at www.juxtasoftware.org/documentation.html (accessed November 23, 2008).

13. University of Virginia, "Project Juxta," *Applied Research in Patacriticism (ARP)*, echo.gmu.edu/toolcenter-wiki/index.php?title=ARP_(Applied_Research_in_Patacriticism) (accessed November 25, 2008).

14. Bethany Nowviskie, "Collex: Semantic Collection & Exhibits for the Remixable Web" (November 2005), www.nines.org/about/Nowviskie-Collex.pdf (accessed April 22, 2008).

15. Robert Tansley, "Building a Distributed; Standards-based Repository Federation China Digital Museum Project." *D-Lib Magazine* 12, no. 7/8 (July/August 2006), www.dlib.org/dlib/july06/tansley/07tansley.html (accessed April 22, 2008).

16. DRIVER: Digital Repository Infrastructure Vision for European Research, www.driver-repository.eu/ (accessed April 22, 2008).

Works Cited

AIIM. "Frequently asked questions (FAQS): ISO 19005-1:2005 (PDF/A-1)." July 10, 2006. www.aiim.org/documents/standards/19005-1_FAQ.pdf (accessed July 27, 2008).

Anderson, Paul. "What Is Web 2.0? Ideas, Technologies and Implications for Education." *JISC Technology and Standards Watch* (February 2007). www.jisc.ac.uk/media/documents/techwatch/tsw0701b.pdf (accessed July 27, 2008).

Andolsen, Alan A. "Will Your Records Be There When You Need Them?" *The Information Management Journal* 40, no. 3 (May/June 2006): 56–61.

Archives New Zealand. *Electronic Recordkeeping Systems Standards.* Wellington, N.Z.: Archives New Zealand, June 2005. www.archives.govt.nz/continuum/documents/publications/s5.pdf (accessed July 27, 2008).

Arthur, Magan. "Intro to Digital Asset Management: Just What Is a DAM?" *CMS Watch.* April 30, 2005. http://cmswatch.com/Feature/124-DAM-vs.-DM (accessed July 27, 2008).

Bantin, Philip C. "Electronic Records Management—A Review of the Work of a Decade and a Reflection on Future Directions." *Encyclopedia of Library and Information Science* 71, suppl. 34 (2002): 47–81. www.libraries.iub.edu/index.php?pageId=3313 (accessed July 27, 2008).

———. "Strategies for Managing Electronic Records: A New Archival Paradigm? An Affirmation of Our Archival Traditions?" *Archival Issues* 23, no. 1 (1998): 17–34. www.libraries.iub.edu/index.php?pageId=3313 (accessed April 12, 2008).

———. *Understanding Data and Information Systems for Recordkeeping.* New York: Neal-Schuman, 2008.

Bantin, Philip, Rosemary Pleva Flynn, Terry Radke, and Stacie Wiegand. "Protecting Organizational Information: Developing Partnerships for Managing University Information Systems." Presentation at EDUCAUSE 2001, Indianapolis, Indiana, October 28–31, 2001. http://net.educause.edu/ir/library/pdf/EDU01115.pdf.

Bates, Melanie, Sue Manuel, Steve Loddington, and Charles Oppenheim. "Digital Lifecycles and File Types: Final Report." *Rights and Rewards Project: Digital Lifecycles and File Types: Final Report.* Leicestershire, U.K.: Loughborough University, 2006. http://rightsandrewards.lboro.ac.uk/files/resourcesmodule/@random43cbae8b0d0ad/1148047621_DigitalLifecyclesV2.pdf (accessed July 27, 2008).

Beagrie, Neil. "Plenty of Room at the Bottom? Personal Digital Libraries and Collections." *D-Lib Magazine* 11, no. 6 (June 2005). www.dlib.org/dlib/june05/beagrie/06beagrie.html (accessed July 27, 2008).

Bearman, David. "Moments of Risk: Identifying Threats to Electronic Records." *Archivaria* 62 (Fall 2006): 15–46.

Besser, Howard. *Introduction to Imaging.* Rev. ed. Ed. Sally Hubbard with Deborah Lenert. Los Angeles: Getty Institute, undated. www.getty.edu/research/conducting_research/standards/introimages (accessed July 6, 2008).

Bishoff, Liz, and Tom Clareson. "Digital Preservation Assessment: Readying Cultural Heritage Institutions for Digital Preservation." Paper presented at DigCCurr2007: An International Symposium in Digital Curation at the School of Information and Library Science at the University of North Carolina at Chapel Hill, April 20, 2007. www.ils.unc.edu/digccurr2007/papers/bishoff_paper_8-3.pdf. Accompanying slides available at www.ils.unc.edu/digccurr2007/slides/bishoff_slides_8-3.pdf (accessed July 5, 2008).

Boles, Frank, and Julia Marks Young. "Exploring the Black Box: The Appraisal of University Administrative Records." In *American Archival Studies: Readings in Theory and Practice*, ed. Randall C. Jimerson, 279–300. Chicago: The Society of American Archivists, 2000.

Borgman, Christine. "Personal Digital Libraries: Creating Individual Spaces for Innovation." Paper presented at the NSF/JISC Post Digital Library Futures Workshop, June 15–17, 2003, Cape Cod, Massachusetts. www.sis.pitt.edu/~dlwkshop/paper_borgman.html (accessed July 27, 2008).

Caplan, Priscilla. "How to Build Your Own Dark Archive (In Your Spare Time): A Talk for the Cornell Digital Preservation Management Workshop." Paper presented at the Cornell Digital Preservation Management Workshop, November 2004. www.fcla.edu/digitalArchive/pdfs/Howtobuildyourowndarkarchive.pdf (accessed July 27, 2008).

Center for Research Libraries. "Core Requirements for Digital Archives." www.crl.edu/content.asp?l1=13&l2=58&l3=162&l4=92 (accessed April 18, 2008).

Center for Research Libraries and OCLC. *Trustworthy Repository Audit and Certification (TRAC): Criteria and Checklist, Version 1.0.* Chicago and Dublin, Ohio: Center for Research Libraries and OCLC, 2007. www.crl.edu/content.asp?l1=13&l2=58&l3=162&l4=91 (accessed April 18, 2008).

*Changing*Minds.org. "Resistance to Change." *Changing*Minds.org. http://changingminds.org/disciplines/change_management/resistance_change/resistance_change.htm (accessed July 27, 2008).

Chen, Su-Shing. "Paradox of Digital Preservation." *Computer* 34, no. 3 (March 2001): 24–28.

Cobb, Judith, Richard Pearce-Moses, and Taylor Surface. "ECHO DEPository Project." www.ndiipp.uiuc.edu/pdfs/IST2005paper_final.pdf (accessed April 17, 2008).

Collaborative Electronic Records Project. *E-Mail Guidelines for Managers and Employees.* Sleepy Hollow, N.Y.: Rockefeller Archive Center, 2006. www.rockarch.org/CERP/pdf/emailguidelines.pdf (accessed July 27, 2008).

———. *Records Retention and Disposition Guidelines.* Sleepy Hollow, N.Y.: Rockefeller Archive Center, 2007. http://siarchives.si.edu/cerp/RECORDS_RETENTION_SCHEDULE_rev2.pdf (accessed July 27, 2008).

Convention Recordings International, Inc., 6983 Sunset Drive South, St. Petersburg, FL 33707. www.conventionrecordings.com (accessed July 27, 2008).

Cook, Terry. "Byte-ing Off What You Can Chew: Electronic Records Strategies for Small Archival Institutions." *Archifacts* (April 2004): 1–20. www.aranz.org.nz/Site/publications/papers_online/terry_cook_paper.aspx (accessed July 22, 2008).

Cornell University. *Cornell University Library Digital Preservation Policy Framework.* December 2004. http://commondepository.library.cornell.edu/cul-dp-framework.pdf (accessed July 27, 2008).

Crow, Ryan. "Open Society Institute: A Guide to Institutional Repository Software." 3rd ed. New York: Chain Bridge Group, 2004. www.soros.org/openaccess/pdf/OSI_Guide_to_IR_Software_v3.pdf (accessed April 18, 2008).

Crystal, Billy. *The Princess Bride.* DVD. Directed by Rob Reiner. Santa Monica, Calif.: MGM Home Entertainment, 2001. Based on the book by William Goldman, *The Princess Bride: S. Morgenstern's Classic Tale of True Love and High Adventure: The "Good Parts" Version, Abridged.* New York: Harcourt Brace Jovanovich, 1973. www.imdb.com/title/tt0093779/ (accessed April 12, 2008).

Cullen, Charles T. "Authentication of Digital Objects: Lessons From a Historian's Research." *Authenticity in a Digital Environment.* CLIR Report 92 (May 2000). www.clir.org/pubs/reports/pub92/cullen.html (accessed July 27, 2008).

Cunningham, Adrian. "Digital Curation/Digital Archiving: A View From the National Archives of Australia." Paper presented at DigCCurr2007: An International Symposium in Digital Curation at the School of Information and Library Science at the University of North Carolina at Chapel Hill, April 20, 2007. www.ils.unc.edu/digccurr2007/papers/cunningham_paper_7.pdf. Accompanying slides available at www.ils.unc.edu/digccurr2007/slides/cunningham_slides_7.pdf (accessed July 27, 2008).

CyberControls, LLC, "Basics of Computer Forensics," www.cybercontrols.net/forensics/attorneyforensicbasics.asp (accessed July 6, 2008).

Davis, Susan E. "Electronic Records Planning in 'Collecting' Repositories." *American Archivist* 71 (Spring/Summer 2008): 167–89.

Day, Michael, Maureen Pennock, and Julie Allinson. "Co-operation for Digital Preservation and Curation: Collaboration for Collection Development in Institutional Repository Networks." Paper presented at DigCCurr2007: An International Symposium in Digital Curation at the School of Information and Library Science at the University of North Carolina at Chapel Hill, April 20, 2007. www.ils.unc.edu/digccurr2007/papers/dayPennock_paper_9-3.pdf. Accompanying slides available at www.ukoln.ac.uk/ukoln/staff/m.pennock/presentations/digccurr2007.ppt (accessed July 27, 2008).

DigCCurr2007: An International Symposium on Digital Curation at the School of Information and Library Science at the University of North Carolina at Chapel Hill, April 18–20, 2007. www.ils.unc.edu/digccurr2007 (accessed July 27, 2008).

Digital Curation Centre. "About the DCC: Vision." www.dcc.ac.uk/about/ (accessed April 18, 2008).

————. "DCC Events." www.dcc.ac.uk/events (accessed April 18, 2008).

————. "Preservation." www.dcc.ac.uk/tools/digital-curation-tools/#113 (accessed April 18, 2008).

————. "Web Archiving Tools." www.dcc.ac.uk/tools/digital-curation-tools/#122 (accessed July 27, 2008).

Digital Curation Centre and DigitalPreservationEurope. *DRAMBORA: Digital Repository Audit Method Based on Risk Assessment.* www.repositoryaudit.eu/ (accessed April 18, 2008).

Digital Data Curation in Practice 2nd International Digital Curation Conference. November 21–22, 2006, at the Hilton Glasgow Hotel, Glasgow. www.dcc.ac.uk/events/dcc-2006/programme/ (accessed July 27, 2008).

Digital Preservation Coalition. "Report for the Digital Curation Centre/Digital Preservation Coalition (DCC/DPC) Workshop on Cost Models for Preserving Digital Assets: British Library Conference Centre, July 26, 2005." www.dpconline.org/graphics/events/050726workshop.html (accessed April 22, 2008).

Digital Preservation Testbed. *Functional Requirements for a Preservation System.* The Hague: Digitale duurzaamheid, 2005. www.digitaleduurzaamheid.nl/bibliotheek/docs/Technical_and_Functional_Requirements.pdf (accessed July 27, 2008).

Dobratz, Susanne, et al. *Catalogue of Criteria for Trusted Digital Repositories, Version 1 (Draft for Public Comment).* Nestor-Materials 8. Frankfurt am Main: Nestor Working Group on Trusted Repositories—Certification, 2006. http://edoc.hu-berlin.de/series/nestor-materialien/8/PDF/8.pdf (accessed July 27, 2008).

Dollar Consulting. *Archival Preservation of Smithsonian Web Resources: Principles and Best Practices.* Smithsonian Institution Archives, July 2001. http://siarchives.si.edu/pdf/dollar_report.pdf (accessed July 27, 2008).

Dollar, Charles. M. *Authentic Electronic Records: Strategies for Long-Term Access.* Chicago: Cohasset Associates, 2002.

DRIVER: Digital Repository Infrastructure Vision for European Research. www.driver-repository.eu/ (accessed April 22, 2008).

Eaton, Fynnette. "Managing Change in an Ever-Changing Electronic Environment." Presentation at the SAA Annual Meeting, Washington, D.C., August 5, 2006. www.archives.gov/era/pdf/2006-saa-eaton.pdf (accessed July 27, 2008).

Ericson, Timothy L. "At the 'Rim of Creative Dissatisfaction': Archivists and Acquisition Development." In *American Archival Studies: Readings in Theory and Practice*, ed. Randall C. Jimerson, 177–92. Chicago: The Society of American Archivists, 2000.

Fedora Commons. "History of the 'Fedora Project' and 'Fedora Commons'™ Names." www.fedora-commons.org/about/history.php (accessed April 18, 2008).

Fischer, Randy. "Florida Digital Archive: Ingest and Dissemination with DAITSS." Paper presented at DigCCurr2007: An International Symposium in Digital Curation at the School of Information and Library Science at the University of North Carolina at Chapel Hill, April 20, 2007. www.ils.unc.edu/digccurr2007/slides/fischer_slides_8-4.pdf (accessed July 27, 2008).

Franklin, Brian. "Trial by File: Five Tools for Managing Formats." *RLG DigiNews* 10, no. 5 (October 15, 2006). http://worldcat.org/arcviewer/1/OCC/200 7/07/10/0000068996/viewer/file1.html#article3 (accessed April 18, 2008).

Gantz, John, et al. *The Expanding Digital Universe: A Forecast of Worldwide Information Growth through 2010: An IDC White Paper*. Framingham, Mass.: IDC, 2007. www.emc.com/collateral/analyst-reports/expanding-digital-idc-white-paper.pdf (accessed July 27, 2008).

Gavitt, Sharon. *Computer Output Microfilm (COM)*. New York State Archives Publication No. 52. [Albany, N.Y.]: New York State Archives and Records Administration. Reprinted online March 14, 2002. www.archives.nysed.gov/a/records/mr_pub52.pdf (accessed July 27, 2008).

Gill, Tony. "Metadata and the Web." In *Introduction to Metadata: Pathways to Digital Information*. Los Angeles: Getty Institute, 2005. www.getty.edu/research/conducting_research/standards/intrometadata/metadata.html (accessed July 27, 2008).

Gilliland, Anne J. "Setting the Stage." In *Introduction to Metadata: Pathways to Digital Information*, online ed., version 2.1. Los Angeles: Getty Institute, 2005. www.getty.edu/research/conducting_research/standards/intrometadata/setting.html (accessed July 27, 2008).

Ginn, Mary L. *Sample Forms for Archival and Records Management Programs*. Lenexa, Kans.: ARMA International; Chicago: Society of American Archivists, 2002.

Google Maps API. www.google.com/apis/maps/ (accessed July 27, 2008).

Greene, Mark. "'The Surest Proof': A Utilitarian Approach to Appraisal." In *American Archival Studies: Readings in Theory and Practice*, ed. Randall C. Jimerson, 301–44. Chicago: Society of American Archivists, 2000.

Hammond, Tony, Timo Hannay, Ben Lund, and Joanna Scott. "Social Bookmarking Tools (I) A General Review." *D-Lib Magazine* 11, no. 4 (April 2005). www.dlib.org/dlib/april05/hammond/04hammond.html (accessed July 27, 2008).

Harvard University Library. *Guidelines for Managing Faculty Files.* August 2006. http://hul.harvard.edu/rmo/downloads/FacultyGuidelines.pdf (accessed July 6, 2008).

————. "JHOVE2: A Next-Generation Architecture for Format-Aware Digital Object Preservation Processing." Rev. 2006-06-01. http://hul.harvard.edu/jhove/JHOVE2-proposal.doc (accessed April 18, 2008).

Harvey, Ross. "Digital Futures Industry Briefing: National Archives of Australia and Council of Australasian Archives and Records Authorities." Presentation at the National Archives of Australia meeting, Canberra, ACT, November 8, 2006.

Hedstrom, Margaret, et al. "'The Old Version Flickers More': Digital Preservation from the User's Perspective." *American Archives* 69, no. 1 (Spring/Summer 2006): 159–87.

Hofman, Hans. "The Use of Standards and Models." In *Managing Electronic Records*, ed. Julie McLeod and Catherine Hare, 18–33. London: Facet, 2005.

Hunter, Gregory S. *Preserving Digital Information: A How-To-Do-It Manual.* New York: Neal-Schuman, 2000.

Hyry, Tom, and Rachel Onuf. "The Personality of Electronic Records: The Impact of New Information Technology on Personal Papers." *Archival Issues: Journal of the Midwest Archives Conference* 22, no. 1 (1997): 37–44.

"Intentional Archives." Archives&Archivists listserv, February 18–22, 2008.

International Conference on Digital Preservation: iPRES 2007. Beijing, China, October 11–12, 2007. http://rdd.sub.uni-goettingen.de/conferences/ipres/ipres-en.html (accessed April 18, 2008).

International Council of Archivists. Committee on Electronic Records. *Guide for Managing Electronic Records from an Archival Perspective.* ICA Study 8. Paris: ICA, 1997. Web link now points to www.ica.org/en/node/30019 (accessed July 27, 2008).

International Council of Archivists. *Electronic Records: A Workbook for Archivists.* ICA Study 16. Paris: ICA, 2005. www.ica.org/en/node/30273 (accessed July 27, 2008).

International Council on Archives. *Principles and Functional Requirements for Records in Electronic Office Environments—Module 1: Overview and Statement of Principles; Principles and Functional Requirements for Records in Electronic Office Environments—Module 2: Guidelines and Functional Requirements for Electronic Records Management Systems; and Principles and Functional Requirements for Records in Electronic Office Environments—Module 3: Guidelines and Functional Requirements for Records in Business Systems.* www.ica.org (accessed August 14, 2008).

"International Internet Preservation Consortium Announces New Mailing List for Web Curators." *Netpreserve.org: International Internet Preservation Consortium.* www.netpreserve.org/press/pr20080519.php (accessed July 27, 2008).

International Organization for Standardization. *ISO 14721:2003, Space Data and Information Transfer Systems—Open Archival Information System—Reference Model, Part 1.* 1st ed. Geneva: ISO, 2003. www.iso.org/iso/iso_catalogue/catalogue_tc/catalogue_detail.htm?csnumber=24683 (accessed July 27, 2008).

International Standards Organization. *International Standard 15489: Information and Documentation—Records Management, Part 1, General.* 1st ed. Reference Number: ISO 15489-1:2001 (E). www.iso.org/iso/catalogue_detail?csnumber=31908 (accessed July 27, 2008).

Johnston, Leslie. "Development of Repository Architecture and Services at the University of Virginia Library." Paper presented at DigCCurr2007: An International Symposium in Digital Curation at the School of Information and Library Science at the University of North Carolina at Chapel Hill, April 20, 2007. www.ils.unc.edu/digccurr2007/papers/johnston_paper_8-1.pdf; slides available at www.ils.unc.edu/digccurr2007/slides/johnston_slides_8-1.pdf (accessed July 27, 2008).

Joint Information Systems (JIS) Committee. "Digital Repositories" Programme. *Repository Metadata and Management Project (RepoMMan).* www.hull.ac.uk/esig/repomman/project_aims/index.html (accessed April 22, 2008).

Joint Interoperability Test Command (JITC). "Records Management Application (RMA)." http://jitc.fhu.disa.mil/recmgt (accessed April 18, 2008).

Jones, Maggie, and Neil Beagrie. *Preservation Management of Digital Materials: A Handbook.* London: British Library, 2001. www.dpconline.org/graphics/handbook/reviews.html (accessed July 21, 2008).

JupiterOnlineMedia. "Blog." *Webopedia: An Online Information Technology Encyclopedia.* www.webopedia.com/TERM/b/blog.html (accessed July 27, 2008).

———. "Wiki." *Webopedia: An Online Information Technology Encyclopedia.* www.webopedia.com/TERM/w/wiki.html (accessed July 27, 2008).

Juxta. *User's Manual for Juxta 1.0.* February 1, 2006. www.patacriticism.org/juxta/wp-content/uploads/2006/02/JuxtaManual.pdf (accessed April 22, 2008).

Kenney, Anne R. "The Cornell Experience: arXiv.org." Presentation at the Digital Curation Centre/Digital Preservation Coalition [DCC/DPC] Workshop on Cost Models for Preserving Digital Assets, British Library Conference Centre, July 26, 2005. www.dpconline.org/docs/events/050726kenney.pdf (accessed April 22, 2008).

Kenney, Anne R., and Stephen Chapman. *Digital Imaging for Libraries and Archives.* Ithaca, N.Y.: Department of Preservation and Conservation, Cornell University Library, 1996.

Lagoze, Carl, and Herbert Van de Sompel. "Object Reuse and Exchange Compound Information Objects: The OAI-ORE Perspective." *Open Archives Initiative.* May 28, 2007. www.openarchives.org/ore/documents/ CompoundObjects-200705.html (accessed July 27, 2008).

Lawrence, Gregory W., et al. *Risk Management of Digital Information: A File Format Investigation.* Washington, D.C.: Council on Library and Information Resources, 2000. www.clir.org/pubs/abstract/pub93abst.html (accessed July 27, 2008).

Lee, Bronwyn, Gerard Clifton, and Somaya Langley. *Australian Partnership for Sustainable Repositories PREMIS Requirement Statement Project Report* (Canberra: National Library of Australia, 2006), Appendix 4. www.apsr.edu.au/ publications/presta.pdf (accessed April 18, 2008).

Lee, Cal. "Guerilla Electronic Records Management: Lessons Learned From Some Time in the Trenches." *Ohio Archivist* 32, no. 1 (Spring 2001): 3–7. www. ils.unc.edu/callee/guerrila_erm.htm (accessed April 22, 2008).

———. "Open-Source Software: A Promising Piece of the Digital Preservation Puzzle." www.ils.unc.edu/callee/oss_preservation.htm (accessed April 22, 2008).

Lee, Christopher A. "Guerilla Electronic Records Management: Records Management Lessons Learned." *Records and Information Management Report* 18, no. 5 (May 2002): 1–14.

Levy, David M. "Where's Waldo? Reflections on Copies and Authenticity in a Digital Environment." In *Authenticity in a Digital Environment,* ed. Charles T. Cullen. Washington, D.C.: Council on Library and Information Resources, 2000. www.clir.org/pubs/reports/pub92/levy.html (accessed July 27, 2008).

Library of Congress. *Metadata Encoding and Transmission Standard.* www. loc.gov/standards/mets/ (accessed April 17, 2008).

Lynch, Clifford. "Authenticity and Integrity in the Digital Environment: An Exploratory Analysis of the Central Role of Trust." In *Authenticity in a Digital Environment: May 2000,* ed. Charles T. Cullen. Washington, D.C.: Council on Library and Information Resources, 2000. www.clir.org/pubs/reports/pub92/ lynch.html (accessed July 27, 2008).

Marsh, Mike, et al. "The Nexus and Praxis of Records Management and Archives: Is There a Difference?" Lecture at the Internationaler Archivkongress: Archive, Gedächtnis und Wissen, in Vienna, Austria, August 23–29, 2004. www.wien2004.ica.org/imagesUpload/pres_186_MYBURGH_B-ARMA01.pdf (accessed July 27, 2008).

Marshak, Robert J. *Covert Processes at Work: Managing the Five Hidden Dimensions of Organizational Change.* San Francisco: Berrett-Koehler, 2006.

McDonald, John. "Managing Information in an Office Systems Environment: The IMOSA Project." *American Archivist* 58, no. 2 (Spring 1995): 142–53.

McGovern, Nancy. *Cornell University Electronic Student Records System Project Report.* Ithaca, N.Y.: Cornell University, 2000. http//rms.library.cornell. edu/online/studentRecords/default.htm (accessed April 22, 2008).

McLeod, Julie, and Catherine Hare. *How to Manage Records in the e-Environment.* 2nd ed. London: Routledge, 2006.

McLuhan, Marshall. *Understanding Media: The Extensions of Man.* New York: McGraw Hill, 1964.

Moore, Reagan, et al. "Building Preservation Environments with Data Grid Technology (NARA Research Prototype Persistent Archive)." Presentation at the Society of American Archivists Annual Conference, Washington, D.C., August 5, 2006. www.archives.gov/era/pdf/2006-saa-moore.pdf (accessed July 27, 2008).

Morville, Peter. *Ambient Findability.* Farnham: O'Reilly, 2005.

Murray, Kathleen, and Mark Phillips. "Collaboration, Best Practices, and Collection Development for Born-Digital and Digitized Materials." Paper presented at DigCCurr2007: An International Symposium in Digital Curation at the School of Information and Library Science at the University of North Carolina at Chapel Hill, April 20, 2007. www.ils.unc.edu/digccurr2007/papers/murrayPhillips_paper_9-3.pdf; accompanying slides at www.ils.unc.edu/digccurr2007/slides/murrayPhillips_slides_9-3.pdf (accessed April 8, 2008).

National Archives and Records Administration, the Arizona State Library, and the Society of American Archivists. New Skills for the Digital Era Conference, Washington, D.C., National Archives, May 31–June 2, 2006. http://rpm.lib.az.us/newskills/ (accessed July 27, 2008).

———. "New Skills for a Digital Era: Case Studies." Paper presented at the New Skills for the Digital Era Conference, Washington, D.C., National Archives, May 31–June 2, 2006, http://rpm.lib.az.us/newskills/CaseStudies.asp (accessed April 22, 2008).

National Archives of Australia. "Xena Digital Preservation Software." http://xena.sourceforge.net/ (accessed July 27, 2008).

———. *Guidelines for Implementing the Functional Specifications for Electronic Records Management Systems Software.* February 2006. www.naa.gov.au/Images/ERMSguidelinesupdated_tcm2-1019.rtf (accessed July 27, 2008).

National Library of New Zealand. *Metadata Extraction Tool.* www.natlib.govt.nz/about-us/current-initiatives/past-initiatives/metadata-extraction-tool/?searchterm=metadata%20extract (accessed April 18, 2008).

———. *The Web Curator Tool.* http://webcurator.sf.net/ (accessed April 18, 2008).

NINES: A Networked Infrastructure for Nineteenth-century Electronic Scholarship. www.nines.org/ (accessed April 22, 2008).

Norsam Technologies. www.norsam.com (accessed July 27, 2008).

Nowviskie, Bethany. "Collex: Semantic Collection & Exhibits for the Remixable Web." November 2005. www.nines.org/about/Nowviskie-Collex.pdf (accessed April 22, 2008).

O'Shea, Greg, and David Roberts. "Living in a Digital World: Recognising the Electronic and Post-custodial Realities." *Archives and Manuscripts* 24, no. 2 (November 1996): 286–311.

O'Sullivan, Catherine. "Diaries, On-line Diaries, and the Future Loss to Archives; Or Blogs and the Blogging Bloggers Who Blog Them." *American Archivist* 68, no. 1 (Spring/Summer 2005): 53–73.

OAISter. www.oaister.org (accessed July 27, 2008).

OCLC/RLG PREMIS (PREservation Metadata: Implementation Strategies) Working Group. "Implementing Preservation Repositories for Digital Materials: Current Practice and Emerging Trends in the Cultural Heritage Community." Dublin, Ohio: OCLC Online Computer Library Center, 2004. www.oclc.org/research/projects/pmwg/surveyreport.pdf (accessed July 27, 2008).

OCLC/RLG PREMIS Editorial Committee. "PREMIS Data Dictionary for Preservation Metadata, Version 2.0." Dublin, Ohio: OCLC Online Computer Library Center, 2008. www.loc.gov/standards/premis/v2/premis-2-0.pdf (accessed July 27, 2008).

Online Computer Library Center (OCLC). *Digital Archive*. www.oclc.org/digitalarchive (accessed April 18, 2008).

———. "Preservation Metadata for Digital Materials." www.oclc.org/research/projects/pmwg/background.htm (accessed July 27, 2008).

Open Archives Forum. "OAI for Beginners—the Open Archives Forum Online Tutorial." www.oaforum.org/tutorial/ (accessed April 18, 2008).

Open Archives Initiative. www.openarchives.org (accessed July 27, 2008).

OW2 Consortium. *ObjectWeb: Open Source Middleware*. http://middleware. objectweb.org (accessed July 27, 2008).

Oxford University Library Services. *Complex Archive Ingest for Repository Objects*. October 2006. http://cairo.paradigm.ac.uk/about/index.html.

Paquet, Lucia. "Appraisal, Acquisition and Control of Personal Electronic Records; From Myth to Reality." *Archives and Manuscripts*: *The Journal of the Archives Section, the Library Association of Australia* 28, no. 2 (November 2000): 71–91.

Paradigm Project. "Accessioning." *Workbook on Digital Private Papers, 2005–2007*. www.paradigm.ac.uk/workbook/accessioning/ (accessed April 22, 2008).

———. "Appraisal and Disposal: Issues to Consider When Making Appraisal Decisions." In *Workbook on Digital Private Papers, 2005–2007*. www.paradigm. ac.uk/workbook/appraisal/appraisal-issues.html (accessed April 22, 2008).

———. *Guidance for Creators of Personal Papers*. 2007. www.paradigm. ac.uk/guidanceforcreators/guidance-for-creators-of-personal-digital-archives.pdf (accessed April 18, 2008).

———. *Workbook on Digital Private Papers, 2005–2007*. www.paradigm. ac.uk/workbook (accessed July 27, 2008).

Paynter, Gordon, et al. "A Year of Selective Web Archiving with the Web Curator at the National Library of New Zealand." *D-Lib Magazine* 14, no. 5/6 (May/June 2008). www.dlib.org/dlib/may08/paynter/05paynter.html (accessed July 29, 2008).

Pearce-Moses, Richard. "The Winds of Change: Blown to Bits." Address presented at the closing plenary of the Society of American Archivists 69th Annual Meeting, New Orleans, August 19, 2005. www.archivists.org/governance/presidential/rpm2005.pdf (accessed July 27, 2008).

———. *A Glossary of Archival and Records Terminology.* Chicago: Society of American Archivists, 2005.

Pearce-Moses, Richard, and Susan E. Davis, eds. *New Skills for a Digital Era.* Preprint of conference proceedings sponsored by National Archives and Records Administration, Society of American Archivists, Arizona State Library Archives and Public Records. Washington, D.C., The National Archives, May 31–June 2, 2006. Proceedings edited by the Society of American Archivists and the Arizona State Library Archives and Public Records, August 28, 2007.

Pederson, Ann. "Australian Contributions to Recordkeeping." In *Understanding Society through Its Records.* John Curtin Prime Ministerial Library. http://john.curtin.edu.au/society/australia/index.html (accessed July 27, 2008).

———. "Basic Concepts and Principles of Archives and Records Management." In *Understanding Society through Its Records.* John Curtin Prime Ministerial Library. http://john.curtin.edu.au/society/archives/management.html (accessed April 12, 2008).

Pennock, Maureen. *DCC Digital Curation Manual Instalment on Curating E-mails: A Life-cycle Approach to the Management and Preservation of E-mail Messages.* Bath, U.K.: Digital Curation Centre, 2006. www.dcc.ac.uk/resource/curation-manual/chapters/curating-e-mails (accessed July 27, 2008).

Pitti, Daniel V., and Wendy Duff, eds. *Encoded Archival Description on the Internet.* Binghamton, N.Y.: Haworth Information Press, 2002.

Prudlo, Maron. "E-Archiving: An Overview of Some Repository Management Software Tools." *Ariadne* 45 (April 2005). www.ariadne.ac.uk/issue43/prudlo (accessed July 27, 2008).

Reich, Victoria A. "Lots of Copies Keep Stuff Safe as a Cooperative Archiving Solution for E-journals." *Issues in Science and Technology Librarianship* 36 (Fall 2002). www.istl.org/02-fall/article1.html (accessed July 27, 2008).

Reilly, Bernard. "Certification of Digital Repositories: A Status Report on International Consensus-Building." *Session 705: Measuring Digital Preservation Readiness: Digital Site Surveys and Certification of Trusted Digital Repositories.* Paper given at the Society of American Archivists 71st Annual Meeting, Chicago, September 1, 2007.

Repository 66. *Repository Maps.* http://maps.repository66.org (accessed July 27, 2008).

Research Libraries Group. *RLG Worksheet for Estimating Digital Reformatting Costs.* May 1998. www.oclc.org/programs/ourwork/past/digimgtools/RLGWorksheet.pdf (accessed April 22, 2008).

Rieger, Oya Y. *Preservation in the Age of Large-Scale Digitization.* Washington, D.C.: Council on Library and Information Resources, 2008. www.

clir.org/pubs/abstract/pub141abst.html (accessed July 27, 2008).

————. "Select for Success: Key Principles in Assessing Repository Models." Paper given at DigCCurr2007: An International Symposium in Digital Curation at the School of Information and Library Science at the University of North Carolina at Chapel Hill, April 20, 2007. www.ils.unc.edu/digccurr2007/slides/rieger_slides_8-3.pdf (accessed July 27, 2008).

Roach, Bill. E-mail to the ERECS-L listserv. December 12, 2004. www.lsoft.com/scripts/wl.exe?SL1=ERECS-L&H=LISTSERV.ALBANY.EDU (accessed July 27, 2008).

Roberts, John, and Andrew Wilson. *International Recordkeeping/Records Management Metadata Initiatives: Report and Recommendations for DC Advisory Board.* http://dublincore.org/groups/government/dcmi_resource_management.pdf (accessed July 27, 2008).

Ross, Seamus, and Ann Gow. *Digital Archaeology: Rescuing Neglected and Damaged Data Resources.* A JISC/NPO Study within the Electronic Libraries (eLib) Programme on the Preservation of Electronic Materials. London: Library Information Technology Center, 1999. www.ukoln.ac.uk/services/elib/papers/supporting/pdf/p2con.pdf (accessed July 27, 2008).

Ross, Seamus, and Andrew McHugh. "Role of Evidence in Establishing Trust in Repositories." *D-Lib Magazine* 12, no. 7/8 (July/August 2006). www.dlib.org/dlib/july06/ross/07ross.html (accessed April 18, 2008).

Rothenberg, Jeff. "Digital Preservation: The State of the Art." Presentation at the Digital Preservation, Technology & Policy Workshop, Koninklijke Bibliotheek, Nationale bibliotheek van Nederland, December 13, 2002. www.kb.nl/hrd/dd/dd_links_en_publicaties/workshop2002/rothenberg.pdf (accessed July 27, 2008).

————. "Preserving Authentic Digital Information." In *Authenticity in a Digital Environment: May 2000*, ed. Charles T. Cullen. Washington, D.C.: Council on Library and Information Resources, 2000. www.clir.org/pubs/reports/pub92/rothenberg.html (accessed July 27, 2008).

Samuels, Helen Willa. "Who Controls the Past." In *American Archival Studies: Readings in Theory and Practice*, ed. Randall C. Jimerson, 193–210. Chicago: Society of American Archivists, 2000.

Serco Consulting. *MoReq2.* www.moreq2.eu/ (accessed April 18, 2008).

Shepherd, Elizabeth, and Geoffrey Yeo. *Managing Records: A Handbook of Principles and Practice.* London: Facet, 2003.

Shirky, Clay. "Making Digital Durable: What Time Does to Categories." Summarized by Stewart Brand (November 14, 2005). http://blog.longnow.org/?p=51&akst_action=share-this (accessed April 18, 2008).

Smithsonian Institution Archives. *Archiving Smithsonian Websites: An Evaluation and Recommendation for a Smithsonian Institution Archives Pilot Project.* May 2003. http://siarchives.si.edu/pdf/websitepilot.pdf.

Smorul, Mike, Mike McCann, and Joseph JaJa. "Pawn: A Policy-Driven Software Environment for Implementing Producer-Archive Interactions in Support of Long Term Digital Preservation." Paper presented at the Archiving Conference, May 2007, Arlington, Va. https://wiki.umiacs.umd.edu/adapt/images/e/ea/Pawn-archiving07-uploaded.pdf. The accompanying PowerPoint presentation can be found at: https://wiki.umiacs.umd.edu/adapt/images/1/1c/PAWN-Archiving07-v1.ppt (accessed July 27, 2008).

———. "The Use of Producer-Archive Network Workflow (PAWN) in Support of Customized Archival Practice." Paper, DigCCurr2007: An International Symposium in Digital Curation at the School of Information and Library Science at the University of North Carolina at Chapel Hill, April 20, 2007. www.ils.unc.edu/digccurr2007/papers/smorul_paper_6-3.pdf. The accompanying PowerPoint Presentation: https://wiki.umiacs.umd.edu/adapt/images/1/13/Digccurr07-v1.ppt (accessed July 27, 2008).

Society of American Archivists. "Publications and Products Catalog." www.archivists.org/catalog/index.asp.

State Archives Department, Minnesota Historical Society. *File Formats, Version 4* (March 2004). www.mnhs.org/preserve/records/electronicrecords/docs_pdfs/erfformats.pdf (accessed April 22, 2008).

———. *Trustworthy Information Systems Handbook, Version 4* (July 2002). www.mnhs.org/preserve/records/tis/docs_pdfs/tis.pdf or www.mnhs.org/preserve/records/tis/tis.html (accessed July 27, 2008).

Stephens, David O. *Records Management: Making the Transition from Paper to Electronic.* Lenexa, Kans.: ARMA International, 2007.

Stephens, David O., and Roderick C. Wallace. *Electronic Records Retention: An Introduction.* Prairie Village, Kans.: ARMA International, 1997.

———. *Electronic Records Retention: New Strategies for Data Life Cycle Management.* Lenexa, Kans.: ARMA International, 2003.

Tansley, Robert. "Building a Distributed, Standards-based Repository Federation China Digital Museum Project." *D-Lib Magazine* 12, no. 7/8 (July/August 2006). www.dlib.org/dlib/july06/tansley/07tansley.html (accessed April 22, 2008).

Taub, Eric A. "The Record of Your Life as a Digital Archive." *New York Times*, August 16, 2007. Technology Section. www.nytimes.com/2007/08/16/technology/circuits/16basics.html (accessed July 27, 2008).

Testbed Digitale Bewaring. *Costs of Digital Preservation.* The Hague: Digital Preservation Testbed, May 2005. www.digitaleduurzaamheid.nl/bibliotheek/docs/CoDPv1.pdf (accessed April 22, 2008).

———. "Decision Model." In *Digital Longevity.* The Hague: Digital Preservation Testbed. www.digitaleduurzaamheid.nl/bibliotheek/docs/Decision_model.pdf (accessed April 22, 2008).

———. *From Digital Volatility to Digital Permanence: Preserving Email.* The Hague: Digital Preservation Testbed, April 2003. www.digitaleduurzaamheid.nl/bibliotheek/docs/volatility-permanence-email-en.pdf (accessed July 27, 2008).

———. *Functional Requirements for a Preservation System.* The Hague: Digital Preservation Testbed, 2005. www.digitaleduurzaamheid.nl/bibliotheek/

docs/Technical_and_Functional_Requirements.pdf (accessed April 18, 2008).

The Basement. "ASCII Table: 7-bit." Basement Computing. www.neurophys. wisc.edu/comp/docs/ascii (accessed April 12, 2008).

Theimer, Kate. "Archives and 'New' Technology." *ArchivesNext.* www. archivesnext.com/?page_id=62 (accessed July 31, 2008).

Thibodeau, Kenneth. "If You Build It, Will It Fly? Criteria for Success in a Digital Repository." *Journal of Digital Information* 8, no. 2 (2007). http://journals. tdl.org/jodi/article/view/197/174 (accessed July 27, 2008).

————. "Critical Competencies for Digital Curation: Perspectives from 30 Years in the Trenches and On the Mountain Top." Paper presented at DigCCurr2007: An International Symposium on Digital Curation at the School of Information and Library Science at the University of North Carolina at Chapel Hill, April 20, 2007. www.ils.unc.edu/digccurr2007/papers/thibodeau_paper_7.pdf (accessed July 5, 2008).

————. "What Constitutes Success in a Digital Repository?" Paper presented at the Joint Conference on Digital Libraries Opening Information Horizons Workshop: Digital Curation & Trusted Repositories, Seeking Success, June 15, 2006, Chapel Hill, North Carolina. http://sils.unc.edu/events/2006jcdl/ digitalcuration/Thibodeau-JCDLWorkshop2006.pdf (accessed April 18, 2008).

Thomas, Susan. *Paradigm: A Practical Approach to the Preservation of Personal Digital Archives.* Version 1.0. March 2007. www.paradigm.ac.uk/ projectdocs/jiscreports/ParadigmFinalReportv1.pdf (accessed July 27, 2008).

Tibbo, Helen. "Researching the Researchers: Finding Out How University Employees Manage Their Digital Materials." Paper presented at the NHPRC ERR Fellowship Symposium, November 19, 2004. http://ils.unc.edu/nhprcfellows/ tibbo.ppt (accessed July 27, 2008).

United States Department of Defense. *Electronic Records Management Software Applications Design Criteria Standard* (DoD 5015.02-STD). Washington, D.C.: Department of Defense, April 25, 2007. www.dtic.mil/whs/ directives/corres/pdf/501502std.pdf (accessed July 27, 2008).

University of Illinois at Urbana-Champaign. *Archon™: The Simple Archival Information System.* www.archon.org/ (accessed April 22, 2008).

University of Minho [Portugal], Department of Information Systems. *Conversion and Recommendation of Digital Objects Formats (CriB).* 2007. http:// crib.dsi.uminho.pt/ (accessed April 18, 2008).

University of North Carolina at Chapel Hill, School of Library and Information Science. *Managing the Digital University Desktop.* www.ils.unc. edu/digitaldesktop/ (accessed July 27, 2008).

University of North Carolina at Chapel Hill, School of Library and Information Science. "Timeline and Results." *Managing the Digital University Desktop.* www. ils.unc.edu/digitaldesktop/timeline/ (accessed July 27, 2008).

University of Virginia. "Project Juxta" *Applied Research in Patacriticism (ARP).* http://patacriticism.org/juxta/ (accessed July 25, 2008).

Urrichio, William. "Moving beyond the Artifact: Lessons from Participatory Culture." In *Preserving the Digital Heritage: Principles and Policies*, ed. Yola de Lusenet and Vincent Wintermans (The Hague: Netherlands National Commission for UNESCO, 2007): 16. www.unesco.nl/images/preserving_the_digital_heritage. pdf (accessed April 17, 2008).

Van Garderen, Peter. *Digital Preservation: An Overview*. Managing Information Assets in the Public Sector, Edmonton, Alberta, October 12–13, 2006. http://archivemati.ca/wp-content/shockwave-flash/digital_preservation_ overview.html (accessed July 27, 2008).

W3C: Semantic Web. *Semantic Web Activity*. www.w3.org/2001/sw/ (accessed July 27, 2008).

White, Martin. *The Content Management Handbook*. London: Facet, 2005.

Wikipedia contributors. "'Web Archiving,' Subsection on 'External Links.'" *Wikipedia: The Free Encyclopedia*. http://en.wikipedia.org/wiki/Web_ archiving#External_links (accessed July 27, 2008).

———. "Baudot Code." *Wikipedia: The Free Encyclopedia*. http:// en.wikipedia.org/wiki/Baudot_code (accessed April 12, 2008).

———. "Binary Numeral System." *Wikipedia: The Free Encyclopedia*. http://en.wikipedia.org/wiki/Base_2 (accessed April 12, 2008).

———. "Creative Commons." *Wikipedia: The Free Encyclopedia*. http:// en.wikipedia.org/wiki/Creative_Commons (accessed July 27, 2008).

———. "History of Personal Learning Environments." *Wikipedia: The Free Encyclopedia*. http://en.wikipedia.org/wiki/History_of_personal_learning_ environments (accessed July 27, 2008).

———. "Institutional Repository." *Wikipedia: The Free Encyclopedia*. http:// en.wikipedia.org/wiki/Institutional_repository (accessed July 27, 2008).

Wikiquote contributors. "Casey Stengel." *Wikiquote*. http://en.wikiquote.org/ wiki/Casey_Stengel (accessed April 22, 2008).

Wilkins, Jesse. "Email Records." E-mail to the ERECS-L listserv. December 21, 2004. http://listserv.albany.edu:8080/archives/erecs-l.html (accessed July 27, 2008).

Woodyard-Robinson, Deborah. "Section 3.7 Costs and Business Modelling." In *Digital Preservation Coalition Online Handbook*, added March 17, 2006. www. dpconline.org/graphics/inststrat/costs.html (accessed April 22, 2008).

Young, Jeanne. "Electronic Records Management on a Shoestring: Three Case Studies." *Information Management Journal* 39, no. 1 (January/February 2005): 58–60.

Zeng, Marcia Lei. *Metadata for Digital Collections*. Lecture notes for Metadata for Digital Collections Workshop, School of Library and Information Science, Kent State University. www.slis.kent.edu/~mzeng/metadata/lecturenote. htm (accessed July 27, 2008).

Essential Tools

Dollar, Charles M. *Authentic Electronic Records: Strategies for Long-Term Access.* Chicago: Cohasset Associates, 2002.
    This book contains a wealth of policy recommendations.

Eaton, Fynnette. "Managing Change in an Ever-Changing Electronic Environment." Presentation at the Society of American Archivists annual meeting, Washington, D.C., Aug. 5, 2006. www.archives.gov/era/pdf/2006-saa-eaton.pdf (accessed July 26, 2008).
    This very simple presentation explains the basics of the impact of change and how to understand and manage resistance to it.

International Council of Archivists. *Guide for Managing Electronic Records from an Archival Perspective.* 1997. www.ica.org/en/node/30019 (accessed July 27, 2008).
    This guide gives an excellent overview of the whole issue.

International Council of Archivists. *Electronic Records: A Workbook for Archivists.* April 2005. www.ica.org/en/node/30273 (accessed July 27, 2008).
    Here you will find an excellent step-by-step guide to the process, when you are ready to actually start implementing a system.

Jones, Maggie, and Neil Beagrie. *Preservation Management of Digital Materials: A Handbook.* London: British Library, 2001. www.dpconline.org/graphics/handbook/reviews.html (accessed July 27, 2008).
    First compiled by Neil Beagrie and Maggie Jones, the Digital Preservation Coalition now maintains and updates this workbook as an online resource. The handbook provides an internationally authoritative and practical guide to the subject of managing digital resources over time and the issues in sustaining access to them. It includes a section called "Exemplars and Further Reading," which compiles resources on such topics as 1) collaboration, 2) outreach, 3) third-party services, 4) rights management, 5) staff training and development, 6) standards and best practice guidelines, and 7) costs and business modeling. While it has a

decidedly British slant, most of what it includes as useful resources remain useful for those not in the United Kingdom.

McLeod, Julie, and Catherine Hare, eds. *Managing Electronic Records*. London: Facet, 2005.

This excellent collection of essays addresses various issues. It includes case studies, which most similar books do not.

McLeod, Julie, and Catherine Hare. *How to Manage Records in the e-Environment*. 2nd ed. London: Routledge, 2006.

As part of a "how to" series developed for people new to the field, provides remarkably readable easy-to-follow and practice-based guidelines at every turn.

Paradigm Project. *Guidance for Creators of Personal Papers*. 2007. www. paradigm.ac.uk/guidanceforcreators/guidance-for-creators-of-personal-digital-archives.pdf (accessed July 27, 2008).

The guide gives detailed advice on managing personal digital materials; a good guide for creators.

Paradigm Project. *Workbook on Digital Private Papers, 2005–2007*. www. paradigm.ac.uk/workbook/ (accessed July 27, 2008).

This is absolutely the most complete document available for your purposes, a font of advice and tools developed by the Personal Archives Accessible in Digital Media (Paradigm) project of the libraries of the Universities of Oxford and Manchester, England. The project explored the issues involved in preserving digital private papers. Through the workbook, which evolved over the life of the project, the participants shared their practical experience in appraising, acquiring, and processing digital private papers into their digital repositories, using archival and digital preservation best practices of the time. They created a published paper version which you may find in a library or from a used-book supplier, but the current iteration exists online only.

Pearce-Moses, Richard. *A Glossary of Archival and Records Terminology*. Chicago: Society of American Archivists, 2005.

This glossary is more comprehensive than the ARMS glossary listed below. While the two overlap in many areas, they do not replace one another.

Shepherd, Elizabeth, and Geoffrey Yeo. *Managing Records: A Handbook of Principles and Practice*. London: Facet, 2003.

This book is basic, well organized, and highly readable.

Sedona Conference. *The Sedona Guidelines for Managing Information and Records in the Electronic Age*. thesedonaconference.org/publications_html (accessed July 27, 2008).

Here is your guide to staying legal.

Trustworthy Repository Audit and Certification (TRAC): Criteria and Checklist,

Version 1.0. Chicago and Dublin, Ohio: Center for Research Libraries and OCLC, 2007. www.crl.edu/content.asp?l1=13&l2=58&l3=162&l4=91 (accessed July 27, 2008).

The *Audit Checklist for the Certification of Trusted Digital Repositories* is unusually readable.

United Nations. Archives and Records Management Section. *Glossary of Recordkeeping Terms.* archives.un.org/unarms/en/unrecordsmgmt/unrecords-resources/glossaryofrecordkp.html (accessed July 27, 2008).

The Archives and Records Management Section (ARMS) has compiled a glossary of recordkeeping terms, which provides generic definitions taken from international sources as well as definitions specific to the United Nations. It is available completely online, with a printer-friendly version.

Beginner Bibliography

ArchivesNext. *Archives and "New" Technology*. www.archivesnext.com/?page_id=62 (accessed July 27, 2008).

While this started as a blog, it has become a valuable resource that contains examples of archives using Web 2.0 features. At the top, it has a series of short videos showing how the various technologies work.

Bantin, Philip. "Electronic Records Management—A Review of the Work of a Decade and a Reflection on Future Directions." In *Encyclopedia of Library and Information Science*, Volume 71, Supplement 34, 47–81. New York: Marcel Dekker, 2002. www.libraries.iub.edu/index.php?pageId=3313 (accessed July 27, 2008).

A good overview of the history of the growth of electronic material in our lives.

Bantin, Philip. "Strategies for Managing Electronic Records: A New Archival Paradigm? An Affirmation of Our Archival Traditions?" *Archival Issues* 23, no. 1 (1998): 17–34. www.libraries.iub.edu/index.php?pageId=3313 (accessed July 27, 2008).

Bantin lays out the conflicting major archival theories on appraisal, acquisition, and description of electronic records.

Bantin, Philip C., and Gerald Bernbom. "The Indiana University Electronic Records Project: Analyzing Functions, Identifying Transactions, and Evaluating Recordkeeping Systems—A Report on Methodology." *Archives and Museum Informatics* 10, no. 3 (1996): 246–66.

This very early article comes from the Indiana University project. In it the authors plainly describe their process and thinking as they set about identifying electronic records to keep and where to find them. That task made them start to grapple with issues of function and business transactions. Read it as a road map for the nontechnical archivist to follow into the issues of appraisal of electronic records. Bantin updates reporting on the project in "The Indiana University

Electronic Records Management Strategy—Revisited," *The American Archivist* 62, no. 1 (Spring 1999): 153–63. This article won the Society of American Archivists' Posner Award for the best article published in volume 62 of *The American Archivist*, 2001. www.indiana.edu/~libarch/ER/lettered6.pdf (accessed July 27, 2008).

Caplan, Priscilla. "How to Build Your Own Dark Archive (In Your Spare Time): A Talk for the Cornell Digital Preservation Management Workshop." November 2004.   www.fcla.edu/digitalArchive/pdfs/Howtobuildyourowndarkarchive.pdf (accessed July 27, 2008).
        Caplan speaks with the voice of experience.

Caplan, Priscilla. *Metadata Fundamentals for All Libraries*. Chicago: American Library Association, 2003.
        This book covers the basics on how we use metadata and includes discussions of some widely used schemes.

Consultative Committee for Space Data Systems (CCSDS). "Reference Model for an Open Archive Information System." 2002. http://public.ccsds.org/publications/archive/650x0b1.pdf (accessed July 27, 2008).
        This is the original OAIS document.

Cook, Terry. "Byte-ing Off What You Can Chew: Electronic Records Strategies for Small Archival Institutions." *Artifacts* (April 2004): 1–20. *See also*: Archives and Records Association of New Zealand (ARANZ), www.aranz.org.nz/Site/publications/papers_online/terry_cook_paper.aspx (accessed July 27, 2008).
        This article covers why you need to get involved.

Cook, Terry. "The Impact of David Bearman on Modern Archival Thinking: An Essay of Personal Reflection and Critique." *Archives and Museum Informatics* 11, no. 1 (March 1997), 15–37.
        Cook provides an excellent summary of the early thinking in the struggle to understand electronic records while he deals more broadly with Bearman's influence on the profession.

Cunningham, Adrian. "Waiting for the Ghost Train: Strategies for Managing Electronic Personal Records before It's Too Late." *Archival Issues: Journal of the Midwest Archives Conference* 24, no. 1 (1999): 55–64. www.mybestdocs.com/cunningham-waiting2.htm (accessed July 27, 2008).
        This is a passionate assertion of the importance of curators to actively work with creators to assure the preservation of their digital materials.

Dollar Consulting. *Archival Preservation of Smithsonian Web Resources: Principles and Best Practices.* Smithsonian Institution Archives, July 2001. http://siarchives.si.edu/pdf/dollar_report.pdf (accessed July 27, 2008).
        You will find this a nicely balanced discussion on the issues involved in website capture for archival purposes. It focuses on policy issues and has a nice

vocabulary section as well as extensive policy suggestions. While written for a specific institution, many others can easily adapt it for local purposes.

Electronic Records Research Committee. "Functional Requirements for Electronic Records Report." Austin: Texas State Library and Archives Commission, 1998. www.tsl.state.tx.us/slrm/recordspubs/index.html (accessed July 27, 2008).

This report gives the reader a set of functional requirements to work with.

Evans, Joanna, Sue McKemmish, and Karuna Bhoday. "Create Once, Use Many Times: The Clever Use of Recordkeeping Metadata for Multiple Archival Purposes." Paper presented at the meeting of International Congress on Archives, Vienna, Austria, August 23–29, 2004. www.wien2004.ica.org/imagesUpload/ pres_174_MCKEMMISH_Z-McK%2001E.pdf (accessed July 27, 2008). *See also*: Monash University. "Clever Recordkeeping Metadata: Create Once, Use Many Times—The Clever Use of Metadata in eGovernment and eBusiness Processes in Networked Environments." Records Continuum Research Group (RCRG). www.sims.monash.edu.au/research/rcrg/research/crm/ (accessed July 27, 2008).

As one of the many research projects currently under way, this one shows a lot of promise.

Hillman, Diane I., and Elaine L. Westbrooks. *Metadata in Practice*. Chicago: American Library Association, 2004.

This book consists largely of a collection of case studies in the use of metadata with digital object projects.

Hunter, Gregory. *Preserving Digital Information: A How-To-Do-It Manual*. New York: Neal-Schuman, 2000.

An early work on the topic; Hunter provides many clear graphics to explain his points and offers much practical advice.

Jones, Maggie, and Neil Beagrie. *Preservation Management of Digital Materials: A Handbook*. London: British Library, 2001. www.dpconline.org/graphics/ handbook/reviews.html (accessed July 27, 2008).

First compiled by Neil Beagrie and Maggie Jones, the Digital Preservation Coalition now maintains and updates this handbook as an online resource. The handbook provides an internationally authoritative and practical guide to the subject of managing digital resources over time and the issues in sustaining access to them. It includes a section called "Exemplars and Further Reading," which compiles resources on such topics as 1) collaboration, 2) outreach, 3) third-party services, 4) rights management, 5) staff training and development, 6) standards and best practice guidelines, and 7) costs and business modeling. While it has a decidedly British slant, most of what it includes as useful resources remain useful for those not in the United Kingdom.

Lavoie, Brian. "Meeting the Challenges of Digital Preservation: The OAIS Reference Model." *OCLC Newsletter* 243 (January/February 2000): 26–30.

This highly readable article explains the OAIS model. Read it before you read OCLC's official publications.

Lee, Cal. "Open-Source Software: A Promising Piece of the Digital Preservation Puzzle." 2002. www.ils.unc.edu/callee/oss_preservation.htm (accessed July 27, 2008).
    Lee's highly readable article explains the difference between proprietary software and open-source software.

Library of Congress. *Metadata Encoding and Transmission Standard.* www.loc. gov/standards/mets/ (accessed July 27, 2008).
    METS is emerging as an important metadata framework.

McGovern, Nancy. "Cornell University Electronic Student Records System Project Report." Division of Rare Books and Manuscript Collections, Carl A. Kroch Library, Cornell University. November 2000. http://rms.library.cornell. edu/online/studentRecords/default.htm (accessed July 27, 2008).
    Though now nearly a decade old, the report provides a list of eighteen recommendations for prudent policies and procedures still relevant to any historical repository that must manage electronic records in a highly readable way.

National Archives, U.K. Government Records and Information Management. "2002 Revised Requirements: Functional Requirements for Electronic Records Management Systems (ERMS)." *Functional Requirements for ERMS.* 2002. www. nationalarchives.gov.uk/electronicrecords/reqs2002/ (accessed July 27, 2008).
    This handbook provides a set of functional requirements to work with.

New York State. *Functional Requirements to Ensure the Creation, Maintenance, and Preservation of Electronic Records.* 1998. www.ctg.albany.edu/publications/ reports/functional/functional.pdf (accessed July 27, 2008).
    The state of New York also provides a set of functional requirements to work with.

OCLC/RLG. *Preservation Metadata and the OAIS Information Model: A Metadata Framework to Support the Preservation of Digital Objects.* June 2002. www.rlg.org/en/pdfs/pm_framework.pdf (accessed July 27, 2008).
    This analysis of how one might implement the OAIS reference model provides a good explanation, but not for the novice.

Pederson, Ann. "Basic Concepts and Principles of Archives and Records Management." In *Understanding Society through Its Records.* John Curtin Prime Ministerial Library. http://john.curtin.edu.au/society/archives/management.html (accessed July 27, 2008).

"Session 304: The Sedona Principles and Guidelines: What You Should Know about the Impact of Current Law and Litigation on Electronic Records Management." Society of American Archivists (SAA) 69th Annual Meeting, New

Orleans, August 18, 2005.

This session provides a clear explanation of the legal perspectives that underlie the guidelines.

Snyder, Kirk, and David Isom. "A 30(b) (6) Can Sink Your Ship: Good Records Management Policies and Knowledge of the Law Will Help Records Managers Keep Their Companies Afloat in the Face of Possible Litigation." *Information Management Journal* 40, no. 1 (January/February 2006): 52–55.

This is one of many good articles in the ARMA journal that addresses, in no uncertain terms, the need to manage electronic records.

State of Victoria. Victorian Electronic Records Strategy (VERS). www.prov.vic. gov.au/vers/vers/default.htm (accessed July 27, 2008).

This provides another set of functional requirements to work with.

Thomas, Susan. *Paradigm: A Practical Approach to the Preservation of Personal Digital Archives.* Version 1.0. Oxford: Bodleian Library, 2007. www.paradigm. ac.uk/projectdocs/jiscreports/ParadigmFinalReportv1.pdf (accessed July 27, 2008).

Thomas presents a final report summing up the findings and recommendations of the Paradigm Project: a must read.

Continuing Education Opportunities and Workshops

Workshops on the management and/or preservation of digital materials have begun to appear in many places, sponsored by many groups. Below you will find just a few. While these all charge a fee to attend, many develop websites that contain a substantial amount of the content presented in the sessions. To locate workshops and camps when this list has become dated, check the archives of the Electronic Records listserv (ERECS-L), an edited listserv about the preservation and management of records in electronic form. You'll find the archives at listserv. albany.edu:8080/archives/erecs-l.html (accessed July 26, 2008).

Cornell Digital Preservation Management Workshop. "Digital Preservation Management Resources." www.library.cornell.edu/iris/dpworkshop/ (accessed July 27, 2008).

Digital Library Federation. "Best Practices for Shareable Metadata." http://webservices.itcs.umich.edu/mediawiki/oaibp/index.php/ShareableMetadataPublic#General_Recommendations (accessed July 26, 2008).

The Shareable Metadata Best Practices has four main sections:

- *Introduction,* which provides useful background explaining the idea of "shareable" metadata
- *Best Practices for Shareable Metadata Content,* which includes general recommendations on authoring "shareable" metadata, documenting decisions made about the metadata, and recommendations on how to author certain classes of metadata elements
- *Best Practices for Technical Aspects of Metadata,* which includes recommendations for technical metadata issues including use of namespaces, XML schemas, and character encoding, and
- *Final Preparations,* or how to check for "shareability" before implementing your OAI data provider. webservices.itcs.umich.edu/mediawiki/oaibp/index.php/IntroductionMetadataContent

NARA Southwest Region. Annual E-Records Forum. U.S. National Archives and Records Administration. www.archives.gov/southwest/agencies/records-mgmt/forum-announcement.html (accessed July 26, 2008).

Northeast Document Conservation Center (NEDCC). "Persistence of Memory: Sustaining Digital Collections of Digital Assets." Cosponsored by OCLC Western Services Center. www.nedcc.org/about/news.pom.php (accessed July 26, 2008).

Northeast Document Conservation Center. "Stewardship of Digital Assets." Cosponsored by Palinet, Solinet, Amigos Library Services, and OCLC Western Services Center. www.nedcc.org/education/workshops/soda/sodadesc.php.

Open Archives Forum. "OAI for Beginners." www.oaforum.org/tutorial/ (accessed July 26, 2008).

A free tutorial which provides an introduction to the Open Archives Initiative Protocol for Metadata Harvesting (OAI-PMH). Working through the tutorial you will

- gain an overview of the history behind the OAI-PMH and an overview of its key features;
- achieve a deeper technical insight into how the protocol works;
- learn something about some of the main implementation issues;
- find some useful starting points and hints that will help you as an implementer.

Society of American Archivists. "Education & Events." www.archivists.org/menu.asp?m=education.

Check the current schedule for workshops in:

- Basic Electronic Records
- Electronic Records: Preservation of PDF Web Seminar
- The Essentials of Digital Repositories
- Electronic Records "Summer Camp"

The University of Arizona School of Information Resources and Library Science Digital Information Management Certificate Program. "Welcome to DigIn!" www.sir.arizona.edu/digin (accessed July 26, 2008).

Zeng, Marcia Lei. *Metadata for Digital Collections.* www.slis.kent.edu/~mzeng/metadata/cemetadata.htm (accessed July 26, 2008).

Other Useful Works

Bantin, Philip C. *Understanding Data and Information Systems for Recordkeeping.* New York: Neal-Schuman, 2008.

"This book is dedicated to providing archivists and records managers with some basic information on how prominent information systems . . . are designed and how they manage data and information."

Bantin, Philip C., and Gerald Bernbom. "The Indiana University Electronic Records Project: Analyzing Functions, Identifying Transactions, and Evaluating Recordkeeping Systems—A Report on Methodology." *Archives and Museum Informatics* 10, no. 3 (1996): 246–66.

The first few pages provide an excellent clarification of the shifting meanings of provenance in the world of electronic records.

Bearman, David. "The Implications of Armstrong v. Executive of the President for the Archival Management of Electronic Records." *American Archivist* 56, no. 4 (Fall 1993): 674–89.

This article contains a detailed discussion of an early lawsuit and includes ten managerial steps for implementing acceptable records management control within existing systems, as well as the functional requirements developed during the Pittsburgh study.

Canadian Heritage Information Network. *Digital Preservation for Museums: Recommendations.* www.rcip.gc.ca/English/Digital_Content/Preservation_Recommendations (accessed July 26, 2008).

In 2002, the Canadian Heritage Information Network commissioned a study on best practices for digital preservation with a specific focus on museums in Canada. While the majority of the study focused on surveying existing literature and identifying common themes in the existing documents on best practices, a set of recommendations and a digital preservation policy checklist were also produced as a result of the study.

The recommendations were divided into action and broader recommendations.

Action recommendations were those that an individual organization could implement immediately while broader recommendations were those that museums could consider implementing in collaboration with other institutions, paninstitutional organizations, and collectives.

CBS News. *Coming Soon: A Digital Dark Age? Digital Memory Threatened as File Formats Evolve.* CBSNews.com, January 21, 2003. www.cbsnews.com/stories/2003/01/21/tech/main537308.shtml (accessed July 26, 2008).

This report provides a sober analysis of the problems of digital information in terms everyone can understand. While it's getting old, it is still valid.

Center for Research Libraries (CRL). *Trustworthy Repository Audit and Certification: Criteria and Checklist.* February 2007. Version 1.0. www.crl.edu/content.asp?l1=13&l2=58&l3=162&l4=91 (accessed July 27, 2008).

This publication adds another to the growing number of criteria and checklists for evaluating TDRs. One of its checklists refers to documents (policies, procedures, plans, etc.) that a repository should keep current. It also argues that TDRs should be prepared to demonstrate review cycles appropriate to their activities and requirements.

Collaborative Electronic Records Project, Rockefeller Archive Center. *E-Mail Guidelines for Managers and Employees.* Sleepy Hollow, N.Y.: Rockefeller Archive Center, 2006. www.archive.rockefeller.edu/CERP/pdf/emailguidelines.pdf (accessed July 26, 2008).

Collaborative Electronic Records Project, Rockefeller Archive Center and Smithsonian Institution Archives. http://siarchives.si.edu/cerp/index.htm (accessed July 26, 2008).

Despite the size and reputations of the two institutions involved, this project started with a couple of dedicated (and frightened) curators who recognized the need to face the issue of digital materials, especially e-mail. They have put together a very detailed guide on e-mail management for their donors. But they have also turned their website into an outstanding one-stop shop for tools and advice on the long-term retention of digital materials at www.siarchives.si.edu/cerp/index.htm. Be sure to check their pages on both "Progress" and "Resources."

Darlington, Jeffrey, Andy Finney, and Adrian Pearce. "Domesday Redux: The Rescue of the BBC Domesday Project Videodiscs." *Ariadne* 36 (July 30, 2003). www.ariadne.ac.uk/issue36/tna/ (accessed July 26, 2008).

This article provides an illustrated examination of the heroic efforts needed to rescue the data from a digital project created in 1986.

Digital Library Federation. "Digital Preservation." www.diglib.org/preserve.htm (accessed July 26, 2008).

"Building on the work of the Commission on Preservation and Access (CPA), CLIR [Council on Library and Information Resources] and the DLF [Digital Library Federation] remain committed to maintaining long-term access to the digital intellectual and scholarly record. They have a particular interest in practical initiatives and in research into most poorly understood areas. This page links to CLIR, DLF, and CPA preservation initiatives, research reports, and related information resources."

Duff, Wendy. "Ensuring the Preservation of Reliable Evidence: A Research Project Funded by NHPRC." *Archivaria* 42 (Fall 1996): 28–45.

"The University of Pittsburgh Electronic Records Project, a three year project funded by the National Historical Publications and Records Commission, identified a set of nineteen functional requirements for electronic evidence. This paper describes the Project's products, including the functional requirements for record-keeping, the production rules, literary warrant, and a metadata model for business acceptable communications."

Fallows, James. "File Not Found: Why a Stone Tablet Is Still Better than a Hard Drive." *Atlantic Monthly* (September 2006). www.theatlantic.com/doc/prem/200609/information-erosion (accessed July 26, 2008).

This article takes a look at the perishability of digital materials.

Hafner, Katie. "Even Digital Memories Can Fade." *New York Times*, November 10, 2004. www.nytimes.com/2004/11/10/technology/10archive.html?ex=125774 2800&en=e07d6277aca5e520&ei=5088 (accessed July 26, 2008).

This author looks at the difficulty of digital preservation.

Harvard University, Office for Information Systems. *Web Archiving Resources.* June 30, 2008. hul.harvard.edu/ois/projects/webarchive/resources.html (accessed July 26, 2008).

A cornucopia of links to resources on a wide range of topics, including e-mail, intellectual property, and metadata, plus a wide variety of tools.

Hedstrom, Margaret. "Building Record-Keeping Systems: Archivists Are Not Alone on the Wild Frontier." *Archivaria* 44 (Fall 1997): 44–71.

This article provides a good summary of the Pittsburgh Project compared to the University of British Columbia project. *See also* Marsden below. It provides a good overview of the technical solutions that had begun to appear, with a caution that most repositories cannot adopt a single strategy, but must tailor a network of solutions to suit their individual needs.

Hedstrom, Margaret. "Digital Preservation: A Time Bomb for Digital Libraries." *Language Resources and Evaluation* 31, no. 3 (May 1997): 189–202. Published originally in *Computers and the Humanities* 31 (1998): 289–302. *Language Resources and Evaluation* continues the journal *Computers and the Humanities* as of vol. 39, no. 1 (2005). www.springerlink.com/content/h73v57h6587k4l7n/ (accessed July 26, 2008).

This article discusses the present state of digital preservation, articulates requirements of both users and custodians, and suggests research needs in storage media, migration, conversion, and overall management strategies. While somewhat dated, the author's points remain valid.

Hedstrom, Margaret, et al. "'The Old Version Flickers More': Digital Preservation from the User's Perspective." *American Archives* 69, no. 1 (Spring/Summer 2006): 159–87.

Experimental research testing users' response to various methods of preserving text and computer games to determine what characteristics users value most in preserved digital materials.

Henry, Linda J. "An Archival Retread in Electronic Records: Acquiring Computer Literacy." *American Archivist* 56, no. 3 (Summer 1993): 514–21.

The story of what a computer illiterate archivist learned about learning about computers as she faced the prospect herself.

Hitchcock, Steve, et al. "Digital Preservation Service Provider Models in Institutional Repositories: Toward Distributed Services." *D-Lib Magazine* 13, no. 5/6 (May/June 2007). www.dlib.org/dlib/may07/hitchcock/05hitchcock.html (accessed July 26, 2008).

This article describes the evolution of a series of models that have helped guide the development of flexible and distributed preservation services for institutional repositories.

Hodge, Gail M. "Best Practices for Digital Archiving: An Information Life Cycle Approach." *D-Lib Magazine* 6, no. 1 (January 2000). www.dlib.org/dlib/january00/01hodge.html (accessed July 26, 2008).

Early work summarizing the emergence of "best practices" for long-term retention of digital materials.

Hyry, Tom, and Rachel Onuf. "The Personality of Electronic Records: The Impact of New Information Technology on Personal Papers." *Archival Issues: Journal of the Midwest Archives Conference* 22, no. 1 (1997): 37–44.

This article looks at some of the issues the archivist in a collecting repository must confront with the electronic media in personal collections.

Kaczmarek, Joanne, Patricia Hswe, Janet Eke, and Thomas G. Habing. "Using the *Audit Checklist for the Certification of a Trusted Digital Repository* as a Framework for Evaluating Repository Software Applications: A Progress Report." *D-Lib Magazine* 12, no. 12 (December 2006). www.dlib.org/dlib/december06/kaczmarek/12kaczmarek.html (accessed July 26, 2008).

A report on the effort to develop a framework of evaluating repository software applications based on RLG's 2005 Audit Checklist, using a common software evaluation scoring method.

Karp, Mike. "How a New Government Rule Affects Your Storage Infrastructure: A New Regulatory Requirement for Storage Managers." *Network World* (August 22,

2006). www.networkworld.com/newsletters/stor/2006/0821stor1.html (accessed July 26, 2008).

Describes the impact of a Supreme Court ruling concerning the qualities electronic records should have to serve as discoverable legal documents.

LaMonica, Martin. "States Struggling to Deal with Digital Documents." CNET News.com (April 25, 2006). http://news.cnet.com/2100-1014_3-6064793.html (accessed February 28, 2008).

CNN takes a brief look at state governments' attempts to address digital materials.

Lee, Cal. "Bridging the Gap: Mechanisms for Legitimate Peripheral Participation." *MAC* [Midwest Archives Conference] *Newsletter* (January 2003): 23–25. www. ils.unc.edu/callee/bridging_gap.htm (accessed July 26, 2008).

Solid strategies for influencing activities in other professions that have implications for archivists and curators.

Lee, Cal. "Guerilla ERM: Lessons Learned from Some Time in the Trenches." *Ohio Archivist* 32, no. 1 (Spring 2001): 3–7. www.ils.unc.edu/callee/guerrila_erm.htm (accessed July 26, 2008).

Some very practical advice on actually getting the job done.

Lee, Christopher A. "Guerilla Electronic Records Management: Records Management Lessons Learned." *Records and Information Management Report* 18, no. 5 (May 2002): 1–13.

This is a revised and expanded version of Cal Lee's article above.

Library of Congress. "Digital Preservation." www.digitalpreservation.gov/ (accessed July 26, 2008).

The Library of Congress has taken a collaborative approach to the collection and preservation of digital information in order to remain relevant and useful to Congress and its constituents in the digital age. In December 2000, Congress asked the library to lead a collaborative project, called the National Digital Information Infrastructure and Preservation Program (NDIIPP), with a goal of developing a national strategy to collect, archive, and preserve the growing amounts of digital content, especially materials that are created only in digital formats, for current and future generations.

The library is working with partners from universities, libraries, archives, federal agencies, and commercial content and technology organizations to accomplish five goals: 1) identify and collect at-risk born-digital content, 2) build and support a national network of partners working together to preserve digital content, 3) develop and use technical tools and services for preservation, 4) encourage public policy to support digital preservation, 5) show why digital preservation is important for everyone.

Lyman, Peter, and Brewster Kahle. "Archiving Digital Cultural Artifacts." *D-Lib*

Magazine (July/August 1998). www.dlib.org/dlib/july98/07lyman.html (accessed July 26, 2008).

This article considers the World Wide Web as a cultural artifact, using it as an example for many others. Points out the validity and weaknesses of the standard metaphors used for the Web and the technologies we have for preserving it, and outlines the technologies that we need but which had not, in 1998, appeared yet.

Lyman, Peter, and Hal R. Varian. *How Much Information?* School of Information Management and Science, University of California at Berkeley, 2003. www2.sims. berkeley.edu/research/projects/how-much-info-2003 (accessed July 26, 2008).

The authors attempt to analyze the amount of information that existed in the world at the time and develop a projection of its growth—dated, but still stunning.

Lynch, Clifford A. "The Integrity of Digital Information: Mechanics and Definitional Issues." *JASIS* [Journal of the American Society of Information Science] 45, no. 10 (1994): 737–44.

This author has a thoughtful explanation of the problem of maintaining the integrity of a record in a networked environment. He uses particularly effective analogies.

Marsden, Paul. "When Is the Future? Comparative Notes on the Electronic Record-keeping Products of the University of Pittsburgh and the University of British Columbia." *Archivaria* 43 (Spring 1997): 158–73.

A well-defined comparison of the differences and the implications in the differences between the Pittsburgh Project's definition of a record and the definition used by UBC. *See also* Hedstrom, "Building Record-Keeping Systems," above.

Michigan State. "Records Management Reports and Guidelines." *History, Arts and Libraries*. Vendor Review Team Final Report. www.michigan.gov/hal/0,1607,7-160-18835_18894-62997--,00.html (accessed July 26, 2008).

Michigan State. RMA Project Grant Proposal. www.michigan.gov/hal/0,1607,7-160-18835_18894-62996--,00.html (accessed July 26, 2008).

Michigan State. RMA Project Monthly Reports (May 2000–September 2002). http://www.michigan.gov/hal/0,1607,7-160-18835_18894-74276--,00.html (accessed July 26, 2008).

Michigan State. Business Process Analysis Reports. http://www.michigan.gov/hal/0,1607,7-160-18835_18894-74284--,00.html (accessed July 26, 2008).

Between 2000 and 2002, the state of Michigan conducted a pilot project for acquiring and implementing a Department of Defense 5015.2-compliant records management application. The reports to the funding agency provide very detailed documentation of both the quantitative and qualitative aspects of the project.

National Archives (U.K.). *Digital Preservation: Advice and Guidance*. www. nationalarchives.gov.uk/preservation/advice/digital.htm (accessed July 26, 2008).

Digital preservation guidance notes provide concise, authoritative advice on specific topics related to the preservation and management of electronic records. Their intended audience is anyone involved in the creation of electronic records that may need to be preserved over the long term, and those responsible for preservation.

National Archives of Australia. *Designing and Implementing Recordkeeping Systems (DIRKS) Manual.* www.naa.gov.au/records-management/publications/dirks-manual.aspx.

This is a remarkably clear and thorough guide for conducting a records survey and establishing a system of records management.

Piasecki, Sara J. "Legal Admissibility of Electronic Records as Evidence and Implications for Records Management." *American Archivist* 58, no. 1 (Winter 1995): 54–64.

Using the history of the legal admissibility of records in a variety of media, the author shows how electronic records have moved into the mainstream and why institutions must manage them well.

Quick, Ken, and Michael C. Maxwell. "Ending Digital Obsolescence." IS&T's 2005 Archiving Conference, Washington, D.C., April 26, 2005, 201–5.

Rist, Oliver. "Home-Brewed E-mail Archiving." *Infoworld* 28, no. 22 (May 2006): 34.

Rist details how a small-business man created an e-mail and instant chat data archive using "off the shelf" components.

Saffady, William. *Digital Document Management.* Lenexa, Kans.: ARMA International, 2007.

This book provides practical guidance and tools for planning, selecting, and managing a document management system (DMS). It also includes worksheets and models for making the case to decision makers.

Schneider, Craig. "Missing Email May Cost Morgan Stanley $10m." CFO.com, August 31, 2005. www.cfo.com/article.cfm/4340197/c_4340354?f=archives&origin=archive (accessed July 26, 2008).

The headline says it all: the perils of ignoring e-mail.

Society of American Archivists, Best Practices Task Force. *Managing Electronic Records and Assets: A Working Bibliography, 6. Electronic "Manuscript Collections."* www.archivists.org/saagroups/bptf/mera-emss.asp (accessed July 26, 2008).

This online bibliography of guidelines, handbooks, articles, books, and reports on managing electronic materials addresses electronic "manuscripts collections" specifically in Section 6.

Society of American Archivists, Metadata and Digital Object Roundtable. www.archivists.org/saagroups/metadata/ (accessed July 26, 2008).

The Metadata and Digital Object Roundtable of the Society of American Archivists provides a place for collaboration and a source for guidance to archivists at all types of repositories as they engage with the digital environment. This website will provide access to information and resources to archivists charged with these duties.

Sphere, J. Timothy. "A Framework for EDMS/ERMS Integration." *Information Management Journal* 38, no. 6 (November–December 2004): 54–62.

Stanford University. *Conservation Online (CoOL): Electronic Records.* palimpsest. stanford.edu/bytopic/electronic-records/ (accessed July 26, 2008).

Stanford has a large collection of Internet-available documents, including some of the pioneering works. While not fully comprehensive, and now plagued by broken links, the site still pulls together some of the best resources available.

Stephens, David O. *Records Management: Making the Transition from Paper to Electronic.* Lenexa, Kans.: ARMA International, 2007.

This is Stephens's most mature book. In this volume he provides a background in records management and then examines the current trends in RIM thinking and the technology and disciplines being developed to support the new perspective. The final chapter extends the trends he has discussed to the archival profession.

Stephens, David O., and Roderick C. Wallace. *Electronic Records Retention: An Introduction.* Prairie Village, Kans.: ARMA International, 1997.

While old and aimed at records managers, the book remains useful to archivists for the clarity of explanation, history of the issue, and glossary.

Stephens, David O., and Roderick C. Wallace. *Electronic Records Retention: New Strategies for Data Life Cycle Management.* Lenexa, Kans.: ARMA International, 2003.

While aimed at records managers, the book remains useful to archivists for the clarity of explanation of the issues involved and the appendices. Fully half of the book consists of laws and regulations from Australia, Canada, and the United States about the retention of electronic records. Building on their previous work and the increased understanding that records managers had developed since 1997, the authors adapted previous advice to the more recent environment, and specifically address the issues they had not addressed in their 1997 work. The authors intend records managers in institutional settings to use the book, but much of their advice can apply to the way you work with donors.

Stielow, Frederick J. "Archival Theory and the Preservation of Electronic Media: Opportunities and Standards below the Cutting Edge." *American Archivist* 55, no. 2 (Spring 1992): 332–43.

Stielow argues that electronic records provide archivists a niche with which to establish a stronger presence among information professionals. He explains why archivists need to understand new technology before fully embracing it and promotes standards as important in the preservation of electronic records.

TechTerms.com. *Tech Terms Dictionary*. www.techterms.com/ (accessed July 26, 2008).

This is a free online dictionary of computer and technology terms that strives to define computer terms, and explains them as well. As they say, "Some of the terms in the dictionary are common and easy to understand, while others are less common and more advanced. For this reason, each computer term includes a 'Tech Factor' rating, based on a scale from one to ten. Terms with low tech factors are basic terms that are good to know, while terms with high tech factors are more advanced and are not used as often."

Testbed Digitale Bewaring. *Costs of Digital Preservation*. The Hague: Digital Preservation Testbed, 2005. www.digitaleduurzaamheid.nl/bibliotheek/docs/CoDPv1.pdf (accessed July 26, 2008).

This document reports on a project to determine the factors that contribute to the cost of digital preservation and how they relate. It is highly readable and contains highly informative comparison charts.

Testbed Digitale Bewaring. *Functional Requirements for a Preservation System*. The Hague: Digital Preservation Testbed, January 2005. www.digitaleduurzaamheid.nl/bibliotheek/docs/Technical_and_Functional_Requirements.pdf (accessed July 26, 2008).

Van Bogart, John W. C., and John Merz. *St. Thomas Electronic Records Disaster Recovery Effort*. Technical Report RE0025. National Media Laboratory (November 1995). www.imation.com/government/nml/pdfs/AP_NMLdoc_StThomasElectronic.pdf (accessed July 26, 2008).

This report covers the recovery after Hurricane Marilyn crossed the Virgin Islands. While dated as to the technology involved, it provides specific details about how Van Bogart and Merz handled the hard drives and other hardware affected by the storm.

Van Garderen, Peter. *Digital Preservation: An Overview*. Recorded presentation at Managing Information Assets in the Public Sector, Edmonton, Alberta, October 12–13, 2006. www.archivemati.ca/wp-content/shockwave-flash/digital_preservation_overview.html (accessed July 26, 2008).

As the title suggests, Van Garderen provides an overview of the issues in this book in an engaging seventy-seven-minute presentation.

More Resources

Alouette Canada: www.alouettecanada.ca (accessed July 31, 2008).

ARMA Electronic Records & E-Discovery. Audio/Video/Software: www.arma. org/erecords/index.cfm?View=Audio (accessed July 31, 2008).

ARMA Electronic Records & E-Discovery. *Information Management Journal.* Articles: www.arma.org/erecords/index.cfm?View=IMJ (accessed July 31, 2008).

ARMA Electronic Records & E-Discovery. Online Courses: www.arma.org/ erecords/index.cfm?View=LC (accessed July 31, 2008).

ARMA Electronic Records & E-Discovery. Publications: www.arma.org/erecords/ index.cfm?View=Publications (accessed July 31, 2008).

Cultural, Artistic and Scientific Knowledge of Preservation, Access and Retrieval (CASPAR): www.casparpreserves.eu (accessed July 31, 2008).

Digital Curation Centre: www.dcc.ac.uk/ (accessed July 31, 2008).

Digital Preservation Coalition, 3. Institutional Strategies: www.dpconline.org/ graphics/inststrat (accessed July 31, 2008).

DigitalPreservationEurope (DPE): www.digitalpreservationeurope.eu (accessed July 31, 2008).

Digitale Duurzaamheid (Digital Preservation Testbed), Dutch National Archives. Digital Longevity: www.digitaleduurzaamheid.nl/index.cfm?paginakeuze=185& lang=en (accessed July 31, 2008).

Electronic Resource Preservation and Access Network (ERPANET): www. erpanet.org/ (accessed July 31, 2008).

Harvard University. Office for Information Systems. Web Archiving Resources: http://hul.harvard.edu/ois/projects/webarchive/resources.html (accessed July 31, 2008).

International Internet Preservation Consortium: http://netpreserve.org (accessed July 31, 2008).

National Archives of Australia. "Digital Records in the National Archives." www. naa.gov.au/records-management/secure-and-store/e-preservation/at-naa/index. aspx (accessed July 31, 2008).

National Archives (U.K.). Archiving: www.nationalarchives.gov.uk/preservation/ digitalarchive (accessed July 30, 2008).

National Archives (U.K.). Digital Continuity Project: www.nationalarchives.gov. uk/electronicrecords/digitalcontinuity/default.htm (accessed July 31, 2008).

National Digital Information Infrastructure and Preservation Program (NDIIPP): www.digitalpreservation.gov (accessed July 31, 2008).

Preserving Access to Digital Information (PADI): www.nla.gov.au/padi/ (accessed July 31, 2008).

SAA Group: "Managing Electronic Records and Assets: A Bibliography: 6. Electronic 'Manuscript Collections'": www.archivists.org/saagroups/bptf/mera-digcoll.asp (accessed July 31, 2008).

SAA Online On-Demand Programs: www.archivists.org/prof-education/online_ ondemand.asp (accessed July 31, 2008).

SAA Publications and Products Catalog: www.archivists.org/catalog/index. asp?keywordID=44 (accessed July 31, 2008).

Smithsonian Institution Archives. Publications: http://siarchives.si.edu/research/ main_pubs.html (accessed July 31, 2008).

U.S. National Archives and Records Administration (NARA). Electronic Records Archives (ERA). www.archives.gov/era (accessed July 30, 2008).

Index

About the Author

Elizabeth H. Dow worked as an archivist describing materials in three historical repositories in Vermont: the Sheldon Museum, in Middlebury; the Vermont State Archives, in Montpelier; and the Special Collections Department of the Bailey/Howe Library at the University of Vermont, in Burlington. In January 2000, she left the university to develop an archives track in the School of Library and Information Science at Louisiana State University, in Baton Rouge.

As Professor Dow started to become familiar with the literature of electronic records, she found she needed to read very widely to understand the whole picture. She also found that most of the thinking and research concerned archivists in institutional archives. She became fascinated by the process of teasing out the parts that apply to curators in a collecting repository and the challenge of synthesizing them for this book.

Dow holds degrees in history from Juniata College in Pennsylvania (BA) and the University of Vermont (MA) as well as degrees in library science from the University of Oregon (MLS) and the University of Pittsburgh (PhD).